All the MISSING PIECES

Pain from my past will not cripple me in the present.

M. ANNE WRIGHT

ISBN 978-1-0980-2517-5 (paperback)
ISBN 978-1-0980-2518-2 (digital)

Copyright © 2020 by M. Anne Wright

All rights reserved. No part of this publication may be reproduced, distributed, or transmitted in any form or by any means, including photocopying, recording, or other electronic or mechanical methods without the prior written permission of the publisher. For permission requests, solicit the publisher via the address below.

Christian Faith Publishing, Inc.
832 Park Avenue
Meadville, PA 16335
www.christianfaithpublishing.com

Printed in the United States of America

Anne is a gifted writer who suffered the painful loss of several family members including her very young son and a stepson through suicide. With humanity, raw candor, and wit, she is able to take readers on a journey of incomparable range and resonance into the most pervasive of family secrets that shroud suicide.

Perhaps it is the stigma about mental illness that distorts our understanding about family and social relationships/structures, interfering with our ability to recognize and help family members before they think self destruction is their only option. If families can openly and honestly confront their own fears about mental illness and suicide, they can grasp the responsibility and power they have to help their loved ones find other ways to end their suffering before it is too late. No family is immune to the possibility of a family member feeling isolated and misunderstood. Anne offers inspiration for everyone in pain—with information and insight that she hopes will shed light on a still stigmatized topic and help save lives.

Helen W Jones APN, C., PhD. Professor Emeritus
from Raritan Valley Community College in Somerville NJ
and therapist in private practice,
H.W. Jones Holistic Health in Flemington, NJ

In a world that often changes faster than our ability to adapt, one unchanging, unshakable, and unbreakable constant is that God IS love. Rather than simply showing love, God IS love. His love is soft & severe, comforting & confronting, sacrificing & searching. From God's first question in the Garden "Where are you?" to Jesus' final cry on the cross "It is finished" we are brought face-to-face with the fierce love of God. His love creates us, pursues us, redeems us, and restores us through Christ. As the Apostle Paul says, there is no conceivable thing that can separate us from the love of God that is in Christ Jesus our Lord. (Romans 8:38 & 39)

Nathan Tuckey, Lead Pastor
South Ridge Community Church

ACKNOWLEDGMENTS

There would be no story without the unsuspecting contributions of my family. My story can be compared to a thousand-piece puzzle. The problem: numerous absent pieces making completion impossible.

To my sister, Chris, my touchstone, who supported me and worked with me to make sense of the senseless life we lived.

For you, my Jason, my special younger son. Your life ended before it began. At fourteen, you knew more about life and people than most people learn in a lifetime.

The only surviving immediate family member is my older boy, my Jamie. A man I cannot thank enough for his support, opinions—even the ones I didn't want to hear—laughter, creativity, and faith in God. My greatest joy. My greatest regret is that you were robbed of the childhood every child deserves.

PROLOGUE

Sluggishly, the murky fog lifted, bringing with it the odor of death. I was unable to move, frozen in place. All about me, a vast nothingness. Something appeared in the distance, a great body of water, still and black. I moved closer to witness a young boy rising from the sea creating a gentle wake. His movement, slow, cautious, and steady. Clear to me he didn't see me even though I was in within his sights. A screech startled me, but not the child. Lumbering past me he stopped, stared. Dressed in a clown's outfit, a big yellow bow tie at this neck, below a huge painted smile. He snarled until he saw the child. Lips parted as he smiled, an evil smile, a sneer that revealed broken, yellow teeth. Saliva oozed onto his clothes. He moved stealthy toward the child who stood frozen in place.

I awoke suddenly, transported back to reality, thankful to be driven from my familiar, unfinished nightmare. Dreams about water, clowns, the young boy who drowned many years ago. There were different versions, but most had the same components. I suspect a missing piece of the puzzle of my life lies hidden in the images.

Mental illness plagued my family. Abuse, uncontrolled rage, searing pain, addictions, and my abject loneliness. I learned it does not discriminate, regardless of your standing. Clergy, parents, siblings, anyone.

I vowed to shine a light on the illness that plagues millions. Mental illness is not a sign of weakness. The bearer cannot "pull themselves up the bootstraps." As with any illness, it needs identification, treatment, and support. And ignoring the signs is disastrous, as I learned firsthand.

From an early age, I knew there were secrets not yet revealed. Perhaps they never would be, but I have learned I will not be hindered by the past crippling me in the future.

Join me as I travel back in time as I looked for pieces of the puzzle of my life. Like me, you will learn we are resilient creatures. And I learned that even when I was giving God the hand, He was there. I was carried, pushed, protected even in the darkest of time. You can not only "survive," a state one should not live in. But you will have joy. Real Joy if you are receptive.

Shall we begin?

1

Our bathroom had an escape route.

"I am talking to you, young lady. Where are you going?" Mother's tone revealed anger and disgust. I had reached the second-floor landing. The bathroom door was to my left. I glanced down at mother. Her lips were pinched tight as she spoke. Drops of spittle lingered in the corners of her mouth. My four-year-old legs propelled me forward. Flesh rubbed together on my chubby legs as I sprinted through the bathroom, Mother following behind. I was in reach of my getaway. Grabbing the glass doorknob, I opened the door. Entering the small linen closet that divided the bathroom from the nursery and my parents' bedroom.

"Dollie, stop running." Heavy footsteps were closing in fast.

I continued circling through rooms until the door to the hallway was in sight. I ran through the room, only to end up back where I started at the top of the stairs.

Mother closed in behind me, my bladder bursting as I reentered the bathroom and sat down on the toilet. I was trapped. If I wet my panties, her anger would intensify. I lowered my head. She entered the bathroom yelling at me as I emptied my bladder.

"Mommy, me sorry." I apologized, chewing on my lip without knowing what I did.

"I told you to watch your sister. You know she throws up after she eats, and you just left her. If she dies, it's your fault." Her face twisted like the gnarly timeworn oak tree out back. "She is just a baby. You're so selfish. Why did you leave her?" The sound of the door slamming as she left triggered something in me, a sense of shame, guilt, and responsibility that would stay with me into adulthood.

Minutes later, she reentered the room. "Dollie, are you finished?" Mother's voice was softer, loving almost. "I need you to keep an eye on your sister." Her voice like a hum, melodic and unusually faint. "You are Mommy's special helper."

"Uh-huh," I called as I slid off the potty, washing my hands and left the space. Chubby little legs scooted down the stairs as fast as they could.

"Now go see how your sister is," she cooed.

I entered the living room where my sweet baby sister, Chris, rested in a small crib. Looking into the crib, I observed a sleeping baby girl. Small bubbles dropped from her tiny mouth onto the pad beneath her curly red hair. Thank God, her oval-shaped head was a temporary condition. "Mommy, she's asleep and making mouth bubbles."

Mother walked toward me, stopping in front of the crib. "Look at that pretty red hair—red hair like every member of my family."

"Mommy, why don't I have red hair?"

She stared for the longest moment without answering my question. "Don't wake her up. You can go if you want. I'll keep an eye on her now."

I made my way to the front porch where I found my daddy. "Come on, Princess, sit on Daddy's lap." As much as I loved being called *Princess*, I hated sitting on his lap. As I stood there, my feet still planted to the ground, he rose from his chair. "Hey, let's go get a milkshake. Okay? It'll be our secret. Don't tell your mother or grandmother." He brought his finger to his lips. He took my hand, and we were off to Delany's, my favorite place filled with penny candies and sweet milkshakes. Once inside, he hoisted me up on the stool, we ordered, and within minutes, I was slurping down the thick banana-laced treat. "Hey, Bill, you know my little Princess, don't you?" Dad asked. The counterman smiled at me.

The air was cool on my skin as we began the five-block trek back home. Dad would swing me and tell me stories. "Home at last, Princess. Don't tell anyone about our little secret." He feigned seriousness raising a finger to his lips. I liked this game of secrets, unlike other games where secrets were not savored but severed.

He climbed the steps toward the door. "Wait out here—I'll see if the coast is clear." I knew he was teasing but also being protective. Comforting like my teddy bear, Mr. Boo Boo de Boo Boo. What was I thinking with that name?

Our family lived in an urban city in New Jersey. In a house built for our family, my grandparents. I loved that house with the front screened-in porch where we sat on the glider watching traffic, bolts of lightning sliced through the night sky and spied on neighbors through windows. The entrance to our house was atop the side porch. Built-in benches rested juxtaposed the massive front door that welcomed us on warm summer nights. We would catch fireflies in jars with holes punched in the lid to allow air to enter.

"Well, I am still alive," Daddy said, stepping onto the porch. "Your grandma is out in the yard working on her roses." Moments later, I saw her round the bend with her clippers, her hair tied up, donning a dress that mirrored all her dresses with a belt of matching fabric and her ever-present apron.

We lived with my dad's mother. I loved Grammy, and even more importantly, she loved me. Memories of her roast leg of lamb, pineapple upside-down cake, and my favorite, tapioca pudding served with a dollop of strawberry jam still seduce me.

"When's Margaret coming back?" she called. "It's almost dinnertime." She hated my mother. Her feelings for her son, my father, were mixed. She protected him, but there was also something unspoken. Another secret, a cover-up—something was missing.

His words were clipped, brisk. "How the hell would I know where she is, but I'm sure she'll be back in time."

"Don't take that tone with me." Grandma's voice sliced the air.

"Shut up, you old hag." He turned toward her. Face crimson. Jaw set.

Grandma looked at me, at her son, then back to me. She turned and disappeared behind the house. There was silence. This was not the moment to say one word to Dad. The fuse was lit. A violent eruption was just below the surface.

Teddy bear daddy was gone. Scary daddy surfaced. Running up the stairs into the house, almost knocking my mother down. She was in the house all the time. I felt the bite of her nails on my shoulders.

"Stop running in the house. How many times do I need to tell you the same thing?" Her face tightened as she spoke.

"Margaret, leave her alone." My grandmother had entered through the back door. Now these two came face-to-face. "Dollie, go upstairs, honey." Grammy ordered. I ran up the steps. The battle had commenced. "She's my daughter—I will say whatever I want to her."

"Margaret, she's just a little girl. Can't you leave her alone?" Grammy pleaded.

Upstairs, I curled up on the big old rocker in my room. As a little girl, I felt like crying, and I didn't know why.

"Enough!" Dad screamed. "Shut up—the both of you."

There was a battle going on, and somehow, I knew I was the catalyst.

The day ended with stiff silence between the adults in my life. Chris was sleeping with angels in her crib, and I was in my bed. Leaning on my elbow, my head rested in my hand. Outside, below the roofline lay Magie Avenue. Random cars and trucks ambled slowly up the avenue toward the red light. Always afraid of missing something, I lay like that until sleep grabbed me and pulled me into the dark shadows.

"I'm going potty, Grammy." My legs swung back and forth. I was startled by a noise. Directly overhead, there was a heat grate. Behind the grate, the face of a clown peered down at me. Panicking, I called out. "Who are you? Go away?" The clown behind the metal grid stared down, eyes bloodshot, painted smile that failed to hide the downturned mouth. "Grammy, hurry!" My screamed echoed off the bathroom tiles. He smiled, revealing yellow, jagged, decaying teeth. Thick mucus slid downward to land on my upturned face. It smelled like those eggs we found hidden weeks after Easter. Abruptly, my body was transported back to my little bed.

"What's the matter, sweetie?" the family matriarch asked, entering my bedroom. "You were yelling in your sleep. Why are you screaming? You'll wake your sister!" My mother's eyebrows were pulled close together.

"Princess, Daddy's here. Don't cry." My body shifted from Dad's weight on the mattress.

That night was the premiere event of a dream that would visit my nightlife for the remainder of my life.

*****

A few days later, I sat on a bench on the front porch with Dad across from me. A neighborhood girl sat beside him, her little dress barely covering her knees. A bandage protected an unseen scrape on her right knee—the outcome of a day of play. The kids all loved climbing under, over, and behind debris left hidden in the rear space of neighborhood garages that served as a safe place during games of hide-and-seek. But the real danger came when we would charge to kill the dragon, tree branches high in the air to serve as weapons.

One sunny afternoon a little girl from the neighborhood sat on the porch bench across from where I sat. I watched as her shiny, braded blonde hair swung as my father tickled her into a fit of laughter. Unwanted, that is.

"Stop, please." She bit her lower lip, struggling for freedom. I knew what she was feeling because that is how I felt when Dad tickled me. He was relentless. My giggles faded. And I would begin to cry. Extensive tickles are very uncomfortable, just like giving me shocks with the fireplace poker. I would watch him drag his shoed foot over the carpet, grab the poker then touch me. I hated it and him in that moment.

Smoke filtered through the front door screen. "Bob, leave her alone," Grandma chided, cigarette dangling from her fingers as she stepped onto the front porch.

Dad rose, freeing his victim. "Get back inside and mind your own business." The neighbor girl climbed down off the bench, scrambled down the stairs and ran for home.

Grandma retreated into the house, but not before releasing one of her infamous sighs. Dad rose. I followed him into the center hall where he and Grammy were engaged in a quarrel. My hands cupped my mouth when he raised his hand to slap her.

"Don't you dare touch me!" she demanded without flinching as she snuffed out the cigarette butt. She stood firm in front of him, void of fear. My tummy began to make noises. He turned, trembling, fist clenched by his side. Grandma's right hand dug deep into her apron pocket. I knew what was coming next. Out came the familiar red-and-white package. Her red-polished fingers pulled out a cigarette from its resting place. Dad headed toward the big screened-in porch on the front, Grandma turned into the kitchen, and I returned to the side porch stoop.

"Are you out here alone? Where's your father?" Mother asked, returning from a walk around the block with my sister.

Thinking of his clenched fist, I responded simply, "Inside." The mind of child is constantly learning, always connecting one link to another. It was then that I realized I had never seen my grandpa. "Mommy, where is my grandpa? My friends have grandpas."

Mother released a long strand of wind, paused, and then in an unusually tender voice, answered, "Your grandpa, my daddy, died when I was just four. I loved him very much, and he loved me too." Her eyes glistened as she spoke.

"Died?" I felt a little sad wave wash over me. Even as a little girl, my heart was tender, easily wounded.

"He got sick, in his chest, and died. No more questions about him." Mom's voice faded. Shifting on the bench, she looked off into space, but something pulled her back. "Your other grandpa, your father's father, was a very nice man. He was run over by a car. Your father had a terrible fight with him, screaming terrible things at him. Grandpa Knight went for a walk to cool down, I guess. The man who hit him said he walked right in front of the car like he was in a trance."

"Was it Daddy's fault?"

Her lips curled slightly as her shoulders rose and dropped.

"What the hell are you telling her that for?" Daddy screamed from behind the mesh. The door opened, and the floor shook as he stomped onto the gray weathered floor. "At least, he wasn't crazy like you and your father."

Chris startled awake from the noise and began to fuss. Dad pushed passed Mother, who was now on her feet, on his way down the front steps. Mother entered the house, heaving a sigh. What had just happened? So many incidents in my life didn't make sense, missing pieces of a broken life. Why did my grandfather walk in front of a car? Was he distracted? After all, he had had a heated argument with his son, our father. I know from all accounts of my grandfather, even Mother, he was a kind, gentle man. Was Dad just attacking Mom with foolish words about her father's death to get even? Secrets lurked in the shadows.

Not until now did I consider his death was a suicide, the first of many?

Grandma appeared and sat beside me. "It's okay, honey." Her frail hand held mine. I began performing my calming ritual, rubbing her long, neatly manicured nails.

"I sorry about Grandpa, Gramma."

Her smile meant to hide the depth of her loss. "I have you now to love. But yes, I do miss Ed. No more talk about it, okay? Guess what's for dinner?"

I sat bolt upright. "What?"

"Spaghetti and meatballs."

"Yay." The previous moments faded as the image of sauce-covered pasta and huge meatballs appeared.

"Help me set the table?" Gramma asked, knowing I would say yes. I loved spending time with her. Together we entered our house. From upstairs, I heard, "Dollie, I need you up here to watch Chris."

Grandma, in her no-nonsense voice, called up, "She's busy helping me with supper. That is, unless you want to help me."

As much as I loved spending time with Grandma, the antithesis was true with Mother. The air stopped moving when these two women were in the same space.

No response, just footsteps on the wooded floor above indicated Mother was entering the nursery.

Grandma winked at me. "Now how about that spaghetti?"

2

My bedroom was nestled in the front corner of the house where the side street and main street intersected. Lights from the cars traveling late at night cast scary but exciting shadows on my walls. Even then, my imagination formulated scenarios where fairies hid, monsters loomed, and the escape was the wardrobe that sat between the two side windows. I knew that if I had the key, I could open the doors and take the shoot that led to safety in the basement, especially if the creatures above dared to venture downstairs.

I would lie in bed and wait. There it was. The familiar sound of the hook sliding into the eye on the door. As customary, I was locked in. Six years old and locked up every night. Chris was safe in her crib, a quiet child.

"Dear God. Bless Mommy and Daddy and Grandma. Take care of me because you are my special friend. God, Grandma said thunder is just you bowling in heaven. Is that true? Because I am really scared of the noise. Do my Grandpas bowl with you? Could you be a little quieter next time? Good night. Oh, thank you for the tapioca pudding tonight. Amen."

I took my position on my right side, a perfect view of the world outside from the third window that faced the main street. As a precocious child, I knew exactly what to do when nature called. The door was locked, but the window was not. God was with me as I opened the window, lifted my nightgown, and stepped barefooted onto the small overhang, a space no larger than three feet wide by twelve inches deep. I pulled my nightgown up and voided in the corner. Cars passed, but no one noticed or reported a child dangerously perched on the little roof. I guess I knew, even at six, that the alternative—calling out to my parents—would create a perilous situation more dangerous than risking a fall into Grandma's beautiful lavender rhododendron bushes that hug the clapboards of our house.

As occurred every morning, on this morning, I heard the sounds of metal against metal, the signal the jailer was ready to release me. By the time I reached the door and opened it, the hall was empty. Mother appeared in the hallway from my parents' bedroom doorway. "Dollie, hurry and get dressed. I need you to keep an eye on your sister. She just ate and already her tummy is bouncing all over."

Before reentering my bedroom, I glanced at the lock. An idea took shape. Tonight would be different. I discovered an alternative to the problem of peeing on the roof. After the day was over, I lay in bed thinking about the events of the day. I soon fell asleep, but the urge to use the bathroom stirred me from my dreams. All I needed was a belt and a chair. I had both. Quietly, not to arouse anyone, I pushed the chair in front of the door. I pulled the doorknob, creating a sliver of an opening, just the width of the belt. Slowly, the belt was eased into the space and pushed upward, catching the hook and lifting it up and out of the eye. Freedom! As quiet as a church mouse, I hugged the wall past the attic door, moved cautiously down the hallway, avoiding the noisy floorboards, and slipped into the bathroom. No more roof-climbing for this little girl. In the morning, the adults would just assume someone else unlocked the door.

The Knight family moved from Grandma's to an apartment complex a few towns west of Grandma's home. What I remember is based on pictures taken by my dad. He was an excellent photographer. Gifted. One picture I especially love is the one with me sitting on the overstuffed couch, knees up, reading the papers. Another picture I am standing behind my sister in her bassinet holding my teddy bear, leaning over to check on her.

The apartment complex was situated on a road that paralleled the river, twisting and turning in unison. Outside, children were playing, but adults milled around the complex whispering. Some pointed, shouldered, and shrugged, while others shook their heads.

"When was the last time his mother saw him?" a blue-haired lady, the same crabby woman who always yelled at us, asked the bald man beside her.

"His mother said she saw him at lunch. He grabbed his toy boat, and off he ran. She reminded him to not to go across the street, as he did a week ago."

"I bet he went to the river to play with his boat. O my God—Earl, you don't think..." Her face twisted.

It wasn't long before police cars, ambulances, and other nondescript cars parked along the winding curb that echoed the snaking river. The little group of children watched as a police officer entered the home of the missing child. Following close behind him, another man, dressed in black, with a high collar, like the priests wore. Everyone in the yard, on the sidewalks, and doorways appeared to be frozen in time.

I sat with my friend on a front step watching the chaos when I heard a blood-curdling scream. I will never forget the sound that emanated from the little boy's mother. Her scream came from a place so deep, so excruciating, it almost sounded inhumane. Everywhere I looked, adults were crying, triggering a domino effect on the little ones. Mother tugged on my arm, ushering me into the house. The moans my mother was making made me cry. Soon, some other mothers gathered in the kitchen whispering. "Oh, dear God, how can this happen? She is so mindful of where her son is at all times—we all are. Did anyone see him headed for the river?"

Ladies in house dresses silently, shook their heads. Reality of the situation had gripped them.

"His little body was discovered in the culvert." Judy's mom's words spoken in a whisper swiping at her eyes. "Poor Sally and Pete." The women cried and held their children close—even I got a squeeze. Eyes rimmed in red, noses dripped as the sobbing continued. Mom rose to look out the window. The entire complex was joined together in grief for a little boy lost. Men gathered near the road.

I escaped into my room but peeked from the door. Other women were gathering waving tissues, softly crying. I wondered what a culvert was, and when my little friend Peter would be home. I guess he was in trouble.

Mrs. Billings voice rose from the kitchen as I listened in. "Oh, God, I can't imagine the pain of burying one of my children. How old was Peter now?"

"I think he was seven—just a year younger than my Gary," another one answered.

"What I don't understand is the location of the body. It was up the river, in the opposite direction of the flow. How did he even get there? It was on the opposite side of the road in the culvert next to the gas station."

Chairs shifted as Mrs. Jones declared it would be best for her to be with her family now. Our apartment soon fell silent. Chris was napping, as was our new baby brother, Bobby. I guess I fell asleep as well because it was the sound of the front door opening that pulled me from my soft sleep. My dreams were filled with strange animal characters dancing in the rain. The little chipmunk went missing though, and we all looked for him. An owl screeched high above in a massive tree partially hidden in the clouds. When I awoke, I climbed out of bed, scampered down the short hall into the living space. Chris was in a playpen, Bobby was in a little seat, and Mom was in the kitchen area that overlooked the living space.

"So what's for dinner?" Dad asked, just returning home. I recalled seeing him earlier walking on the sidewalk that ran parallel to the river. Neighborhood children were playing, and as Dad passed the boys and girls, he tickled the little girl. Dad was such a handsome man with dark hair. He looked like a banker, distinguished and wise. Quite the opposite was true. He drove a bus and barely made it through high school. He ran his fingers through my hair as he passed. "How's my little Princess?"

I loved being a princess to someone. "Bad day, Daddy."

He walked to Chris and tweaked her cheek, triggering a huge smile. Bobby was picked up and tossed in the air. Giggles and drool fell from his lips.

Creases marched across mother's brow as she turned to face him head on. "Did you hear about Peter?"

"Of course. Awful. Are we still playing cards with the Joneses tonight?"

Mother took a few steps forward and reproached him. "Cards? Do you really think I want to play cards tonight? What's wrong with you?"

With lightning speed, he crossed the room and slapped her hard. I cried, as did Chris. "See what you did?" he yelled, his face crimson. "You made me hit you. I just thought it would do us good to get out. There is nothing that can be done for that little boy now. I don't want to spend the entire night talking about him. It's over." He turned and stormed out of the house. I don't know when he came home, but I know it was very, very late. Heavy footsteps walked past our bedroom startled me. I listened for conversation when he entered the bedroom. Silence.

Our little baby brother began to cry so Mom rose to tend to him, her cheek red from dad's abuse.

Dreams nagged at me about Peter and his untimely death all my life. Dreams about water, my father, and me. Feelings about something very bad.

Many years later, I attempted to learn more about the incident but met a dead-end. My resource even led me to call the local newspaper to check their archives.

"When did the drowning occur—what year?" the reporter asked.

"About thirty-four years ago."

"Do you have a name of the child?" Her voice now brittle and brief.

I was beginning to feel foolish for coming so unprepared. "All I have is the first name. Peter. He was around seven."

She snapped at me. "Lady, I need a lot more info than that to even begin to search."

"That's all I have. Well, I guess that's it. Thank you anyway."

After a lengthy pause, her tone, her next words spoken with an air of concern. "The odd thing is you are the second person to call today asking about that child."

Hairs on my arm stood at attention. Who called? Why? I had spoken to a few folks about my curiosity regarding the incident. Could one of them had called? Replacing the phone, my head was swirling with questions. A missing piece of the puzzle of my life.

Time passed, and the complex returned to our normal routines. Visiting Grandma on Sundays was a time I loved. The aroma of roast leg of lamb permeated the house. After dinner, the family gathered in the living room. Grandma was holding my brother who held a book, Chris played with dolls on the floor, and I sat on the couch, a mature seven-year-old fingering a magazine.

"Margaret, did you have his rash checked out by the doctor?" Grandma's voice dripped with accusation.

"It's just a heat rash. I think he will live. Besides, I am putting a lotion on it."

Grandma's body curved forward to plant a tender kiss on Bobby's check, but he quickly wiped it off. "Don't worry, Grandma's here."

"Your mother and I have some good news." Dad began, grabbing everyone's attention.

I looked away from my magazine. "What is it?" Even Chris stopped playing with her doll for a second. "Is it cookies?"

"No cookies, but something much bigger and better. We are all moving to a new house, a brand-new house. It's being built just for us. So how's that sound?"

Bobby clapped, and Chris shrugged. But I was thrilled. "When will we move? Next week?" I asked.

"Dollie, it is going to take a long time to build the house," Mom interjected.

When we first learned we were moving to a brand-new house, I had no idea what awaited us.

"And some more news is that all of you will be going to stay at a boarding school." I had no idea what a boarding school was, but Grandma got up and left the room at this news.

A few months later, we did exactly that. Three children were shuffled into the family car to a boarding school.

"You will need to stay at this school while our house is being built. It won't be too long." Mother's face, paler than usual, was absent of any emotion. Her red hair was darker now, shoulder length, and worn as most ladies did in the '50s. She returned to face forward in her seat in the car. Chris and I remained stone silent.

A U-shaped drive led us from the street directly in front of the brick, nondescript building. The blue and gold sign off to the side read, SAINT JOSEPH'S HOME FOR BOYS. Dad stopped beneath a large portico painted sharp white. Suddenly, through the double doors, an angel appeared. She was dressed from head to toe in white. Around her tiny waist was something that looked like a rope hung. She glided toward us with a smile that displayed glistening teeth. She appeared to glow and floated like liquid silver.

Her right arm extended; she took my brother's chubby little hand in hers. "So I guess you are Bobby—what beautiful red hair you have. I have red hair too." Bobby's face twisted as he tried to get a peek in the little space between her hassock and skin. "Well, I know your name, so I guess it is only fair you know mine. I am Sister Catherine. And who are you?" she asked my sister and me. We mumbled our names. "So nice to meet you. I promise we will take good care of your brother."

Mother ushered us back into the car, and Dad joined Bobby and Sister Catherine as they disappeared behind the doors. Minutes later, Dad returned. Alone. My stomach spoke out loud, and then inside my chest, a butterfly danced. Chris hugged my hand tight. This was not a boarding school. It was an orphanage. A place where children without parents lived.

The image of my pintsize brother's curly red hair bouncing in the light as he toddled off will forever be branded in my mind. He smiled, waved at us, and off he went. I feared that was the last time I would see him.

Dad entered the car wordless. Mother looked at him as if searching for something. He glanced at her, turned the key, and the car roared as we drove away, leaving my three-year-old brother behind. I recall nothing of the drive. Was it a ten-minute drive? Ten hours? My mind coasted, summoning up images of happy times, pretty places, Grandma's tapioca pudding—anything but the reality I was living.

"Here we are," Dad stated flatly. The major road departed as he steered onto a paved driveway that cut through a high fence with rambling vines and bushes and large thorns. Our Buick moved slowly up a long, winding drive toward a large stone structure. It reminded me of a castle I saw in one of my books, except it didn't welcome. There was an absence of color. Gray skies, gray building, and the great shadowy gray of our spirits. Something was wrong, terribly wrong. Parents don't bring their children to an orphanage while their house is being built. Do they?

Dad was wearing slacks and a shirt and his favorite loafers. Mom, a belted dress. We could have been headed off to visit family, but instead, we were entering a cavern of damp stone and marble. A razor of dread cut through the space.

"Where do we go now?" Mom asked. She stood stone-still like the numerous statues peering down on us.

Before we saw her, the echo of her shoes on the marble floor announced her arrival. Dressed all in black except for a white biblike article of clothes across her chest. It also embraced her neck to climb over her head, atop of which rested a black drape-like material. She was much older than the previous woman we saw earlier. Her smile was fabricated, lacking depth or sincerity.

My dad shook her hand. "Mr. Knight, I presume."

"Yes, this is my wife, Margaret." The women shook hands. Mother was stoic, like her counterpart.

Chris and I stood there. No acknowledgment by the nun. "I am Sister Mary Margaret," she said as we were led into another dark, damp room with windows and crisscrossed panes in the far corner. Chris's eyes were huge, and she placed her hand in mine—only to wet her pants.

"I'll take care of her." Mom grabbed Chris's small hand. But Chris held fast to my hand, her eyes pleading with me to come.

"Let your sister go." Mom directed the command at me. I complied, but Chris held fast. Mom loosened her fingers. "Can you tell me where—"

"There is a bathroom down the hall to the left. Oh, don't forget her suitcase so she can be changed." Her tone was curt, her face void of any compassion or warmth. "Does she still wet her pants?" she asked.

"No, I don't know what happened. I guess we were in the car too long without a bathroom break." Dad laughed. "And I guess the sodas didn't help."

Sister Mary Margaret looked down at me. Her eyes ran up and down my body. She appeared to be fixated on my hair.

"Please, be seated." Dad and I folded into large, ornate, dark wooded chairs. Sister began to talk with Dad. I began to drift off. All I could think about was home. I wanted to go home where furniture was soft. Flowered wallpaper adorned my room, toys were perched on shelves or in the orange toy box. This place felt like death. No matter how bad life was, it was better than this place.

Mom and Chris reentered the room. My heart hurt seeing Chris's red-rimmed eyes. She broke away from Mom to run to me. She climbed onto my lap, headed down, her trembling body screaming with fear. After a while, the nun rose. "I guess that's it. You have seen where the girls will be staying, and we have their beds all set up. Feel free to visit whenever you desire, but please, just call first. I am certain you wouldn't want to pull your oldest out of class, or younger girl from some fun activity."

My parents stood.

"I will give you a few minutes with the girls while I let everyone know they have arrived." She left without so much as a simple acknowledgment of two young girls whose world just folded in on them like a Venus flytrap.

I turned to them both. "Mommy, Daddy, please, I want to go home"—pause—"now."

Our parents shifted positions, glancing at each other and then looked down at me. "Dollie, you are going to have to keep an eye on your sister. You are the big girl," Dad said, his voice soft.

Mom squatted down. She was now eye level with Chris. Her gaze went from my sister to me and back again. "Your sister will take care of you until we come get you. Dollie, watch over her. You are the oldest."

We said our goodbyes. Their promise to come back soon settled into my heart and stayed there for the eight-month duration. Eight months to a child is an eternity.

The nun reentered the room. "Everything is ready for your girls. It is almost dinnertime, so perhaps you should leave now."

Quick kisses on our cheeks, and off they went.

A dark-skinned man entered the room. "Jose, take their suitcases up to the dorms. This one"—she pointed at mine—"goes into the older girl's dorm. The other one into the younger girls."

We passed a large bathroom with a bank of sinks and toilets that smelled of antiseptic. The nun immediately separated Chris and me. As we were ushered down the hall, at the far end, another nun waited at the door. "You will be in here," she said to me, pointing to a large room with row upon row of plain metal beds. Bedspreads were off-white, worn, and stained. "You can wait in here. I will be right back. I need to deliver you sister to Sister Catherine."

Chris started to cry, and my lower lip quivered. "We'll have none of that, young lady." Chris's hand was pulled from mine. Just like that, she was gone. I stood there, looking around. Not unlike the bathroom, the room was void of any real color. White cabinets lined one wall, the other a row of windows, the back was bare except for a lone table and chair. A door, on the far side of the room, opened. Another black-clad woman entered.

"Margaret, I am Sister Elizabeth, and you will be sleeping here." She pointed to a bed in the middle of the second row. "Follow me." I obliged. Standing in front of a white cabinet now, she continued, "This is where you will keep your things. We told your parents that you will be wearing clothes supplied by the orphanage. Of course, you can keep your underwear and nightgowns. Now, unpack."

I sensed this woman was as unhappy for me as I was. Her fingers ran through my hair as she passed, a trace of concern, perhaps. I felt the space consume me in its expanse and unfamiliarity. Cold, stark, and unwelcoming. There would be no hugs from Grandma here, no cookies, no friends—just the unfamiliar sounds of an ancient crying building.

"Sister, where is Chris? I always take care of her. She needs me." In that moment, I needed her as well. "I want to go home. Please call my daddy and tell him."

"You will be fine—now settle down. You don't want to get in trouble your first day, do you?"

"Please, I want to go home." My voice echoed in the space, but my cries evaporated into the cavernous room like smoke in the wind.

I was alone.

3

"Line up, children," a nun called.

My life became a series of snapshots. Chris and I living separate lives—one photograph. Our brother Bobby removed from the equation, slipping from my memory—a faded photograph. My parents gone from us—an overexposed shot.

We were out in the play yard. That was the time of day I searched for my sister. On a rare occasion, I would see her off in the distance. Her beautiful curly red hair gleaming in the sun like copper. But there were rules. We needed to stay in our groups. When she saw me, instinctively she would start to run. So I began to hide from her sight to protect her from punishment. But I would check for her as often as possible.

Children gathered around, fighting for position. I wondered what was happening. The girls were squealing with anticipation. So, like any seven-year-old, I jumped into line. All I could see from my vantage point was a nun seated in a chair upfront. Another sister beside her carried a large bag. None of the girls spoke to me, but I had become accustomed to this behavior. I jumped when my shoulder felt a squeezing sensation.

"You need to step out of the line." Sister Mary Margaret looked down on me.

"Why, what did I do?"

She pulled on my arm, tight enough for me to feel uncomfortable. I obliged.

"This line is for girls getting their hair cut. Your parents made it very clear we were not to cut your hair." She flipped my hair.

All the girls had the same haircut. All short, lacking any style. Some of the girls looked like boys.

I moved so I could get a better look. A pretty little girl with hair the color of coal sat in the chair. Her thin legs waved back and forth. Her smile revealed missing front teeth. The scissors moved rapidly, and before long, she was finished. Standing up, she turned to her left. She was handed a small bag of jelly beans.

"Thank you, sister." She ran off giggling. Without hesitation, the next child jumped into the chair.

I watched as the girls had their hair cut in a bob, a mirror image of the girl in front of the line. Little clones. One by one, each child received jelly beans after their trim. My mouth watered. I loved jelly beans. I ran off to sit beneath a tree, alone. The grass was sparse, but it was a great spot to catch a glimpse of Chris without her spotting me. Like me, she was alone, her back against the building. So, caught up watching Chris, thinking about the day we would leave this place, I never heard them approach.

"Here you go," a nameless woman dressed in black said as she dropped the delicious treats on the dirt. She was surrounded by a dozen or more girls. The colorful candy rolled across the ground, landing near my foot.

Children gathered around me, laughing as I crawled in the dirt for the sweet treats in the soil.

"Kinky hair, kinky hair," one girl called. Soon, I was surrounded by children taunting me. The nun only watched, never stopping the children. I thought, why would a woman, married to God, take delight in my suffering?

Day after day, there was isolation, the result of hatred from the other girls. Missing my sister was the worse, though. I worried about how she was doing all the time. I was supposed to take care of her, after all. I assume the seeds of my abandonment issues were planted in solid soil in that place. All the children knew that someday I would be leaving their future uncertain. Jealousy drove them to ignore or tease me. If I only knew then what my life would be like, I might have opted to stay.

"Ouch!" I rubbed my head and looked up to see four older girls surrounding me.

"I want some of that hair!" One of them tugged me from behind. "She has *special* hair!"

"Stop!" I cried.

One of the older girls, perhaps twelve, approached with her hands behind her back. "I think I want some of that hair." From behind her back, she pulled out a pair of clippers. "Hold her down." Laughter continued, louder now. Hands held me down as she approached, snapping the clippers open and closed. Unexpectedly, the scissors fell silent. My abuser ran up the lawn followed closely by her clique. In the distance, I watched as her hassock swooshed briskly walking in my direction. Sister Anna, another kindly woman, approached.

"Margaret,"—I was not called Dollie in this place—"what's going on down here?" There was genuine concern in her question. Sister Anna was sweet, gentle, with a pretty face, although her skin was so pale, she looked sick.

Head bowed, I spoke to the ground, shifting from one foot to the other. "Nothing."

She approached me, took my hand, and with the other hand, tilted my chin upward. "Margaret, are you sure those girls weren't hurting you? Tell me the truth. God is listening, so don't lie."

Even though I knew she was kind, I also knew the kids would step up the attacks if I told.

"No, sister, we were just playing." I knew she knew I was lying, but she said nothing. Her lips formed a smile as she turned and ambled away up the lawn. The torment continued with threats to cut off my hair or to crown me with the same thorns that were forced into Jesus's head as he hung on the cross.

"This whole place is surrounded by the bushes with lots and lots of thorns." The freckled-face girl taunted me. "All we need to do is go and cut a few branches and make a crown to sit on your curly long hair."

It was on a cool spring day, and I summoned the courage to see for myself if these bushes existed. I approached the hedge, as if it would come alive and grab me. Directly in front of the ominous bush, I stared at the thorns. I felt sad thinking about how much that would hurt to have them in my head. I started to cry, all by myself, as far from the building as I could get.

I hated time spent inside in the gymnasium. I felt trapped, exposed, and vulnerable. On one day, the rain forced us down into this damp space used for volleyball, running, and just being kids. This space stood apart the older structure, obviously built just for the purpose of providing a place for us to go when the weather was bad. Off to the side, a set of dirty, uneven, dark, concrete stairs led downward to a room where the janitors kept their pails and cleaning items. There was also a bathroom hidden from any visiting parents. Dim lighting, stench of urine, mold, and mildew permeated the air. But it was the sight of a rat that struck terror in my being. I avoided this space as much as possible.

Sometimes, my vows were all in vain. Being a small child, my bladder was tiny too, so I made my way to the bathroom. A major storm was forming outside, and I was alone in the dimly lit restroom. I was in the stall closest to the door, listening for the sounds of unwanted vermin. A fly buzzed near the drain in the floor. What I heard next was someone enter the room. I listened to footsteps slowly walk toward the stalls and stop outside mine as I was about to leave. The door opened just as I leaned forward to push open the stall door. Directly in front of me stood an older girl with shockingly frizzy red hair. I recognized her from past encounters. For a moment, she stood there in front of me. Her gaze fixed, her mouth set, her fingers twitched on her thighs. I thought she was going to beat me up. I wish she had.

"Get back in there." Her voice was low and authoritative. My mouth was dry as I opened it to protest. "Now!" she said as she pushed me back. I fell onto the toilet seat.

"Please don't hit me!"

She laughed at my pleading. She entered and closed the door. There was to be no physical assault this day. Instead, she directed everything that came next. I was threatened to do as she told me. So frightened, I complied. She removed her panties and directed me what to do. Then she touched me. It wasn't until years later that I realized I was sexually assaulted.

"You better not tell anyone, or you will be sorry." Her hand formed a fist, eyes narrowed as she turned and left me alone. Alone and crying. I had fallen into a hole where nothing made sense. Who could I tell? Maybe Sister Alma, but what I did was bad—too bad to tell her or anyone. Ever.

I placed the event deep in a vault in my memory bank where it remained dormant. It lingered there until many years later when I saw a girl, a new girl, at my school who looked like my attacker. On that day, I told my mother everything. I believe from the look in her eyes, she was sorry it happened, but nothing was said or done to comfort me.

"Sister Alma, when are Mommy and Daddy coming to take us home?" My persistent questions were wearing her down. She would usually disappear when I asked the question. It was as if she had a secret.

She squatted down, took my hands in hers, lips turned upward as she said, "Honey, soon. I promise you. I will come and tell you the minute I know. Okay?" Her essence was what held me together, offering a promise of something better. She showed me there were people who were gentle, loving, kind, and God-fearing. She was my light in the darkness.

On the infrequent family visits, usually post our childish pleadings, our parents repeated the same chant as Sister Alma. "Girls, it won't be much longer. The house is almost finished." They promised us. I observed that they too wore the same look as Sister Alma. I wondered if we would ever go home.

"When we come to get you, the house will be all finished. Maybe we'll get a pool—how does that sound?" Dad promised his terrified daughters who were currently living in hell. After they left, especially late at night, in bed, I would try to picture the house. We had been in this place for over six months.

At night, the nuns forced us to sleep under the covers. I couldn't breathe. If any girl were caught with her head out, we would feel the wrath, a paddle. That instrument of pain was evident to all as it hung prominently on a hook on the wall, a constant reminder of the cruelty of some of these women. The nuns slept in a room off the main room. I could hear them talking and whispering at night. They were especially noisy on their nightly rounds.

Clink, clink, clink. The sound of their rings as they hit the metal bed, a reminder: they were on patrol.

"Margaret, get your head under that cover. Now!" *Whack.*

I tried so hard to obey, but I just couldn't breathe under those heavy blankets. As soon as they passed, I lifted the cover just enough to get air.

One night, deep into the night when all was still, the sound of screaming awakened all of us. The rooms and hallway were suddenly illuminated. All about the room, girls began to cry. Nuns appeared from everywhere.

"Be quiet now," the nun in our room warned us. Our dorm had two women who slept in their bedroom, a room none of us ever viewed. "Get back into your beds—there is nothing to get excited about. If you don't, I promise you I will give you something to cry about."

The screaming got closer and closer. The sounds of pure terror emanated from a little girl, as if she had seen the bowels of hell. Suddenly, at the door of my dorm, I saw my baby sister in her little nightgown and bare feet crying out, "Dollie! Dollie! Where are you?"

Spotting me, she attempted to run to me. I rose to go to her, but a nun grabbed her, taking her away still crying, calling my name. Her voice faded as the lady in black took her away.

My arm was yanked hard to keep me in place. "She is just having a nightmare. She will be fine—now get back to bed."

"But she needs me. Please."

A thin finger pointed to my bed. Quietly, I retreated. That night, I kept my head under the blankets to mute the sounds of my crying.

I learned many years later about the nightmare Chris had had that night, and all she wanted—needed—was her big sister.

We were two little girls lost in a world where they didn't belong.

Years passed, but like a moth circling a light, I couldn't let go of the *why?* It was Mom whom I first approached. I remember the day. Mom was calm, puttering around the house with an aura of calm. Despite her countenance, my experience knew that her moods changed as rapidly as notes in a song.

"Mom, can I ask you a question?" my words spoke in a whisper. I sat in a chair across the room. On this day, a day like any other, my mother remained calm with soft upturned lips.

Seating herself, her speech measured, she began, "Dollie, your father has some severe mental health issues, and, of course, he has that terrible temper. That is what led him to be put away. I wanted to keep you girls and Bobby safe, but I really feared for my life. It was not a good time for you kids to be here." Smiling, I thanked her, rose, and left. It didn't make sense to me.

Sometime later, I ventured into dangerous territory when I asked Dad the same question. I couldn't have been more surprised when he answered with a smile and wink. "Honey, I think you know that your mother is crazy. She needed to get some help, and it was not a time for you kids to be home. That was it. Subject changed. Neither parent ever said to us they were sorry for what they put us through, but it was not expected. They each blamed the other. So what was the truth?

More questions without answers that made sense. I knew there were unspoken truths, puzzle pieces left out of the puzzle that was our life. Life for us would be like a thousand-piece jigsaw puzzle lacking too many pieces to see the real picture.

4

Sister Alma, hands folded in front of her, stood juxtaposed the rear door leading into the gym. Like a cat on the prowl, she stretched her head for a better look. *What was she looking for?* I wondered. I was seated under what had become my tree, a sanctuary from torture. Spotting me, even from this distance, I could see her smile. Her index finger beckoned me to come.

My heart quickened as I hurried to join her. "Margaret, come with me." Together we walked across the grass toward a spot unoccupied of children. Squatting in front of me, her hands took mine in hers. "Your mom and dad are here. Honey, you are going home."

"Really? Now? Are you sure? Where are they? Where's Chris?" I fired questions at her like fireworks propelled high into the night sky.

"Come with me. Your sister is already with them." She kept my hand in hers. "Why are you crying? You should be happy."

I was in shock, the shock of a little girl who had lost hope.

We walked down the hallway last seen eight months earlier, except at that time, we were heading in the opposite direction. "I *am* happy." My tears faded, and from somewhere deep within me, a rising giggle tickled me, rose and bubbled out.

The nun stopped midway in the hall. Squatting down, she looked in my eyes. She was intent as she said, "Margaret, don't carry any tales, okay? Promise me?"

Not knowing what she was talking about, I agreed not to carry any.

"That's my good girl." She rose and patted my head.

Reaching the end of the hallway, we reentered that dark, ornate, damp room. Unlike the first time in this space, I noticed nothing except our parents and Bobby. Mom and Dad were seated in the same overelaborate chairs where they sat many, many months ago. Standing beside them was my baby brother. He looked so different now. Time had honed his language skills.

"I want to go back to see Sister Anne," he said clearly, affirmatively. "She misses me."

He was taller now, almost four. He was so cute with that fiery red hair, and nose dotted with freckles. He was not excited to see me—in fact, his eyes were filled with fluid. His gaze shifted from me to Chris and back again. Chris and I hugged, giggling uncontrollably. Bobby began whimpering. I learned later he loved where he spent the past eight months. In fact, he had a bit of a crying episode as our parents took him from the arms of a very loving nun. He went to heaven, and we landed in hell.

Time appeared to have altered our parents as well. Not much, but there were differences. Mom's hair was longer and styled differently. Dad's dark hair hosted tufts of white at the temples. In this moment, they both projected a sense of calm. Had something been altered?

Dad rose and walked around the table. "How are my little girls?" he asked, taking a long look at us. "I sure missed my princesses." He leaned in and hugged us close.

Mom smiled but stayed seated. "I bet you two can't wait to go home—to our new home." Mom's smile was never one that came from deep within, more of a "say cheese" smile-surface without depth. This time, there was an authenticity. It felt like we were family. I felt safe.

There were papers to sign, and then the little estranged family walked out together. Down the cobblestone path that led to the top of the long driveway. There she sat, our big, black, shiny Buick. We were going home. Chris and I hopped in the back seat. Our parents and Bobby were in the front. Dad started the engine. I popped up and turned to look out the rearview window. The foreboding building and surroundings grew smaller and smaller as Dad drove down the winding drive. *I will never go back there*, I thought. A promise I broke several decades later. Chris and I grasped each other's hands tight as the memories began to fade. My pretty redheaded sister and I bonding in our little private world. Our little bodies were electrified with anticipation as we jiggled restlessly in the seat. We peppered our parents with questions. Bobby slept in the front, exhausted from crying.

"Are we almost there yet?" I asked.

"Can I sleep with Dollie?" Chris demanded as she cuddled closer to me. "How big is the house? Do we have a yard? What color is it?"

Turning around, Mom smiled, "Be patient—we'll be there soon enough." She turned back and looked out the side window. "Looks like rain. It's getting really dark."

"Yeah, I think you're right," Dad answered, turning on the directional signal. The big shiny Buick pulled out onto a major highway.

Leaning forward, I rested my chin on the back of Dad's seat. Night was falling. Lights from passing cars were hypnotizing. Peace at last. We were going home. Home. What would that be like?

"Just a little longer, girls."

"Daddy, when we left, Sister Alma told me not to carry any tails. What does that mean?"

Dad gave a sideway glance at Mom.

"What tails? I don't have any tails," I continued, the image of wiggling tails in my head. I started to giggle.

"Sit back, honey. I don't know what she meant. Maybe she was just teasing you," Dad answered. The drive was long; we were tired, and night had fallen. Bobby was soundly sleeping on Mom's lap after whimpering that he missed Sister Elizabeth. At a time when no seat belts were required, kids sat on laps, stood up on the seats, and even slept in the back window.

"Girls, time to wake up. We're here," Mom said. Bobby rubbed his eyes at the sound of her voice.

We stumbled awake. Chris and I pulled ourselves up to take a look. "This is our new house? Chris, it's red."

Our new home was in a subdivision, the type that was so popular in the early '50s. There was Ellen Estates, Marvin Estates, and so forth. Sounds impressive, living in an estate. Unlike a true estate, Ellen Estates consisted of a hundred homes, identical in size and style. Our house had eaves though, which was a little different. This was the deluxe model. I loved that our house was red. A few other houses had dormers. Ours was one of three on the block with the little protrusion in the roofline where windows looked out on the neighborhood. Middle class at its finest.

We were frozen, our mouths hung open but muted as we entered an upstairs bedroom. The space was large with little nooks derived from the slanted ceilings. One side of the room, a double bed with a pink chenille spread. The other space, a smaller cube held a desk, bookcase, an antique radio, and two dressers. But the best part was the wallpaper with tiny pink roses, buds, and vines.

Chris crawled up the bed, jumping up and down. My baby sister was possessed by some inner joy monster. The little girl whose voice was silenced one dark night in that dreadful, dreary place had found her voice.

In our eyes, our new bedroom was even more beautiful in the morning. Natural light from the windows flooded the room. Outside the rear window grew a tree adorned with tiny lacy leaves that reminded me of palm trees.

"Dollie!" Chris exclaimed, rolling over in our comfy bed.

My body turned to one side. We were face-to-face. "Good morning." Our grins reflected our joy. The nightmare was over.

Both of us tumbled out of bed, barefooted and headed out into the hall. The door on the right led to our brother's room. Bobby's room was perfect for a little boy. Sailboats on a sea of blue sailed around the space. His bed was empty.

"Let's go," Chris ordered in new commanding voice. I smiled.

"Who made you boss?" My voice was almost musical as I teased my sister.

Bobby was at the kitchen table with Mom and Dad. We joined them for a breakfast of French toast, juice, milk, and sausage.

Our parents' room was downstairs. There was a modest living room, dining room, kitchen, and the only bath in the house.

We settled into our new life. Dad went to work. Mom created beautiful ceramics that cooked in her kiln in the basement. We played. Out back, a big yard awaited three high-energy children. And a cellar where I hung rope from one pole to the other and tried tightrope walking. Once a week, the basement doubled as a theater for the Knight sisters. We had numerous performances for neighbors.

"Sisters, Sisters, there was never such devoted sisters. Many men have tried to break us up but no one can. Lord help the mister who comes between me and my sister, and Lord help the sister who comes between me and my man." The Knight sisters sang in unison.

At this point in our performance, we raised fists at each other with the final line. We donned real high silk hats that we snapped open. That was our featured performance.

Late afternoon in early fall, Chris and I headed out to play in the woods behind the house. Just a row of wooded vacant lots, but to us, a mystical forest. We even had a secret cave. Deep in our "underground chamber," we perched on wooden crates. Our hole in the ground was fully equipped. Not only did we have cups and saucers made of plastic for our "meals," but we had candles and a flashlight for illumination. There was a large cardboard box that served multiple purposes. At times, a perch we put our supplies inside, or we covered it with a tablecloth—an old towel—that served as our dining room table. We even had a milk bottle that we placed flowers in. On the wall, our art hung. Pictures of flowers, animals, houses, and children playing. An old rickety stool was used to stand on to ensure the enemy was not approaching. I could conjure up all sorts of monsters for us to pretend to fight off.

"Dollie, give me a cookie," Chris demanded. I moved the carton, turned upside down, served as storage for our treats as well. Handing her one of Mom's delicious chocolate chip cookies, I took one for myself. Mom baked the absolute best chocolate chip cookies. As we chomped on the crumbly delight, we both heard the sound of falling leaves being crushed. Someone was approaching. My finger raised to my lips to silence my sister. "Shush, someone is coming," I whispered beneath the roof of the earthen cave.

"I am really scared," Chris whispered.

"Please, be quiet," I whispered as I stood up to peek out of the slit in the wood. I retreated rapidly back in the safety of the cavern.

Chris smashed her little body into the corner. "What did you see?"

"Shush, they're going to hear you. I didn't see anything." Once again, I hoisted myself up. Ever so slowly, I rose toward the sliver in the wood.

Sounds of passing footsteps circumvented our hiding place. "Agh, damn her, what the…" His words were swollen with alcohol. We heard him amble around the space where we lay quiet. There was a soft thud that I suspect was someone stumbling and falling in the leaves. Our little game had taken a turn—something ominous was happening. A groan, followed by a cough, a cigarette smoker's cough was expelled. He moaned, cursed, and moved about, possibly attempting to stand. Soon the sounds began to fade, and once again, there was silence outside. It was clear, whoever this was, had left.

"Dollie, no wonder Mom doesn't like us playing in the woods alone," my sister whispered.

Chris and I remained silent for a long time. Listening for any signs the stranger had returned. Without warning, the wooden roof flew off, followed by the most horrific scream that emanated from the creature. The green face had red eyes and black teeth. The monster was very short—too short. It was our stupid brother Bobby in a mask. Chris screamed, and Bobby broke into laughter. When she started to cry, he felt badly. "Come on, Chris. I am sorry. He won't do it again, I promise," he pleaded, holding her by her shoulders to consider her face.

Those wooded lots gave all of us so much joy. Using our creativity, we traveled to faraway places. The unwelcome visitor never returned. For a while, most of life was good. Mom didn't seem angry at me any longer—at least not as much as when we lived with Grandma. Chris and I were in school now. And Bobby was happy and content except for the occasional temper tantrums.

My father's tickling intensified, especially when Mother was not around. As I aged, I really didn't like it. My pleas to stop only intensified his fingers from poking me all over. I was his only target, not like at my grandma's house where he focused on other little girls.

On my tenth birthday, I was tucked up in my room, listening to our Philco floor model radio. I smiled, wondering what country would be talking to me tonight. Moving the knob, my little hand danced back and forth over numbers that signified stations. I held steady over 110.6, allowing the crisp British announcer to deliver the weather forecast. There would be rain in London tomorrow. I began to travel mentally to England, picturing the ancient buildings, cobblestoned streets, the Queen. A man's voice from below shattered my dream state. The radio was silenced. I proceeded to leave my room to investigate. My steps were slow and deliberate as I inched down the stairs. It was Dad.

"I am not dealing with her." He was screaming at my mother. I assumed the "her" was my grandmother, mother's mom. There was no love lost between these two. Dad crossed the room to where mother was standing. Even from where I now stood, I could see his neck muscles jumping. Knowing Dad like I did, this was the precursor to an explosion. "Your mother is not going to step one foot in this house. Do you understand me?" His hands balled up. "I don't care if it is Dollie's birthday. Your mother is nothing but trouble, a busybody with too much to say."

"Bob, she is already on her way—there's nothing I can do." Mom screamed. She turned and walked down the hall. But Dad followed her into their bedroom. Sadly. These fights had been escalating. Once again, I was the catalyst today. I mean, it was my birthday, the reason for my grandma's visit. On a daily basis, I was the target for her anger.

Chris was standing in the living room by the front door. Her thumb deep in her mouth, she sucked hard. Her beautiful brown eyes were enormous. Bobby sat on the couch with his feet pulled up to his chest. No one spoke.

"I'll kill you." Although we couldn't see Dad's face, we knew it would be crimson. Someone turned on the switch. He had lost control. Rage was now the driver of this runaway train. A train that would soon derail, leaving in its wake bruised and crimpled bodies. Perhaps not just physical, but the remnants of this type of war are scars so deep and long-lasting, they remain a lifetime.

A dreadful sound, like a pumpkin being dropped to the floor, came from the bedroom. All yelling stopped. The three of us scrambled to the couch. Waiting. Waiting to be killed, waiting to be beaten, waiting to learn Mother was dead. Waiting…waiting. Minutes passed.

Dad sounded like a little boy when he spoke. "Margaret, I am so sorry. Please, please forgive me," Dad cried out through tears. Our mother was silent. We barely heard the sounds of the door opening or his footsteps through the living room toward the front door. His head hung low. At the door, he paused, turned back, opened the door, and left. He said nothing to us, but the look on his face spoke volumes.

I slid from the sofa. Each step felt as if I were wearing cement boots. This feeling in my chest was not uncommon, but still frightening to a young girl about to learn what lies on the other side of the door.

"Stay there, Bobby, sit down. Please. Turn on the TV." His temper was ignited, as it always was when I had the nerve to order him around. Thankfully, he did as told and plopped down on the floor. Chris just looked up at me, pleading. Pleading for comfort. Pleading for understanding. Pleading with her sister to make it all right.

I felt like I was walking in cement boots as I proceeded toward the bedroom. Grabbing the knob, my chest tightened and my breathing quickened. Beads of sweet formed on my brow. A gnawing like a rat on a piece of bread gripped me. What was it? Guilt? Wasn't I told I was the big sister, but my siblings were in the other room, traumatized in their separate ways? Slowly, I turned the knob and stepped into the darkness of the bedroom. Before me, a room turned upside down. My eye caught sight of a huge hole in the wall on the far side of the bed. The sight terrified me.

"Mom, where are you?" As I rounded the bed, I saw that Mom was on the floor, the bruise already forming. With my assistance, she was able to stand up. Once on the bed, she started crying a soundless cry. I helped her clean up, made supper, made certain Bobby and Chris brushed their teeth before bed. The house was still. Dad was still not home.

I climbed the stairs, falling into bed. For hours, I lay in bed replaying the day. If only I could wash away the memories that ambled across my mind like the ocean tides wash away sand.

Dad was taken to jail that night. He never returned to our home again.

Happy birthday, Dollie.

5

Time passed slowly. My role shifted. Without warning or desire, I began to morph into the role of parent.

I lay in bed, looking out at the trees, thinking to myself about my life and the lives of my siblings. What would become of us?

To make ends meet, Mom needed to go to work. Dad paid the mortgage, insurance, our uniforms, and our private schooling. She worked at Bamberger's in Plainfield. A department store, the type that is a mere memory to most today. Each floor was announced by an elevator man with a uniform and a cap. They even had a gourmet bakery. Mom would gather up unsold bakery items at half price at the end of the day and bring them home.

Sundays, we spent with Dad, a relief from the negativity that felt like a whirlpool pulling us down Monday through Saturday living with Mother. I liked going to church even though the hours preceding service were anything but spiritual. Mom would yell at Dad about money, being late, arriving too early, just about anything. Any fear she had of Dad was fading. In return, Dad shouted back. This is how we prepared ourselves for mass in the Knight family.

Weekdays we attended a public school in our town before transferring to a parochial school in third grade. My self-esteem was diminished—a reflection of the image of what I saw every day in my mom's eyes. Wearing glasses, thick glasses, since I was a young child did not add favor to the image I held of my physicality. Praise was nonexistent at home, no matter how hard I tried. During that period, coming from a broken home was the same as being broken. And at night, when the secrets of my life broke into my dreams,

I knew I was different. Not different in a good way, though. The Knight children were different.

It was morning in class when it began.

"What is it, Margaret?" a response to my raised hand.

Attempting to focus on her face, I answered, "Mrs. Painter, I can't see."

I could hear children's whispers, then the room fell silent after Mrs. Painter spoke. "That's enough, children." She walked to my desk and squatted to my level.

My head was down in shame and fear. "Can you see anything? Look at me, honey. Okay?"

"It is like looking through dark water." With that, my hand was taken in hers and led to the front of the classroom.

"Wait here, I will be right back." She had ushered me to the front door of the classroom. You could have heard a pin drop, a rarity with third graders. Little Dollie, who tried to stay out of sight, now stood exposed in front of everyone. Spotting an eighth grader in the hall, she said, "Go to my classroom and stay with the children until I get back. Maybe you could read them a story."

"What, why?" the kid asked.

"Because I said so. Go!"

We went our separate way.

Gently she ushered me into the glaringly white room, the nurses' office, with an offensive odor that reminded me of a dental office. Although I saw nothing, I just knew there was a nonverbal exchange between the women. I recalled from previous visits she wore a stiff white uniform and a cap that looked like an upside Styrofoam cup with a black stripe. "Let me take a look, is that okay? What is your name, honey?"

She was as gentle as an angel guiding me to the table. In a whisper, I responded, "My name is Margaret." Her actions allowed me to feel safe. Feeling safe was even more important than seeing I felt in that moment.

A light was moved in front of my eyes, then held steady. "Honey, I don't see anything. Did you hit your head recently?" I nodded my response. "Well, I think you'll need to see your eye doctor." Her cool hand stroked my arm.

I heard this kind woman speaking with my mother on the phone in the next room. Mom arrived some time later, and I was released into her care. At home, she had me sit on the sofa while she made several phone calls. The absence of concern was obvious. Maybe she was just upset about my vision that was creating her terse tone to those on the other end of the phone. Somehow, my vision loss became all about her. She expounded over the phone about how difficult getting me to the doctors would be.

"I have so many problems, I really don't want to deal with this now. There are bills to pay." She moaned. The impact on her. The cost to her. The strain on her. Additional tearful calls to family and friends dripping with self-pity. Not an utterance of concern for me or the possibility of the impact of blindness would mean to my life. This was the foundation for the formation of isolation and aloneness.

After a trip to the eye doctor, hospitalization, and testing, I was released home. The discharge diagnosis, I learned later, was hysterical blindness—a condition that causes you to show psychological stress in a physical manner. Sometimes we see something that is so disturbing, our body attempts to block the image.

What caused the condition? Another missing piece of the puzzle that was my life. I have flashes of memory about Dad and me, but nothing concrete.

*****

Soon, all of us were enrolled in the new Catholic school in our hometown. Each of us had a very different experience. I excelled academically over the years. Everything came easy for me. Frequently, I wore the merit pin or the religious pin. High honor indeed.

Chris, who followed, did not fare as well. In one of her classes, she had the same teacher I did. A lay teacher with long shiny nails juxtaposed to her gloomily dressed counterparts.

The first day of class, the teacher made an announcement. "I will call your name and when I do, take the next empty seat." She rattled off a few names, then she announced Chris's name, who took a seat in the fourth row.

"Dollie, Ms. Angello had me sit at your old desk." She was so excited to tell her big sister, who responded in typical loving fashion with a shrug.

Bobby hated school and acted out right from the beginning. He too was very bright, but he didn't fare well with authority. Not even when that authority was a nun. "I hate that nun. She told me to sit down and be quiet. All I was doing was getting something out of my jacket. She made me stay in at lunch. I hate her."

"Don't say *hate*," I chastised. "School just started—give her a chance." Mom was at work so I was in charge.

I was in the kitchen when Chris walked into the room a few days later. Bobby had retreated to the solitude of his room. She climbed up on a chair, allowing her chubby legs to dangle beneath her uniform.

"Where were you?" I asked.

"Dollie, Ms. Angello moved my seat to the very back." Her voice quivered as she spoke, so I instinctively took a seat at the table.

"Why?"

Her sobs tore my heart. "In front of the whole class, she said only smart kids sit in the front. The only reason she put me in the front is because she thought I was smart like you. She said she was wrong and pointed for me to move. All the kids laughed at me."

Anger, protection, and embarrassment engulfed me. Her words triggered feelings I held for this teacher even when I was in her class. There was something superficial, unauthentic about her.

"She is wrong about you, Chris. I never liked her. You are not the first person she has embarrassed."

She stood up to get something from the refrigerator before answering. Her slumped shoulders and bowed head screamed of surrender. She was raising the white flag of defeat at eight years of age.

"Sit down." She complied and took a bite of wet cookie that had been dipped in milk. I was witnessing the birth of an eating disorder. "Did I ever tell you what she said to me?"

She shook her head.

I continued: "In front of the entire class, she said I was different because I came from a broken home. She proceeded to explain *broken home* and the numerous causes. All eyes in class were pinned on me, mouths open. It was if they were seeing me for the first time. I was broken."

Beautiful brown eyes were hypnotized with my story. "Really, she said that to you?"

"Uh-huh."

A huge smile formed. "Yeah, she is a jerk." Sisters united against the wicked third-grade teacher.

Stamped forever in her soul those words "You certainly are not as smart as your sister." On that day, so long ago, my little sister gave up on school. She stopped trying and spent classroom time staring out the window in class drifting away to places where she could be free, feel safe, and not be ridiculed.

A few days later, the loudspeaker above the classroom door crackled; a woman's voice announced, "Margaret Knight, please report to the principal's office." Children shifted in their chairs to glance in my direction. Trips to the principal's office was a common event for this eldest of the Knight tribe.

Sister Lucy nodded. "You can go."

I rose, left the sixty-student classroom, and headed toward the all-too-familiar principal's office. I loved Sister Mary. She had a silent wisdom. I knew she knew about the life of the Knight children.

She stood up as I entered, an unusual act for a nun, but a sign of respect. "Sit down, Margaret." I sat down across from her. The room had warm wood tones on the wall, bookcases, wooden files, a statue of Saint Mary, paintings of saints on the wall, and several leather chairs with studs around the arms. "Sister Lucy says your grades are excellent, as usual. How is everything else?"

"Fine." I offered her a warm smile. I knew she saw through my gesture.

"Sorry to pull you out of class, but your brother was late again. He didn't get to school until after eleven. Do you know what happened to him?"

I told her I didn't know.

Standing up, a lazy smile formed. "Margaret, thank you. I am sorry to pull you out of class. Keep up the splendid work." Her hand cupped my crown lovingly.

"Thank you, Sister." I left the office with regret. Regret that I couldn't stay longer with this dear woman. This loving lady whom I wished I could stay and tell her the truth about our home, but well, that was not possible. In retrospect, I am certain she was acutely aware of our home life.

Mom's accessibility was limited. Not because of work but because her mental illness was taking a front seat. My role as a mother figure escalated on a more mature level. A role I liked. I became the repairer of problems, the glue that held our lives together. I carried this characteristic into adulthood.

It was late spring afternoon. A cloud of watery droplets suspended in the air, hovering over the earth, before resting. The mist made it impossible to go out, so we were all stuck inside. We heard the sound of the door open to the stairwell. In future days and months, a sound we would come to fear.

"Girls, come down here." Mother's tone was flat, expressionless.

Bobby's room had been changed after Dad left. The room that was to be the dining room was now where he resided. We referred to it as the back room.

"Have a seat, girls. I have something to tell you. I already spoke with your brother." She began in that same flat tone. No emotion. "Your dad is coming later. Bobby is going to stay with him at Grandma's."

Chris cried out, "Why?"

"You can't send him away," I added.

"Sister Alma called me last week. She told me all about your brother, about all the trouble he's been in." A brief pause before she continued. "I don't know why you didn't tell me?" She looked squarely in my direction. Her dislike for me was growing almost as much as my guilt.

On my feet now, it took just a few steps before I was standing directly in front of her. "I don't understand. How can you just send him to live with Dad? You know he has a temper and is capable of physical harm when he gets upset. Mothers don't act this. It's wrong." Like our father, Mother housed a contained rage. Was this the moment it would be released? I knew I was pushing her, but the injustice of the moment blinded me. I stepped back, and she stepped forward.

"You don't tell me what to do or what not to do. Who do you think you are? You don't belong in this family." She focused on Chris and yelled, "Your sister is the Thing. That is what she is—a thing." She erupted, spewing poisonous venom over me so close, spittle ejected onto my face.

Chris began crying, and Bobby remained in his room.

"You're spitting on me," I yelled dramatically, wiping my face with the back of my hand. "Come on, Chris, let's go back upstairs. Bobby, you want to come up?" Silence loomed aloud from behind his closed door.

Chris and I ascended the stairs. She was still whimpering, and I was still angry and scared. In this family, children were disposable. A brief time later, I heard Dad's car in the driveway.

Walking to the window, I remarked, "I bet that is Dad." Chris joined me. Together we watched him walk toward the house. Minutes later, we heard muffled voices rise and ebb. The next sound we heard was the front door opening. We watched our brother as he walked to the car with Dad. Before he got in, he looked up at the window where his sisters stood. His eyes shifted downward. And that was that. Bobby was gone.

Later that night, Mother called us for dinner. She had cooked a nice meal, was pleasant, and even kidded a bit. Of course, she was pleased; after all, a problem was removed from her plate. "Dollie, Sister Alma told me what a nice young girl you were. She likes you very much." I suspect the comment was a blend of honest pride—and jealousy. Even though I knew the root of her comment, it felt more comfortable than her earlier outburst that ended my being called the Thing.

She was in a fairly good mood the remainder of that night, even asking us if we wanted to make Jiffy Pop. We loved to shake that metal tray with the aluminum canopy. Soon, the sounds of popping corn could be heard, and the canopy would expand into a giant metal orb of the yummy treat. "Bring the popcorn in here, girls. Let's watch TV together." I thought she was going to burst into song; she was so relaxed. Tonight, she was Donna Reed instead of Joan Crawford.

Chris and I became witness to Mom's decline into madness. In retrospect, we both thought our brother was the lucky one. Dad ignored any problems created by his son. Bobby became the favorite, even with my beloved grandma. I was cast from my throne by my absence. Grandma prepared his favorite meals, cleaned his clothes, heaped praise upon him, and I am certain, was his protector from Dad if needed.

We were not so lucky. Mom's depression led to sleepless nights, erratic behavior, obsessive thoughts, paranoia, and dark moods. Despite having our own rooms now, Chris and I would often still sleep together. Security in numbers against what often occurred in our house. This was our private time to laugh, tell stories, or torture the other. There was the time I hit her in the face with a huge Powerpuff like Milton Berl did; unfortunately, that resulted in a trip to the emergency room.

"I am so sorry, I was just kidding." My words spoken with deep remorse.

"Why would you do such a thing to you sister?" No amount of rebuttal on my behalf was effective.

Another time, I convinced her to hold five quarters in her mouth. "I don't want to," she moaned. But she did as her big sister suggested and promptly almost choked on them. They showed up a few days later in the toilet.

But what I loved best was to scare her. Stories about clowns with jagged teeth who tied children up in the basement, or the monster under the bed, all told with sound effects were effective. On me. I would become scared resulting in Chris convulsing in laughter. After I calmed, we would share in the ridiculousness.

There was another reason we slept together even as we grew. Protection. Support. Comfort. United defense. We had a soul connection that was spiritual, lasting, and unbreakable that transcends understanding. We were as different as clouds and sunshine; nonetheless, connected where it mattered. In our hearts.

I was twelve or thirteen when I arrived home from school to discover Mother perched on a stepladder. Still in bedclothes, hair disheveled, and a cup of instant coffee resting on the counter within reach, she almost toppled over attempting to grab the cup of swill.

"What are you doing?" I asked.

Masking tape in one hand, cup of swill in the other. She slurped on her drink, swallowed hard. "What's it look like I am doing?"

"I have no idea. Really. We are out of milk." Placing the empty glass on the table, I asked again. She remained silent.

Chris entered, signaling me that Mom was acting strange. Folding herself into a chair, she shook her head as she squinted. Interpretation. Stop. Don't ask. Remain quiet. My teenage defiance took hold, stirring my mouth into action. I couldn't help myself as I asked, "Mom, what the heck are you doing? Why won't you tell me?"

"I know you two don't care, but I do. You see these holes in the blinds—I don't want someone peeking in at me. So I am covering them with tape."

"What holes? I don't see any holes."

She pointed to the small miniscule holes between each blind where the cord weaves in and out.

As I rose, my wise sister pulled on my blouse in a last-minute effort to silence me. She failed. Again.

"How could someone see through those holes? The windows are too high up for someone to see in. That is, unless they placed a ladder against the house. How could anyone see through those pinholes?"

Even I knew I had crossed the line with that last comment. I knew the minute that last word left my mouth, I was in trouble. As expected, Chris fled as Mom disembarked from the ladder.

"Crazy? You think I am crazy? Get up there, now." She was so close to me, her spit hit my face. I was pushed toward the stepladder and climbed. "Now, look through the holes." Of course, I could see nothing. There was just enough space for the cord with a little wiggle room. "Do you now see what I mean? I am not going to chance someone looking in on me at night."

I remained silent, stepped from the ladder, and left the room as she continued her rant, spending hours covering the holes with tape.

Mom's paranoia and fear grew as time went on. There were times when we were out and started to talk about anything; she was convinced people were listening and would use what we said against us. To me, the saddest and most bizarre thoughts, beside the tape, was thinking a man who lived down the street on the opposite side was looking in her bedroom window from his house. This feat was impossible. But rationalization had departed, replaced with delusional thinking. What was more insane was trying to hold a rational conversation with her. When I think back, it was so sad for all involved.

Mom's nights were spent awake wandering the house. She would get up to make her decaf instant coffee. Two young women lay in bed as quiet as possible. Listening. The nightly event was too familiar. We waited, praying tonight would be different. On good nights, we would hear Mom going to the kitchen a few times, then head back to bed. It was only then we felt safe enough to fall asleep. But then there were the dark nights. In a drug-induced state, she would rise from bed and stumble down the short hallway to the kitchen. Kitchen cabinets would open, then close. Footsteps indicated her return to bed. Time had passed, and with it the growth of irrational behavior.

"I hope she stays in bed," I whispered.

"Me too." Chris took my hand. Even now, as young women, we held fast to the other.

Sadly, on nights like these, within a few minutes, she would be up again. Her steps, heavy on the wooden floor, like someone marching to war. Often, she would mumble to herself as she entered the kitchen. No longer were the cabinet doors opened and closed. Now the cabinet doors were slammed. Rage was about to escape. This ritual would be repeated several times; with each event, we could feel her building to a crescendo of madness. The pressure cooker was about to blow its lid. On her way back to bed, we heard her stop on the far side of the door.

"She stopped. Oh, God, please make her go to bed," Chris whispered. The light from our alarm clock, resting on the dresser, informed me it was after 1:00 a.m. Children our age should be asleep, and yet, we lay here awake. Waiting. The fact we had school in the morning was of little importance to Mom on nights like these. The poor soul was so lost in her fantasies, any regard for her daughters was lost in a cloud of confusion.

I felt my body stiffen as the all-too-familiar sound of the doorknob jiggled. Then it stopped. This time, the sounds were by the front door. She was probably checking for the tenth time that she locked it. There it was again. This time, the door to the stairwell opened.

"You two get down here, right now," my mother bellowed.

Her nightgown lay limply on her body, all life drained from the fabric. Night and day, she lived in that filthy, coffee-stained garment. To pass her, we needed to press our backs against the wall and through the door. Her impulsivity produced a feral fear, the fight-or-flight phenomenon in me. Would we pass without incident or get slapped, pushed, or, even worse, verbally abused? Physical insults to the body heal—those to the psyche often last a lifetime in the basement of our minds.

She barked an order to me alone. "Get yourself into that bathroom." She had spittle running from the corners of her mouth as she spoke. "Do you call that clean? Get down there and clean that floor."

"I'm tired. We have school in the morning," I protested. Her actions were obscene. I found my courage and continued, "I cleaned the bathroom today before you came home from work. Mom, I don't want to clean it again." Her jaw tightened as she took a step toward me. I backed up into the area, grabbed a cloth and cleanser, and began to clean an already-clean floor.

Mother looked at Chris. "Come on, let's get you to bed. You must be tired."

Chris turned toward me and mouthed, "I'm sorry."

"Chris, you come here. Stay away from that *thing*." Unsteady her steps as she entered her bedroom, Chris in tow. My sister's role was comforter. Mine was a maid. Soon, the crying would commence.

"I saw carpenter ants again," Mother said. "They're destroying the house, and I have no money to do anything about them." She wept.

I released a sigh while scrubbing the tile as I thought, *Here we go again, the dreaded carpenter ants.*

Chris would pat her hand to calm her down. Often, when my work was done and if she was in the mood, I would be allowed to retire. If not, I would be assigned another chore. My sister was not as fortunate. She would be up until Mother fell asleep. Poor Chris, who needed sleep to help her with school, stayed up playing nursemaid to Mother. This was the ritual.

Tonight, it was going to be different: my voice of protection was aroused and would never be silenced again. The step moaned beneath my weight as I began to go to bed.

"Chris, stay with me." mother cried out, halting my sister in her tracks.

Without warning or thought, "She needs her sleep. Mothers don't get their children up at night. It's crazy. You're the mother, not me." I surprised myself as I spoke forceful words at my mother. Words like that were the missiles in the never-ending war between mother and myself. This was when I became a right fighter. A March on Washington, a stand on the South Lawn of the Whitehouse fully ordained right fighter. Another trait carried into adulthood. My compulsion to speak up to right the wrongs of the world did evolve into satisfaction, but the antithesis occurred equally, creating angst and even mistrust and betrayal. Mother thought everything I did was for personal gain.

"Mind your business, she's fine."

"Dollie, I'll be fine. Go to bed and take care of yourself," Chris called out to my back as I opened the door. I could tell she was upset with me for stirring her up—poking a hornet's nest with a stick.

"Go to bed, Thing. Take care of you because that is who you care about. You are so selfish." That was the good night I received from the woman who brought me into this world.

Mom was hooked on prescription drugs. She claimed the need for sleep and the dreaded toothache were the only reasons she took them. I knew this to be a delusion. A visit to friends or family was a shopping trip for Mother to stock up on whatever she found in their medicine cabinet. After a time, work was impossible for her. Demons invaded our poor, ill mother.

I loved her. Hated her. But primarily, I feared her. That fear never left but grew over the years. I was always waiting for the other shoe to drop. The odd thing is Chris never feared her as I did.

Motherhood creates a myriad of feelings. But love is at the center. There is nothing like the joy we receive watching our children grow. Each stage of their lives is celebrated. We scream out as they catch the ball, laugh as they belly-flop into the pool, cry with them when they're hurt or sad. Mom never experienced the joy of motherhood. We were a cross to bear, or a little person to meet her needs, her insatiable needs.

6

I was a young teenager when I heard Mom's footsteps on the stairs, making my heart quicken. A common reaction. Life was calm, but as I learned, it took very little to change her mood.

For some reason, I was in Bobby's old room sitting on the bed. I think I was studying or reading when she entered. Like an eraser on a blackboard, most memories of that event are a blur. Another missing piece of the puzzle of my life.

"Mom, what?" I asked. No answer. Moving toward the window, she stood directly in front of me. In her hand, something caught the sunlight. It glistened.

"I am going to kill myself because you are so bad." I stared at her, and all I saw was a blunt affect, eyes fixated on me. She had crossed over. Gone from reality. I lost the ability to speak at first. Fear gripped me as I tried to find the right words. "Mom, what did I do?"

Her hand moved to her wrist. "You don't care about me. It's all about you. Going out with friends, laughing and talking back." Visibly unstable, she continued her montage of how I failed to meet *her* needs. I was no different than any other teen—in fact, I had more on my plate taking on the mother role.

"You are evil," she said, her fingers wrapped around her pulse.

"Mom, what are you talking about?" I asked in a whisper. My head was spinning, my stomach churning, my thoughts racing. I saw what was in her hand. She played with the razor blade.

"You would love it if I were dead, wouldn't you?"

My mouth was so dry I couldn't speak. I sat there like one of Chris's lifeless dolls. Speechless. Motionless. Terrified. And so sad.

Nothing left for me but heavy defeat. Something died within me that day. My memory has grown dim like a fading lightbulb. But eventually, the threat ended. Those words, "You are so bad, I am going to kill myself," would be with me forever. My life force was gone. My body fell limp. No tears. No verbal exchange. No anger. If I could just die and sleep. That's what I want, sleep.

She fell silent. Although her gaze was directed to the spot where I sat, she didn't see me. Something in her mind took over, as she was no longer in the room but far away caught up in another tangle of mangled thoughts. Eventually, she left. I melted into the mattress.

We all bring our unresolved pain into the present to cripple us. Forever I will hear those words echoed. When I went for a job. Or when I applied to college, or went on a date, or attended church. Everywhere I went, those words hammered at me, beating me down: *I am going to kill myself because you are so bad.*

As would be commonplace, this threat of self-destruction became a tool in her arsenal. She sought attention like a gnat seeks the light. Like the gnat, self-destruction is the result of this behavior.

Dad began to pick us up on weekends, a real break in the climate of the storm that was now our lives. We got to see our brother Bobby, a treat—even though he picked on us and had his own life now. Grandma would always cook and bake for us. Pineapple upside-down cake with real whipped cream. My mouth waters just recalling how delicious her homemade tapioca pudding was. She would add a dollop of strawberry or raspberry jam. I would get scolded for sneaking down in the middle of the night for an extra bowl or two.

At Grandma's, we were allowed to be kids. On this typical weekend day, we laughed, visited friends, and told stories on the side porch.

"I'm hungry," Bobby whined.

"You are, aren't you?" Grandma stood in the doorway. Despite her age, she was still remarkably pretty with silver hair and alabaster skin. Even as she wiped her hands on her apron, she stood with a regal air. "Get washed up," she ordered. We complied and took our seats in the little breakfast nook at the far end of the kitchen. We were seated with me across from Dad. The food was served, and Grandma took a seat.

"Spaghetti and meatballs, my favorite," I said, mouth full of meatball.

Gram laughed. "You have a hollow leg, young lady."

I smiled as I squirmed in my seat to get a glimpse out of the open window, desperate to see if the new pool was finally full of water. The crystal-clear water shimmered over the surface, creating a kaleidoscope of reflections on the bottom. I began my love affair with water early on. I was troubled and wooed by it.

"Hey, Dad, can we go in the pool after supper if it's filled to the top?" I asked.

"Sit still and eat. We'll see," he grumbled.

"Bob, shush," Grandma answered protectively.

He glared at her. Grandma was clean and kempt, and Dad was the complete opposite. A torn gray T-shirt lay limply across his chest. His socks, well, they could be worn for days. I am certain his actions were for cause and effect.

"Why don't you throw that shirt in the garbage? You look like a bum," Gram said.

Bobby stood up and looked out the window. "Well, can we swim?"

Dad's fist connected with the tabletop. Everyone jumped, except Grandma. Instead, she glared at him with quiet disdain and regret. "Yes, you can go in, but you all need to wait an hour. Okay?" Grandma answered without hesitation.

The sound of a toppling chair reverberated in our ears. Dad was fully enraged. But we knew we were safe with that little tough Irish lady in the room. The power she had over him was uncanny. Like a small child, he left the room. "They are not your children. When will you mind your damn business?"

Waiting for us to go swimming was torment. But after an hour, we climbed the ladder and jumped, dove, or slipped into the pool.

"This is so cool. Throw the ball, come on, Chris, and throw it to me," Bobby called, filled with childlike wonderment.

She lifted her arm to toss it, but once again, her mature sister knocked it from her hands. "Why did you do that?" she yelled as I held the ball over my head. I was far too old for such childish nonsense, but my life had too much responsibility with little opportunity to just have fun. My quest for childlike joy stayed with me for the remainder of my days. I treasure the simple gift from God that of sheer delight at all that is ours just for the viewing.

"Get her!" my brother yelled. My siblings launched an attack, but I held the ball high.

"Get off my back. You're hurting me." Bobby just laughed. Soon, we were both submerged beneath the water. My lungs betrayed me, and I rose to the surface.

Coughing, spitting water, rubbing my eyes, I yelled, "You are such a jerk. You almost drowned me!"

Bobby just laughed. Deep down, I knew I was asking for it.

Rounding the corner to the backyard were two neighborhood friends.

"Wow, when did you get the pool?" Sheila questioned.

"How deep is it"? Warren chimed in.

Chris climbed up the ladder, perching herself atop. "Dad got it a few days ago. This is the first time we used it. It took so long to fill. We used the garden hose."

"My father dug down in the dirt, so it is much deeper in the center," Bobby chimed in as he swam to the center where he stood on the bottom. His head went beneath the surface, a demonstration of the depth. "See, it really is deep."

"Do you guys want to come in?" I asked, presenting a flirty smile in the direction of Warren. My crush changed as rapidly as notes in a song. He probably didn't even notice. "I have a bathing suit you can wear Sheila, if you want to come in."

"Okay, sure." She offered a toothy smile at the dark-haired male in our midst. I doubt he was interested in either one of us. Warren was a man of sixteen, and we were just children.

We splashed around with our friends for hours. It was a party in a pool. Laughing, diving, jumping, splashing, and tossing the ball.

"Bobby, turn on the backlight, okay?" I asked. With lightning speed, he climbed the ladder and hit the switch Dad had installed.

The effect the spotlight created on the wiggling water was mesmerizing. I could have watched for hours. Chris had gotten out and was sitting in a lawn chair, leaving the small band of aquatics behind. "Brr, I am really cold."

"Why don't you come in, Buddy? Are you a chicken?" Bobby began clucking.

Buddy the older man (he was nineteen) lived next to Warren just across the main street. He was so cool, always playing guitar and singing folk songs. He introduced me to Mr. Bo Jangles.

"Play something for us, Buddy, okay? Please?" I asked.

His fingers began to tighten the strings, "What do you want to hear?"

"Anything of Pete Seeger's."

Soon, music filled the yard, illumination danced on the water, the sky grew dark, and my beloved fireflies danced amongst Grandma's roses and the honeysuckle. The moon was high in the sky. I had the rhythm of summer in my bones.

"Okay, time to get out," Dad called. "It's almost eleven. You girls can change in the garage. I set it up for you as a dressing room. Bobby, you can change in the basement."

Begrudgingly, we scrambled out of the pool. Sheila and I went through the rear door of the garage and flipped on the light. "Look at my skin—it's all pruned." Sheila laughed.

The garage had two windows on either side. Dad had fixed a shelf, a mirror, and hooks for our clothes. Everything needed to change into and out of our bathing suits. An opaque paper covered the window, allowing light in but blocking visibility. Our skin glistened as we hurried to dry. Now it was the girls' turn. Chris, my friend, and me. Chris still had her baby fat around her tummy. There were tiny little buds forming on her chest, the promise of waiting adulthood.

"Warren is so cute, don't you think?" Sheila giggled. Her body was partially covered with a towel.

Grabbing a smaller towel from the hook, I said, "Yeah, he's okay. But I like Buddy. He is so cool with his guitar. My hair is going to be so frizzy now." I towel-dried my hair.

In typical fashion, we snapped each other with damp clothes, giggled, imitating singing groups of our generation, holding brushes for mics.

"Shush! What was that?" Sheila whispered.

"I didn't hear anything. You're crazy." Then I heard a brushing against the side of the garage. It sounded like a branch scraping the metal siding. My imagination stirred. As in typical mature young women fashion, we screamed. Outside, we heard feet scamper across the yard that faded as they moved away from the structure. We rushed to the window just in time to see the shadowy figure rounding the corner of our house and disappeared.

It was many years later when I learned that it was our father. In a letter my brother wrote me, he also informed me that this man I called father was guilty of other indecent acts. He drilled a small hole in the door to the bedroom that I used when I visited him. It was covered with a paper calendar on the outside—odd but effective. All he had to do was move it, and he had a clear view of his daughter.

Sheila and I sat on the side porch. The streetlights glowed. A gentle breeze touched our end of...

"Dollie, I want your father to stop tickling me," she said, her voice low. "I don't like it. I am too old, and his hands go, well... He is not tickling me—he's..."

I could feel the flush on my cheeks, a sign of humiliation and recognition of what I already knew. I had felt it as well. Tickling hands that "accidentally" touched private places.

Barely audible, I offered a promise. "I... I am sorry, Sheila. I will make it stop." A long, contemplative pause before I spoke again. "Did you say anything to your mother?" I held my breath, waiting for her response.

"No." I believed her. A large family with strong Roman Catholic influence would have taken action against my father and quite possibly forbidden my friend to visit with me. We would feel the sting of such a separation. We never spoke of it again.

Taking on family sins became my destiny. The next day, we all headed off to church, like all good Catholics do. Church was only two blocks away, so we walked. After the service, returning home, I walked beside my grandmother. "Grandma, I need to tell you something." I felt comfortable speaking with her. Dad, Chris, and Bobby were far ahead of us and would not hear my words.

"What is it?" she asked. But somehow, I sensed she was acutely aware of what words I would speak. I told my grandmother what Shelia told me the night before.

Before she spoke, she released a great gust of air. She stopped; her body twisted. Well-manicured hands tipped in blood-red polish fell onto my shoulders. Her eyes as narrow as her lips. "Dollie, did he ever do anything to you?"

"No!" I lied. We both knew I was lying. I had witnessed my father's explosions too many times not to self-protect. How she handled it, I don't know. Discretion became his modus operandi from then on. To my knowledge, my father, a featured player at his church, never touched my friend again. At least, she never mentioned it again. A man who would never miss church on Sundays, who was close friends with a few of the priests, abused his daughters and ignored his son.

When I was about thirteen, Dad took us to Florida. He had friends who invited us. Dad could be so nice at times, but like others in my life, one never knew when the mood would change. The memory of this trip was wonderful. We swam in the clear Atlantic Ocean, went boating on the family's little vessel, crabbed, and even went for a ride in the Goodyear Blimp. That trip was just for me and Dad because I had an unfortunate visit from my friend that prevented me from swimming, gave me cramps, puffed me up, and, well, created a very whiny young woman. From high above, we floated like a feather in the wind. Below ocean was clean azure blue. We viewed shadowy figures of sharks so close to where swimmers played.

"Honey, look, I think that is a whale." I leaned to see where Dad was pointing. Just below the ocean surface, a massive figure slowly rose to the surface. Even at this distance, I could see the spray of water released into the air through his blowhole. A flip of his tail, then he dove below the surface.

"I will never go in the water again." I giggled. I wished this feeling would last. Life was just moving along as it should for a young woman. Living each second, staying in the moment, giving and receiving love and experiencing new and exhilarating moments. I will never forget floating high above the Florida coast in the Goodyear blimp. This experience was likened to our family. From the vantage point of the bather below, everything looks good on the surface, but just below, danger lurked.

This trip occurred at a key point in my life. I was in love. There was an intense agony of a first love. His name was Elvis. I vowed to love him forever. Period. So on this vacation, Dad had another surprise for me. It was late afternoon in Florida, so I was sitting on the Lanai on a wicker chair. The cushions, typical for Florida, had parrots in all stages of flight. Huge palm leaves with red flowers served as the background. "So what do you want to do tonight?" Dad asked. I was still coming down from my fantastic day. My siblings were out with Dad's friends playing miniature golf. I was happy to be with my dad when he was like this, calm and caring, funny and protective.

I grabbed my soda from the faux bamboo table. Even with the ceiling fan on high, it was so hot. "I don't know. I am sort of tired, and it's so hot."

Flopping onto the chair across from me, with the same outrageous pattern as mine, Dad kicked off his loafers. His arms reached around the back of his head where his fingers interlocked. "Well, I guess you won't want to go downtown then. There is a concert, and I just happened to buy a ticket for you. But if you are too tired, we can just stay here."

I came alive. "What concert?"

"Just some guy named Elvis Presley. Have you heard of him?"

I flew out of my chair. "Really, Dad? You're not kidding me, are you? Please, don't be kidding me."

Reaching into his pocket, he pulled out a solitary ticket.

"Let me see." I grabbed it right out of his hands.

He stood tall. "I would suggest, young lady, you get showered and dressed. We only have a few hours, and it is a bit of a drive."

I squealed and rushed into the back bedroom. A short time later, showered, in my shorts and light makeup, I entered the living space of the bungalow where Dad and his creepy friend stood. I sure didn't like the way these men looked at me.

I opened the screen door and ran to the car. Chris and Bobby were off with the wife of Dad's friend to go crabbing. My fingers manipulated the ticket in my hand as I waited with hundreds of giggling teenyboppers. Ponytails swayed, lipstick was applied, cat-eyed glasses gently pushed up on the bridge of noses. We all had one thing in common. Love. Love for Elvis. I jumped in line, remembering my pledge to love this man for the rest of my life. I thought of Dad and what a wonderful thing he did for me, especially knowing he didn't like Elvis.

It felt like forever before I was seated and he appeared. The screaming commenced, drowning out some words. But I am certain, when he sang "Hound Dog" and pointed, it was me he pointed to. At least, that was the story I told my friend Sheila when I got home. She learned the truth decades later via the Internet.

7

Mom's brothers appeared at our front door unexpectedly one day.

"Hi, Uncle Joe, what are you doing here?"

I could hear Chris's footsteps running down the stairs. "Hi, Uncle Jack. Hi, Uncle Joe. I didn't know you were coming. Did you?" Her gaze shifted from the men to me. "Does Mom know you are here?"

"Whoa, slow down," Uncle Jack ordered. He had retained some of the red in his hair, whereas Uncle Joe's was fading. Joe sat in a chair, while Jack remained standing. "No, your mother doesn't know we are here. Your father called us last week, so we thought we should check on what is happening. He said your mother has been feeling depressed. Dollie, what can you tell us?"

Without hesitation, I described Mother's behaviors. I did my best to provide an accurate picture. Drugs. Outrageous behaviors. Paranoia. Midnight runs to the store for cashews or cigarettes or whatever she desired. For us, her children, this was our norm. Seeing my uncles here, I thought help had arrived.

"Is she in her room?"

I nodded.

"Dollie, this place needs to be cleaned. Look at those cobwebs." Why was he telling me? Oh, that's right, I was the mother figure. I was embarrassed for her. Dirty sheets, hair, clothes, cigarette butts everywhere, and the stained coffee mug.

Behind closed doors, we heard the men talking, asking questions, offering comfort, and making suggestions. Uncle Joe spoke loudly, "What are you taking?" He paused. "Drink the coffee, Margaret."

"I'll drink if and when I am ready. You were always Mother's favorite. Joe could do no wrong," she slurred. A familiar montage was about to begin about Grandma's favorite son. That was how Mom handled life. Jump off the tracks like a runaway train.

"If you keep this up and keep saying the things you do, you know you are going to be put away, don't you?" Uncle Jack stated. He sounded authoritative, no-nonsense.

The chatter, whispers, and movement went on for hours. At times, we heard Mom crying, which was commonplace in our home. Crying about herself and carpenter ants but never about us. After a time, my uncles left Mom's room.

"Dollie, do you have anything to drink?" Joe asked, absent of any hint of what was coming next.

"Just coffee, instant coffee."

"Oh, God, no. How can anybody drink that swill? Never mind. We need to talk," Joe said.

Chris remained silent as she rose and retreated in Chris-like manner.

Uncle Joe, leaning on the hutch, began to speak. "How long has she been like this? What pills is she taking? She said she only takes medications to help her to sleep." His face was taut, muscles twitched.

It felt like an interrogation. Dampness covered my hands. "She's been sad for a long time." I opted for the simplest answer. "She doesn't like me very much either. I don't know why."

The elder brother sat beside me. "What about pills? Dollie, she can barely speak. She is filthy."

Without warning, I felt fluid slide down and over my cheeks. "Okay, okay, don't get upset. Come on, Dollie," Joe said.

Jack jumped in. "We just want to help."

"Is she still taking pills? She told us she wasn't."

"She lies about it. To everyone—including herself. Mom goes to different drug stores, doctors, shops, and even goes through the medicine cabinets of relatives and friends."

Uncle Joe moved closer; his face softer now. Is it possible he actually saw me? Could he see past Mother at what this was also doing to me and her children? He sat in the spot Uncle Jack just vacated. Joe headed into the kitchen. From where we sat, quietly, we could hear cabinets open and close. This continued for a half an hour as the younger brother asked me about school and my areas of interest. It was so nice. He cared.

"Well, I can't find anything," Jack stated, back in the living space. "Dollie, does she have any hiding places?"

Calmer now, I rose. Both men followed. Mom, asleep now in bed, a lit cigarette in the ashtray, was unaware of the intrusion. I pointed at the light fixture where shadows of pill bottles rested. Then, opening up her closet door, I reached into the shoe bag, pulling bottle after bottle from her dark hiding place. An oatmeal cylinder painted with flowers, a gift from me to Mom, now held a booty of pain meds, sleeping pills, and other medication to relax, stimulate, elevate, or whatever the need of the day. A real smorgasbord of legal drugs. The scavenger hunt continued. Upon completion, Jack bagged them up. He said he wanted to take them with him to dispose properly and safely.

"What's happening? Turn the damn light off." Mom rolled to face the wall. The same wall that caught her head years earlier from Dad's wrath.

"Why are all the drapes closed? It's like a damn cave in here." Uncle Joe opened the dark, heavy drapes. Artificial light was the only source of illumination, day or night.

"Mom is afraid someone might peek in," I answered.

The drapes were opened. "There, that's a little better."

Outside, a veil of darkness was descending. The men both took seats. "Dollie, we need to be leaving soon. But before we go, we need to decide what to do next. Your mother cannot go on like this. We will need to get her help."

Jack joined in. "There are places she can go, like a hospital to be taken care of. Of course, that means she will be away for some time. Or possibly, she can stay home and go see a therapist. Of course, we need to talk with a doctor first to see what options we have. Dollie, she is your mother. We want to know what you would want us to do."

Did they actually ask their niece, a young girl still in grade school, to make a decision about the fate of her mother? As much as I hated our lives, I didn't want to have her sent away. What would happen to her? To us? A grown-up's decision left in the hands of a child.

With her words "you're so bad I am going to kill myself" etched forever in my white matter, now, I was asked to make a decision that could actually prevent her from harming herself. We had lived with her threats of self-harm for so long, we became numb to her words. But what if she really meant it?

"I really don't want her to go away." My words were well-thought-out, but what if that was the wrong decision? "What would happen to us?" I guess memories of the orphanage stumbled into my mind as a real alternative.

"She needs help, Dollie." The men looked at each other. "After we speak with her doctor, we will decide what is best for her. Listen, we better get going. Call us if she gets worse, okay?"

I nodded and kissed the men goodbye. The door closed behind them, and the problem remained mine, at least for now. Time marched on for the three Knight children, now young men and women. Hormones on fire. The transformation from the safety of parochial school to public was intimidating. Safety lay in the comfort of the same faces, the same classroom, and the sameness offered comfort. Lacking stability in the home, I sought the comfort of familiarity. Dad wanted me to go to an all-girl Catholic high school. I was not interested.

Friends tediously chose courses, often very different from mine. Secretarial for the girls, general courses for the boys, with a healthy dose of shop. My lofty goal, the lure of nursing, so I chose college prep. This would mean my days would now be with strangers. The same strangers who at one time tortured me as I passed.

If we were all painted orange, the Catholic school teenagers couldn't have stood out more. Chairs scraped the floor, laughter, chatter, banging as the period bell rang. Good Catholic teens remained in our chairs until permission was given to leave. Teachers were addressed *mister* or *missus*. But never without a title.

Late one afternoon after a date with a senior, I arrived home. It had been a good day. Stepping into the dimly lit living room, my form cast strange shadows. I didn't see my sister immediately as my eyes adjusted in the reduced light. Even in this situation, I could see Chris's face—she was ashen. Frozen in space. Void of emotion. A human statue.

"Chris?" I moved toward her. "What is that awful smell? It's dreadful." Silence. No emotion. Stoic posture. I reached out and touched her. "Chris?"

Without a word, she ambled toward Mother's bedroom. She stopped. She opened the door and stepped aside.

My eyes burned in the darkened room. The mound under the blanket remained motionless. With a flick of my finger, a dim light partially illuminated the space. Like a needle to a balloon, the happiness I felt minutes before disappeared. "Mom." Nothing. "Mom." Silence.

As I ambled around the bed, I spoke to bulk that stirred slightly. "Mom, what happened? What is that horrific odor?" Reaching the far side of the bed where she lay, I stopped. She was asleep. Dead asleep. A burned-out crater was within inches of her head. My stomach's contents rose, and I swallowed hard. I could see she was breathing and began to stir. I stared down, not knowing what to say or do.

Struggling to focus, she slurred. "Well, I see you finally decided to come home. Did you have fun? Did it occur to you I needed you here?" Steeped in sarcasm, she continued. "Everything is about you. You don't belong in this family. You think you are so perfect."

These assaults continued. I turned to leave. "Yeah, Mom, I think I am perfect." I too could throw out the sarcasm. The truth was I thought very little about me. But when I did, *perfection* was not a word that entered my head. *Loser. Ugly. Worthless.* Those are words I used to describe myself.

I began to leave as the abusive comments were fired at me like a machine gun.

"Sure, run away like you always do. At least your sister stays with me. Thank God I have one child who is loyal and caring." As she rolled over toward the door, she hollered, "Chris! Chris! Come here. I need you."

Reaching the door, I turned around one last time. I felt defeated, blended with an all-too-familiar anger. Especially upset hearing her call out Chris's name. My tone surprised me when I spoke, "Mothers do not act like this. Why are you blaming me? I did nothing wrong. What do you want? My grades are good, I care for the house, and Chris, and I even sold my favorite new white coat I bought to pay the electric bill. What more do you want?"

No response, of course.

"I want a mother, that's what I want. Leave Chris alone." Since I was a small child, I felt pressure, too much for far too long. Even a pressure cooker would blow its lid if there wasn't a valve to release the steam. I wanted to shine a light into the shadows of darkness that prevailed in our home. I prayed Mother would not get up. I needed to assimilate all that has happened. God answered my prayers. She rolled over, her back to the door.

Chris sat at the kitchen table. "She is so drugged up, she must have fallen asleep with a lit cigarette. The bed was on fire when I got home. God only knows what would have happened if I went over to Cathy's." Her words spoken without even a hint of emotion.

"I want to leave. Get out of here for good." The words came out louder than planned. I started to think about the decision to allow her to be treated while she remained in the home. A mistake? Was this all my fault? I walked around my sister to take a seat. We could hear Mother's cries for my sister to go to her.

"Dollie, I feel nothing for her. Nothing I do makes any difference. Night after night, she wants to talk. Always the same. Always about her." She paused before continuing. "Or you. I don't know why she treats you as she does. But of course, she blames you for her troubles. Or the carpenter ants. Or Dad. Or the neighbors. Never herself. Dollie, this sounds terrible, but for a brief minute, I wanted her to die because it felt like that was the only solution. I am so unhappy. I feel trapped."

All teens start to pull away from parents, that's normal. Birds push their babies out of the nest. Mother held on with her talons.

Chris and I spoke for a long time. We shared our mixed emotions for our mother. Love. Hate. Fear. Frustration. A melting pot that has bubbled to the surface now spilling it contents.

8

The sequence of events for the next few years is a blur, like walking in a blinding snowstorm. Mother and I fought often and hard. Usually in defense of what I felt was right. If I felt something was wrong, I spoke up. Often with negative results for me. I was not abrasive, but I would say what I meant without being mean when I said it. The divide between my mother and me became a chasm without a way to the other side. Chris remained silent.

"Don't you dare go out that door." I felt the spray from her mouth land on my cheeks. She was that close to me. "I said no, you're not going anywhere." Pain rose in my cheeks from the well-appointed slap.

I pushed past her. Where was I going? Anywhere but here. Daily fights, daily slaps, anger, crying, name-calling, dirty house unless I cleaned it. She did speak with a therapist, but it didn't last too long, and I knew she wouldn't be as honest with her as she was with everyone else. Her vision of life was delusional.

Outside, the days grew cool, and the leaves wore coats of russet, scarlet, gold, and brown. Expectations of change dared to bring joy into our world. Each season, a new beginning, except here in our little world. The weather changed outside, but inside, the climate remained arid and colorless.

"Get down there and clean that floor. And look at that bathtub. You can't do anything right." Her grasp on my flesh burned as she pushed me along the hall. "Is that clean?" Pushed into the tiny bathroom, I stared at her. Defeated. This ritual abuse was winning. I am certain folks just saw Mother as a woman struggling to raise her daughters. She gave away freely all her troubles to anyone who'd take them. No one really knew what went on in our home. To me, it felt as if no one really cared.

"It looks clean to me, Mom." My voice a whisper, defeated. And emotionally tired.

"Well, look again. Chris, get in here. Now! Does that look clean to you?" she barked.

Chris stood at the entrance of the room. Dark eyes pleading with mine to fix it. All she could do was shrug—any other response would fail.

Mother turned, pushing past Chris. We heard her in the kitchen opening and closing cabinets. Doors slammed. This symphony of the cupboard doors rose to a crescendo. She was no longer in control—her disease was directing her actions.

"Let's go." I grabbed Chris's arm, grabbed Mother's keys off the hook and dragging Chris, I tried to escape. Scrambling to get to the front door and freedom, Mother intercepted us. There was a struggle, but we managed to free ourselves. Mother was compromised by her medications, possibly sleeping pills or narcotic pain pills. We managed to get the door open and stepped out onto the stoop. The fall air against my skin stirred my senses. I felt alive, in a good way. Clean fresh air filled my lungs, unlike cigarette smoke that permeated every surface of the house.

"Chris, hurry," I called.

I ran around the car, and Chris hopped into the passenger's side. The sight of Mom in pursuit, hair askew, threatening, scared me on a level not felt before. In full view of the neighbors, failure to protect herself from judgment, she proceeded to bang on the windows. Mom looked insane.

"Oh my God, what are we doing? Where the hell are we going to go?" Chris's attempts to suppress her laughter failed. She was out of control laughing, tears streaming down her cheeks. She was bordering on hysteria.

Outside, Mom was screaming, crying, and pounding on windows: a dichotomy of the events inside the car. The insanity of this scene being played out for the neighbors, the embarrassment of it all, and the uncertainty of the outcome also created a desire to laugh.

Through gasps for air, my laughter now out of control, I attempted to speak. "Chris, stop, we need to figure out what we are going to do."

I have no idea why we started to laugh, but once we started, we couldn't stop. Hysterical laughter is not born of humor but fear, disbelief, and confusion.

Leaning on the steering wheel, our escape plan was formulated. Our mother circled around the car and was now leaning on the trunk, arms crossed in front of her. At the sound of the engine, she was determined to block our egress.

"Now what do we do? Please, we have to get out of here. There is no way we are going back in there now," I stated firmly, signaling with my head toward our red house. I saw Mother in the rearview mirror leaning on the back of the car, cigarette smoke circling her head. Screaming loudly, "You are not going anywhere. Not now, not ever." Now she was hitting the trunk with her bare hand.

"I have an idea." My voice was far more confident than I was feeling. "I think I have enough room to go forward, make a sharp turn to the right, miss the apple blossom tree, drive across the yard and out onto the street."

There was little room for mistake. The tree was set off between the driveway and the curved sidewalk on a little patch of grass. This was not going to be easy, if even possible.

Biting her lip, she asked. "Do you think you will make it? There is not much room. If you hit the tree, we…" She looked at me for assurance.

"Can you believe this?" My response offered a hint of the ridiculousness regarding the scenario. "This is a team effort." Once I put the car in gear, I need to step on the gas as fast as possible to keep from hurting her or hitting the tree as we made our great escape.

Once again, nervous laughter rose up. What must the neighbors think, yet no one came out of their houses? I heard the neighbor on the right tell the mailman one day, "Don't worry about her. She is crazy and never answers the door." I remember that I actually went over to her house to tell her off in defense of mother.

My grip tightened on the steering wheel as Chris sat bolt upright. She was the lookout to ensure the coast was clear as I drove the getaway car.

"Are you ready?"

"Yeah. As ready as I will ever be."

"When I say three, I am going to hit the gas. Okay? One. Two. Three." I put the pedal to the metal. The car lunged forward, barely missing the tree as I made a sharp right turn, drove across the front yard, another right, and we were on asphalt. Free. I could see Mother in the street in the rearview window.

"Now what?" Chris asked. I remained silent, lost in thought. I cannot recall where we went that night. It is amazing how our mind can block out certain events that are too painful. Or insignificant. I knew we would need to go back, but for now, we were free.

Years later, I learned Mother's account of that day was far more ominous. Apparently, she told family and anyone who would listen that I tried to kill her. I started the car and aimed it at her.

Early one morning, I was on my way to work. My heart raced with fear. I knew that soon I would be found out for the failure I believed I was. Years of criticism blocked any positive thoughts to roll into my being like a stick in a spoke of my bike. Positive thoughts withered; self-devaluation was nurtured.

I never told anyone about what I am going to write here. On that day, fear blocked my rational thinking completely. Thoughts of avoidance filled my head, but there was nothing I could do but go to work. Then it happened. My hands tightened on the steering wheel. I chose a spot and drove off the road. My intentions were not to harm myself, but avoid going to work where the feelings of inadequacy loomed above me like a vulture over a carcass. How pathetic is that? My feelings were not based in fact. The truth is I was successful wherever I went, but I always felt I was a little girl in a grown-up world, playing at being mature. I never even told that story to my sister. So, alarmed by the memory, I called a friend to unburden myself of this additional food for a crippled soul.

"Anne, I have had many students tell me they thought about doing exactly that rather than face work or school or some other fear. The thought is not uncommon. You just acted on it. Don't be so hard on yourself," Helen spoke in her familiar, supportive manner. A nurse, educator, and therapist, a wise woman who obtained her PhD later in life. A role model, indeed.

"I too have friends who made the same statement. Helen, what a sad statement that one would hate their job or feel so incredibly inadequate that venturing off course was the only answer. Crashing into a tree was actually considered by so many." Feeling somewhat better about myself, at least in that moment, I allowed myself to smile. Sort of an act of forgiveness.

"I suspect callouts are not just made because of illness but an injured ego." My wise friend, always able to speak words tempered with truth and tenderness.

9

"Your father was dishonorably discharged from the service." My mother reveled in dishing out terrible facts about those she should love. And this summer day after the Fourth of July was no different. "I learned he had some type of breakdown during training. He punched an officer in the face. At least that is what I heard through the grapevine." She smiled as she shared the story.

She rose, turned toward the stove, and filled a teakettle with water. Then she placed it on the flame. Her cup was given a heaping spoonful of instant coffee. Gosh, that stuff even smelled disgusting. She returned to her seat.

"When I checked, I was informed that a woman, who claimed to be his wife, came to pick him up the day he was released. It wasn't me, so I have no idea who the woman was. I don't know anything about the incident that led up to the assault itself, but I suspect there is a lot more than we will ever know. His family did everything, including lying, to protect the Knight family image. Everything from that day forward was kept hush-hush with his family."

More secrets. More questions. More missing puzzle pieces. Why would Dad flaunt his army experience if he was dishonorably discharged? Did he really hit an officer? Why wasn't he arrested?

The kettle on the stove whistled. Mother rose, poured the steaming water into her cup, and reached into the refrigerator for milk before she folded into the chair. "As you know, I don't get along with your grandmother, but she was right. Your father has always had free hands with girls. His mother knows his history."

High school was an ocean of loneliness. Sure, there was the occasional wave of hope when some kids would befriend me. Unfortunately, the wave would break due to deep-seated lack of esteem; it would crash, tossing me into an island of isolation. The few friends I had lived lives in such sharp contrast to mine I could no longer identify. I became a chameleon, able to become what those around me wanted me to be. My unhappiness was universal. I was an average-looking girl, nice figure, curly brown hair, and beautiful skin. No one really noticed me, invisible. Well, at least that was how I felt. I was certain I didn't exude confidence.

Daily hearing the door open, my stomach tightened with compulsion to reintroduce lunch. I fought the feeling, swallowing hard. The queasy feeling remained. Mother was home, and with Mom, one never knew *who* would show up. She glanced about, approving of the appearance of the home. Would this mean a good night?

"Where is your sister?" she asked, standing in front of the stove. The medications the therapist had her on provided a more stable being. Although her behavior was still unpredictable, living with someone with a borderline personality disorder means one is always walking on eggshells.

"Across the street at Kathy's, I think. I need to ask you something," I continued.

She turned from the stove, sat down, and stared at me. "Well? It better not be unpleasant because I have had a terrible day. I don't want to deal with any of your foolish problems tonight." Mom was able to work again. I prayed the distraction would serve as a release elsewhere. Customers. Bosses. Coworkers. Traffic. Anything that would save her children from her insane wrath.

What else is new? I needed to be careful now. I could uncage the lion with what I was about to ask. "I want to quit school." I held my breath and waited. Her response was not one I anticipated. But with Mom, that was the ride we were on, never knowing what to expect. All she said was okay. I was asking to throw away my life, and she said okay.

So that was it. I quit school. A bright, focused, goal-oriented young woman walked away from a future into a world of self-pity. A self-fulfilling prophecy in the making. I was living down to Mother's expectations.

Later that night, Chris and I talked for hours in our bed. "Mom takes the easy way out. If you leave school, you can do more around the house, get a job, and help financially. Dollie, I understand how you feel, but it makes me sad. You are throwing away your life. Giving up on yourself."

I started to cry. I knew I was about to make a mistake of monumental proportions. Just hearing my sister, a girl who hated confrontations, speak to me like she did was an indicator of her love and concern for me.

A long period of inactivity set in. The few friends I had faded away after being told repeatedly I wasn't available. Now I did have some brilliant ideas. One was to be a model. At 5'3", I was not a candidate—plus, I was average appearing. Then I had the brilliant idea of joining the Peace Corps. I tried secretarial school. Hated it. That was Mom's suggestion. So I quit.

"You can't just sit around all the time, Dollie. You need to get a job. We need the money."

Eventually, I began to work as a certified nurse's aide. I really liked helping others. The facility was for children with mental and physical disorders. The excitement of rushing to the side of a bed of a child having a grand mal seizure and rendering aid was wonderful. I felt alive. Needed. Appreciated. But the real bonus was housing was supplied. No more listening to Mom complain about taking me to work. I was independent. I loved the charge nurse. All the young gals admired her. Her humor, her support, and especially her patience with a group of goofy teens was refreshing. We were admired. A tall woman who wore a cap that appeared as if she turned a paper cup upside down and stuck it on her head.

Her smile lit up a room. "Morning, ladies. Come on, let's get report so we can get started." The eager young women gathered around the nurse's station.

"Okay, any questions?" She waited. "I have a little surprise. We need to do some education on new treatments for wound care. Are any of you interested in coming to my house tonight?" We were invited into her private home. "We can have pizza first and talk. How does that sound? The directions will be available later, and I will leave them in that basket." She pointed to the metal carrier on the corner of the desk. "Come around six. Now scoot, get to work."

We turned on our heels. Chattering and laughing down the hall toward our assigned children.

"Margaret, can I see you for a minute?" Even though I had done nothing wrong, a lifetime of being blamed gave me pause. I walked back to where I stood seconds before. "Let's go to Mrs. Olson's office." As I ambled down the drab halls with scars in the bland tawny wall paint, various scenarios played in my mind. Surely, bad news would soon be delivered. After all, the lack of explanations signaled something ominous would soon be delivered. "Here we are," she said, standing in front of a door, tapping lightly on the door.

Inside, a voice called out, "Come on in."

Never having seen the inside of this office, my eyes darted around the room. Not unlike the woman before us, it was cold, lacking warmth or personality. No family pictures, plants, void of anything that spoke of the character of this woman. Quite the contrary. Worn white paint-covered walls and ceilings. Two of the ugliest chairs I had ever laid eyes on sat in front of her desk. Sort of a baby poop brown with worn patches on the arms. Probably from years of people rubbing nervously against her threads. Iridescent overhead lighting lit the room, making it appear more like an operating suit than an office. To the right of desk, in a far corner, rested a table lamp with colored glass things hanging from it. Garish and out of place in the space.

We entered and were asked to take a seat by this woman. Her hair was pulled back so tightly that her face appeared taut. Mrs. Olson smiled—a rarity—and began to speak. "Margaret, we have been talking a great deal about you. We feel you have a special gift for nursing." She smiled at me. "We have never made the offer I am about to make you. If interested, we would like to pay for you to go to nursing school. You can continue to live here, work when able and when finished. Well, we can always use woman like you."

I had lied about high school, and obviously, they didn't check. I asked for time to think about it, saying I would need to check with my mother. Without an education, this gift would go unopened. A few days later, I fabricated a reason for turning down their offer. My heart was breaking. In that place, I finally fell in love. A reason to get up. A passion for healing. I was somebody to be reckoned with. The honor they bestowed upon me was evidence. Healing of a nearly destroyed esteem had begun to be healed. Standing in front of a full-length mirror, I vowed to fix my chassis. My exterior needed to reflect the new and improved me. A fire was ignited. Hair, makeup, and exercise made for an attractive young woman.

Living in the quarters provided at the hospital was like a sorority. I made friends who loved the same things I did. Out in the real world now, my weekends were spent 'down the shore,' as we say in Jersey. One friend had a Honda 50cc scooter. How I loved the feel of the independence it afforded us. So fun. We drove all over on that thing with me laughing in the back as we rounded corners and drove over metal bridges that caused the bike to wiggle precariously. I loved it. I felt alive. I knew I wanted my own.

One afternoon, I spotted my friend in the nursery. I entered. "These babies are so cute," Wilma Jo remarked. "Because I'm pregnant, I get to work in the nursery all the time."

"When is your baby due again?" I asked this older woman in her late twenties. She was truly a woman of the world to me. Divorced, two children, one on the way. I was wet behind the ears, as my grandmother would say.

"Four weeks."

Crossing around to the other side, I observed the little one in the crib. He looked perfectly normal but had some developmental issues and, sadly, was blind. My heart broke looking down upon that precious little being.

My friend stroked his head. "Looking at this little guy kind of scares me. I never thought about it much until I started working here."

"I understand, but the odds are in your favor for a perfectly healthy baby." I paused, lost in thought about this baby's future, or lack thereof. At least, his parents were committed to his care. They came daily with smiles on their faces. They would say things like, "He is our gift from God, our special gift."

I wasn't certain if they were crazy or really held a faith in things not seen, the promise of a loving God. I had not met such a God. The God I knew was punishing, distant, more interested in catching us doing something wrong than in loving us.

"Did I tell you I am moving to Rhode Island after the baby is born?" Although I had friends now, a newfound confidence, this lady I really loved, the thought of her moving away left me feeling a little off balance. She continued: "I had an idea. Please don't think I am crazy, but I wondered if you might want to move with me?"

"To Rhode Island?"

"No, to Italy. Of course, to Rhode Island! What do you think?"

My imagination soared at the possibilities of a fresh start, far away from my past. "Yeah, that would be great." My face felt warm from the excitement.

A few weeks later, I was packed and leaving for Rhode Island. A new life, near the ocean, with my best friend. After telling my dad about my new plan and how I'd get around town, he wasn't as excited as I thought he'd be.

"Dollie, this is really stupid," Dad scolded. "The thought of you riding around on a motorcycle is so dangerous. It really is stupid."

Smiling at him, I assured him I would be okay. My youth blinded me of any potential danger. All I saw was the vision of me riding around on my new white Honda 50 cc motorcycle. It was more of a motor scooter, but I loved it, that feeling of freedom. Separation from constrictions. And, as a bonus, my hair always looked great and straight for some reason. I do suspect road dirt was the key. Helmets were not required back then.

I lived in a three-bedroom apartment with my friend and her three children on what she called the wrong side of the tracks. On the first floor was a carpet-cleaning business, and on the second, the owners of the business with their children. My friend lived on the upper level. It was a quaint place with a little deck out back.

My stay with my friend, however, was short-lived. Working now with a steady paycheck allowed me to move out. Without an education, my career choices were limited. My career was as waitress at the town square drugstore. There were two counters, each shaped like a U that protruded into the store. Thirty people could be seated at one time. A very popular place for breakfast and lunch. The store and surrounding area was typical Norman Rockwell early Americana. A gazebo sat in the center of the square surrounded by a plot of grass with walkways snaking through it on the way to the wooden structure.

One evening, I rode my scooter to a huge house on the best street in town. Elm Street boasted of beautiful large Victorian-style homes. Elm Street was the first right turn off the square from my employment location within walking distance.

I climbed the stairs. The porch was white with a blue ceiling, and wicker furniture was placed in groupings with plants everywhere. My hand forced the brass knocker to strike. I was so nervous. The door opened to reveal an aged woman, frail with deep blue eyes and snow-white hair. "Yes. Are you Dollie?"

I nodded.

"Well, please come in, dear. Let's go into the kitchen and have some tea. Do you like tea? I made shortbread cookies today we can have as well. How does that sound?"

I smiled in agreement. I liked this woman instantly. Her kindness poured out of her like sweet nectar. We sat beneath a window table at the far end of her massive kitchen.

"So you are interested in the apartment?" she asked. Once again, I nodded, still enamored by this generous, kindly woman. "Has the cat got your tongue?" She giggled at her little joke.

I smiled as I said, "No, I guess I am just feeling a little nervous."

"Nonsense! What does a sweet thing like you have to be nervous about? Let's talk, tell me all about yourself. I do know you are from New Jersey, and you work at the drugstore. My friend Mabel, the lady you met at lunch last week, told me about you. But tell me more. And then I will tell you about how this old lady got to be a landlady in this mansion. How does that sound? If it goes well, you will be my next tenant."

So that was how my interview went. Her husband, a wealthy banker, died several years back. The huge empty house swallowed her up. There was a hole in her world where her husband once lived. Her friends and financial advisor suggested converting a portion of her mansion into beautiful apartments, renting them to a woman. She really didn't need the extra money, but not having a family, I suspected she enjoyed the sounds of life in her now-quiet world.

My first apartment was on the best street in town. A lovely Victorian, surrounded by lavish lawns, colorful gardens, embracing aromas, and ancient oaks and maple trees. In the rear of the house was a weeping willow with a thick canopy of arching branches resting on the lawn. Lying beneath that tree felt as if I were in a tent composed of slim leaves and fuzzy yellow flowers. Oh, and when the breeze lifted her flowering limbs up, she appeared to be dancing. Of course, the roots were playing havoc below the surface on the waterlines.

My new home was, as I named it, the Penthouse. Three flights up the massive stairwell. Each floor held one unit. Even now, I smile remembering the warmth and security of my little nest. Internal shutters could be closed if desired. The view from my tower allowed me to see the street below and even a slice of the grass on the town center. It was fully furnished. There was a cute kitchen with a massive window where I could sit and see my tree out back. The living room, bedroom, and a little spare room were enough space for a young single woman. After a life of tumult, I was close to heaven in my tranquility.

Summer had arrived, and that meant, hit the beach. "Leave it to you to end up on the most exclusive street in town," Wilma Jo stated without a hint of jealousy. She shifted on the blanket to catch the rays on her back.

Rubbing suntan lotion on my slim legs, I responded, feigning an air of aristocracy. "You forgot, it is the Penthouse, after all."

"She obviously doesn't need the money, or she wouldn't have rented to you on your meager earnings." (Pause.) I got a sitter so we can go to The Sands tonight." Her beautiful teeth flashed. My friend was all about having fun. "I think Johnny might be there. Do you think Sam will come over?"

Shading my eyes, I tilted my head upward. A threatening cloud suddenly blocked out the sun. "Do you think it is going to rain? The weather reports this morning said it would be warm and sunny."

"You didn't answer me."

"Yeah, he'll be there." Sam was my latest boyfriend. A Scottish lad from Connecticut. I guess one could say we were going steady. He was my first real boyfriend. I did date a few guys in Rhode Island and some from New London, where the subbase was located. But those navy men were not known for their truth-telling abilities. Then there were the boys we met at The Sands, a dance club on the beach for the tourist crowd. They were just dancing partners, nothing more.

Later that evening, now tan from the beaming sun, we found ourselves at The Sands. "It's a little warm in here tonight. Would you get me something to drink?" I asked Sam. He headed off toward the bar at the far end of the room. Wilma Jo and I went onto the deck, as it was much cooler there. The moonbeam melted into the sea. It appeared as liquid silver in this light.

"He is so serious tonight—even more than usual. What's up with him? He's got a bug up his butt." There was the all-too-familiar crispness in her voice. She didn't like him very much, and when he got like this, well, her dislike couldn't be camouflaged.

"Here you go. I got you a gin and tonic." Sam handed me the drink. "It is beautiful out here, isn't it? And a lot cooler than inside."

Wilma Jo headed back inside. "I'll leave you two alone."

We danced and talked, and then it was time to go home. Sam had already left. He needed to be up early the next morning. We made a date for the following Friday.

Riding along the coast on my scooter around the winding narrow roads was fun, but with a hint of fear. Tonight, my friend was on the back taxing the engine. If there was any hill of any significance, she needed to get off and walk. But there were no hills that night. I dropped her off and headed across the tracks toward home. Dogs barked as I passed, always a heart stimulant for this lady. Canines loved to chase me, nipping at my ankles.

To avoid noise, I got off the bike down the road and pushed it home, up onto the drive. I was surprised to see lights ablaze in Martha's suite. Entering, I viewed a note propped on the stairwell that led to my apartment. Recognizing the owner's handwriting, my fingers fumbled with the message. This cannot be good. I feared the note was to announce an increase in my rent. I was barely surviving as it was.

It read *"I hope you had a good night. Please knock on my door when you get home."* My watch read 11:45 p.m. I knocked, the door opened, and there she stood, my landlady. A pink chenille robe, satin slippers, and bobbie pins in her hair. "Come on in," the elderly socialite requested.

She ushered me into her parlor. It boasted of a beautiful brocade sofa, matching chairs, and a marble cocktail table. A magnificent pink-tinted marble fireplace was flanked by an iron vessel that held wood on the other side and antique brass tools resting in a stand. Doilies covered the furniture, tables, and even the mantle. A room dedicated to a long past era.

"Have a seat, dear. I will be right back." A few minutes later, she returned carrying a white tray. She leaned over and placed it onto the table directly in front of where I sat. She moved cautiously around the sofa—her shuffling gait was prevalent tonight. A sure sign of fatigue for this dear woman in her eighties. I viewed the cane she occasionally used resting against the wall by the door.

"I know it's late, dear, but would you like some tea? It's decaffeinated. And, of course, some cookies. Your favorite."

The teapot was covered with rosebuds, a mirror image of the teacups, saucers, and dessert plates. Her veined hands lifted the pot and poured each of us some tea. And then, with the grace like a feather in a summer breeze, she held the delicate dish of cookies and tea cakes in front of me. I willingly picked out a few, laying them onto a dish. I was waiting for her to reveal the reason for this late-night surprise tea party.

"Mrs. Sanders, these are delicious. Thank you." I wasn't lying. This lady loved baking, and it was reflected in the product. She used the finest ingredients.

"Dear"—her slim hand caressed my arm—"how about you start calling me Aunt Martha?"

"I'd like that, Aunt Martha. You are like family to me in many ways." I so loved this woman although, I must admit, I felt inferior to her. Not because of anything she did, but the old interjects that played in my head.

After a few minutes of idle chatter, she let out a very unladylike yawn. I laughed out loud. Midnight was long past her bedtime. "Listen, I hope what I am about to say doesn't upset you. But I know you struggle with your finances. Many years ago, I was in the same position until I married my wonderful husband." She paused. "So I want to lower your rent by thirty dollars."

Unable to speak, I was so moved, I released an expulsion of air. I was overcome by the sweet, generous actions of this lady. "Thank you so much. That will really help."

She rose and walked to the left front corner of the room. Now standing in front of a corner cabinet, she played with a side panel. To my surprise, it popped open. From where I was seated, I could view the contents. There were stacks and stacks of money. The cabinet was lined with a metal of some sort. I assumed to protect the contents in case of a fire. Legal-looking documents and what appeared to be a jewelry case were visible. Removing a paper, she crossed the room.

"This is the lease. I will have a new one for you tomorrow. Now I need to say good night. This old lady is about to fall asleep." She walked me to the door, and before I left, she placed a feather-like kiss on my cheek. "Good night, dear."

"Good night, Aunt Martha. Sleep well."

From that day forward, she was Aunt Martha. She would leave food on the steps for me. Always with a note that would read "I have leftovers I thought you might enjoy." No one I knew ever had an entire cake as a leftover. I felt loved and cared for. Aunt Martha was one of the many angels placed in my path. Perhaps to compensate for the absence of caring parents.

I arrived home late one gray, frigid night; my breaths hanging in the air like a cloud. I climbed the steps leading to the double doors into the manor. Dead silent was the night. Shadows stretched across the lawn from illumination that poured from the windows.

What was this feeling deep within? The feeling was so uncomfortable and unsettling. Creaking steps beneath my weight only added to my discomfort. Without thought, I stopped and turned back down the steps I had just climbed. For reasons unknown to me, I turned left at the base. There was a crunching sound as I moved along the pathway that led to the rear of the estate. A sense of dread, like watching a scary movie, gripped me as I advanced toward the back of her house. A feeling of concern, not necessarily fear, overwhelmed me as I rounded the west side of the mansion.

A soft whimper rose near the steps leading into the back door. In the faint light, I saw a form. I rushed to the area. My Aunt Martha lay on the cold concrete. Her breathing was erratic, speech incoherent. I covered her with my coat, went inside, and called an ambulance. Back outside, I placed a seat cushion under her head and held her hand, listening for the sirens in the distance.

"Aunt Martha, help is on its way." She answered with a moan. "Where do you hurt? Can you breathe okay?" Even in the dim light cast from the kitchen window, I could see the terror in her eyes. "I will stay with you until help comes. You will be okay." If she did fall, the internal injuries for a woman her age could be extensive.

What happened to this dear lady was unclear. She had money, lived alone, and was far too innocent for her own good. She opened her heart and home to anyone who needed her. A creature of habit—anyone who observed her knew her pattern. No matter the weather, she took her bag of garbage out every night to dispose of in the receptacle outside. I offered to do it for her, but she insisted to do it herself. A very independent woman. I loved that about her. There was the real possibility someone waited for her to gain access to her home. Or her aging body failed her, she fell and lay at the bottom of the back stairs. The truth is if I didn't come along, she would have died. My feeling delivered me to find this dear lady.

God planted her in my life. Her kindness, her generosity, and in return, God allowed me to be there for her when she needed me. These "feelings" continued all my life. Like a close friend, I honored them because they were a nudge from God to take action. Even when my faith was rooted in sand.

Rhode Island was a turning point in my young life. Coastal roads often felt me driving on their surface on my little Honda. I danced on the beach, went to the Sandpiper, dated, and even became engaged. I think I knew almost immediately I was not in love with this man and was certainly not a suitable candidate for marriage. I was in love with life, and exploration of this new way of living was important. So I broke the engagement, and eventually, I returned to New Jersey with a heightened awareness of self.

10

Years marched on. I made friendships, worked, moved out of my mother's house for a time, and lived with a girlfriend. Her family, the antithesis of mine, was as comfortable as a soft pair of slippers. I loved being there.

"So are you ladies going to the shore again this weekend?" Mr. Amorevole asked, a string of spaghetti hung low from his lips.

My friend, Teresa, or Terry, looked at me. "Yep. Leaving right after we eat."

As promised, after dinner, we were headed down the shore. This weekend would be like any ordinary weekend. We had no idea where we would sleep, but just like previous adventures, we were always offered a place to stay. It is a miracle we weren't raped or beaten up, but somehow, none of that happened. Just two kids hanging out with other kids.

I met my husband Jim down the shore. We danced to Aquarius at the house he and his friends rented, hit the beach, and had fun. Crashing at the boys' place was safe since Terry knew many of the guys from high school.

"Make love, not war" was the chant of the time. Terry and I were faux love children—not into the drugs or sleeping with anyone we met. But we did wear love beads, dance to strobe lights and split our fingers in the peace sign whenever we could. Terry and I did, on occasion, drink in excess and then get behind the wheel. What we thought funny was incredulously stupid.

Jim and I dated for several months in an on-and-off relationship. He pulled me in with those soulful eyes, and I was hooked.

After several months, we became engaged and married on Valentine's Day, my idea. As anticipated, Mom hated him. She became a constant source of irritation in our marriage, like a pebble in our shoe. Nothing pleased her about him.

Chris continued her duty as the peacemaker. She stayed with Mom. Bobby, however, discovered drugs. After all, it was the dawning of the Age of Aquarius. Harmony and understanding, no more falsehoods or derisions, and golden living dreams of visions. That was the promise.

Bobby smoked pot, played his guitar, and went to art school. He was the quintessential love child. Dad never said a word about his drug use, despite the fact he smoked in the house, and the odor of grass was prevalent. It was easier for our father to ignore anything unpleasant. I loved my brother, his independence, his outrageousness, and his art. I admired him in many ways. Now that he was living with Dad, he had his own set of problems.

Jim and I moved into our first apartment after we married. Our first apartment was upstairs to our landlord. It reminded me of my room at home, with eves, windows, and the cutest little kitchen. Seven months into our marriage, I made an important phone call.

"Mom, did you hear me?" I asked. I knew the answer before she even responded.

There was silence with my news. I held my breath, waiting for her excitement. Waiting for her to gush over the news of my pregnancy. I hadn't told Jim yet, as he was still at work.

"I heard you," she finally responded.

"That's it? That's all you've got to say? What's wrong with you? You are going to be a grandmother."

Her sigh of exasperation and disgust was distinct. "What do you want me to say? You know how I feel about your husband."

Folding into a chair like a deflated balloon, a gush of air released into the air. "Never mind. Is Chris there?"

"No."

"Mother, please don't tell her anything. Please. I want to tell her myself. At least, she will be happy for me." Without waiting for a response, I hung up. I knew she would tell my Chris. Not only about my pregnancy but the usual complaints about me as a daughter. Having a baby just meant my attention would be shared by yet another being.

*****

My beautiful boy was born in July. I couldn't believe it when this perfect being was placed in my arms. Could it be? Was I actually going to take this flawless being home? Was he mine? Never had I felt this joy before. We named him after his father, Jim, but I called him Jamie. I saw instantly soft strawberry-toned hair. My boy had inherited the Irish gene.

My joy was doubled when we moved from our tiny apartment. First into a little house down the shore, and then into my dream home. A yellow stucco house on the corner. Ivy climbed up the fireplace, and a sweet curving walkway welcomed guests toward the maroon front door. To the left, an open porch sat below a massive window. The floor was flagstone, and white pillars supported the overhang. In the summer, our place was the center of activity. Folks would come over after boating to play cards and drink gin and tonics. We even had block parties with neighbors and friends supported by local police who barricaded the road. I couldn't wait to show my favorite person my home, my sweet Chris.

Chris stayed with Mom. Her life was one of existing. Existing to make Mom happy, or at least, quiet her down. She paid a heavy price for her continual avoidance of confrontation. Friends from work took up some of her time; she had a few dates, but a good deal of time was devoted to Mom's needs.

"Can you come visit, Chris? We would love for you to see our new home. I love it." I spoke into the phone, unable to contain my joy. "It is painted yellow, has country clapboard cabinets in the kitchen with a brick floor. I love the porch, and we can sit out there and talk the night away after Jamie goes to sleep. Hey, maybe we can go out in the boat, just you and me. I am getting so excited just thinking about it."

My brows lowered as my sister declined. Once again, Mom needed her, convinced there was someone watching the house. Locks were installed that would have kept out the military. It was clear Chris was floundering, stagnant in her growth, but her needs were invisible to our mother.

"She called the other night and sounded okay," I offered, then continued, "but when I mentioned inviting you for the weekend, she screamed at me. I was reminded how she needs you, how I am selfish, Jim was a lousy husband, and she ended by calling me the Thing."

I listened to Chris as she recanted our mother's misguided feelings about me. "Dollie, she is more needy now than ever. She wants me to go everywhere with her. Signs of her crippling paranoia have a stronghold on her. Although her narcissism is of long standing, she is much worse now, Dollie. You are the primary target for her anger. I have something to tell you. Please, don't get upset."

"Chris, you're scaring me." My mouth had dried up as I tried to speak.

"Well, remember I told you about my date? Well, when I got home, she had taken pills because I left her. She was released the next day but needed to see her therapist. Apparently, she told the doctor it was an accident. I told them what she told me that night, but because she didn't take enough to cause harm, she was released." Chris's voice trailed off. "Oh, the house is locked up like Fort Knox and darker than ever." I had much to say but that was for another time, not tonight.

Years later, she was given the diagnosis of a borderline personality disorder. Classic symptoms of the disorder were evident for years. Emotional instability, unstable and intense personal relationships, abandonment issues, intense anger.

Why was I hated by this woman? Chris thought she was jealous of me. No, that is not the answer. It was deeper and exposed early on. Her eyes mirrored her feelings when she looked me.

11

Five years later, we moved our little family one final time. We moved from the shore in Jersey to the mountains of the Poconos.

A chalet-style house sat on massive land. Mountains as far as the eye could see, ponds and lots of nothingness. Just a little family with a five-year-old enjoying the land. The one tiny drawback was the unpaved road that led up to our home and continued a mile to the facility for the criminally insane. Initially, we had no phone because there were no phone lines. Often, I was alone as night until my husband returned from work. From every window, nothing but a black void. Few vehicles passed our home due to the rough road—only an occasional truck of neighbors to the west.

On one such evening, Jim came home and entered through the slider. A shotgun rested against a wall, and I was icing my shoulder. "What the hell is going on? Why is the shotgun here?" he asked. "What's wrong with your arm?"

I guess just seeing him, I felt compelled to cry. Holding it together was no longer necessary. Jamie was tucked away in bed and sleeping now. Between gasps, I told the story that would soon spread throughout the valley, like dust from our road in the summer.

Jim sat next to me on the sofa as the fireplace burned behind us, releasing a rich fruity aroma into the air.

"Okay, Annie Oakley, what happened?" he teased, attempting to extinguish my trepidation.

"I was sitting on the sofa with Jamie. We were watching TV. Jamie noticed the car first and asked me why that car was sitting outside in the dark. I put on a robe, walked to look out, and there it was. An older car, dents all over it, parked on that road that faces our cabin just off to the left." The road was unpaved, like the road in front of our house. It went up around the subdivision. There was no need for a vehicle to be parked there. None.

"Jamie started to get upset because they would turn their lights on and off, open and shut their doors, walk around the car, and yell out. I am certain they were drunk. So, as all the folks around here said, I did as I was told. I got your gun, loaded it, stepped out onto the porch, pigtails and all, lifted the gun, and fired into the air."

Jim started to laugh. "You've never fired a weapon. How did you do?"

Lowering my robe, I exposed my right shoulder and my gunslinger's wound—a huge bruise on my shoulder from the kickback.

"Oh, and as promised, the local farmers hearing the gun came charging down the road. I could see by their smiles they were getting a huge kickout of my predicament. Oh, and the game warden came as well to ensure there were no poachers."

Jamie waddled out in his footed pajamas, rubbing his eyes. "Daddy, Mommy shot the bad men."

With that statement, we both started to laugh. "Honey, let's go back to bed. Daddy's home now."

We loved our life in the Poconos. Long walks, sleigh riding down the mountain, snowmobiling, father-and-son skinny-dipping in one of the two ponds on the property. Arriving home, my husband would strip down, and he and our son would slip into the pond, leaving clothes on the ground. Before long, the two would be bouncing about with their white butts in the water. And in the winter, we would walk in the snow to our neighbor's house, about a half-mile walk on the snow-covered pathway. Our son would play with their boys as the adults sat around the kitchen table.

On one such night, the air was clean, sweet, and cold. Each step we took made a crunching sound, breaking the silence of trees frozen in place. Nothing stirred. The lights in our neighbor's ranch home cast a glow on the frozen snow. The smiles expressed friendliness, characteristic with the farming community of which they were part. "Come on in, have a seat. I made some venison meatballs with brown sugar." Elaine placed the bowl on the table with some bread. Lots of homemade butter, French fries, baked beans, applesauce, and a bottle of wine.

Bill, Elaine's hardworking husband picked up the bottle. "Have you ever tasted dandelion wine?" I started to laugh, thinking he was kidding. "Well, you get yours first." I was poured a hefty glass from the large bottle. I lifted the glass to my lips without any anticipation of what wine made from weeds would consist of. Well, all I can write is both my arms went numb, as did my lips and legs. Weed wine is a killer.

In this environment of community, our marriage began to thrive. The absence of outside influence was a fresh start. Surrounded by the beauty of the area fostered renewal of spirit. Mother's influence continued in her effort to sabotage our relationship, but if I didn't let her, it wouldn't have had an effect. As soon as our phone was installed, the calls began.

"Well, what time did he get home last night? Leaving you alone with that place just down the road, what kind of a husband is he?" Most communications began with a demeaning statement from Mother. The truth is Mom was never happy with my joy. But when I complained about something, my husband for example, well, she was on board. Regrettably, I am ashamed to admit, Mother's comments began to take root. I began seeing him through her eyes, and there were some problems surfacing as the months passed. Being alone so much was difficult. Cracks began to form in our relationship. Besides Mother's input, I suspected we both needed to take ownership. The one commonality was we both loved to play, but were not completely prepared for the grownup part of marriage, at least I wasn't. We were forced to move from PA back to NJ. We talked of separation several times and lived apart but always seem to come together.

This separation was different. I was living in the home of my youth. Chris was still living with Mother. She was in her thirties, had never married, nor had children, and she quit school—yet she stayed with Mom. As a peacemaker, she knew any effort to move away would cause a reaction from Mother that she was not built to live with. She hated conflict, avoidance at all cost. Plus, denial of her abilities that took root in third grade fostered a lack of self-worth. A woman, an insensitive teacher's words helped to mold the being she would become. With a lilt in her voice, the words "the front row is for my bright children. Move to the last row where you belong" sealed her fate. She was good for one thing. Taking care of Mother, and even in that, she felt she failed.

Mom was now working as a governess. The irony of this can only be compared to a blind person being asked to teach painting. Our mother was lost in so many ways and unable to meet the needs of her own children—yet, she was now caring for others. I am certain in many ways she did an adequate job, but she held a distorted reality.

Mother, with her desperate need to be loved, was caring for a small child. For reasons known solely to Mother, she confided to Chris. Her confession was disturbing on so many levels. Apparently, she slapped the sleeping baby awake. His cries allowed her to use the excuse when needed to comfort him. So that is what she did.

Mom was not at home a good deal of time; a gift for me who was presently living at home due to my separation from my husband. Working as a governess meant she lived with families. It was during one of her time away from home, my Jason was conceived. A virus, fever and all that goes with illness, knocked me off my feet. I was too sick to care for my son, plus, I feared he would become ill.

"Hi, Jim, listen, I am running a fever and really feel terrible. I really can't take care of Jamie, and I am afraid if I get too close, he will get it too. Would you please help me?" I asked into the phone. My temperature was 102, and I ached everywhere. I needed help. Mother was on an assignment. Chris and I were always so thankful when she was away. Drama was limited. But she was away now working. Jim was staying with his mother a few towns away.

"I'll come after work. Is that okay? Need to get some clothes and make a few stops."

He stayed a few days, helped get Jamie off to school, and took care of me. My temperature lifted. And on that day, my beautiful Jason was conceived. We called him the virus baby. Nine months later, on the fourth of July, it was hot and promised to be perfect for fireworks. Unable to afford to live on my own, I was still with Mother and Chris. Her next-door neighbor had invited us over for BBQ.

"Wow, you are huge, Dollie," Pat stated, eyeing me.

Carrying a dish of potato salad, I set it down on the table. "I promise not to have the baby and ruin your day," I teased, accepting a glass of lemonade. "Gosh, is it hot. Don't you just love New Jersey summers?" I chugged the cool glass of sweetness.

Wiping her brow, she teased. "Well, if you do, I will deliver it, right here, on the picnic table. Don't worry, I will remove the hamburgers first." A finger touched my swollen belly. "Your mother said you were having a difficult pregnancy. I know it has been hard on her."

My difficult pregnancy was difficult on Mother. Interesting. I wondered how she would deal with my delivery. I withdrew from her touch. Why is it that everyone suddenly assumes it is okay to touch pregnant women? I didn't like it very much.

"I developed gestational diabetes. Therefore, fatigue is so much worse than with Jamie. I hope the delivery is not as problematic as it was with Jamie. Back then, the obstetrician told me I would need a C-section, but I went into labor before it was scheduled. Poor Jamie looked like a cone head after the birth." We laughed.

Mom crossed over into the neighbor's yard. She placed her chocolate chip cookies onto the table. Everyone loved her cookies. They were the Tollhouse recipe, but she really creamed the butter, spooned them perfectly onto the cookie sheet, and added ingredients that would please the recipient. Walnuts. Raisins. White chocolate bits.

"How can I help?" she asked of Pat. "Are you prepared to deliver this baby if Dollie goes into labor? Actually, her due date is upon us." Mom's smile was without heart. In all the pictures of her, especially holding her children, she looked pained, not joyful. Her countenance today was in direct opposition to the one we saw behind closed doors. She had a quick wit, a family trait passed on to her children, a gift, indeed, I opened often to offset pain.

My mother always made me feel as if I was walking through a minefield. "Uh-oh." I looked down at the fluid spilling onto my shorts. Unfortunately, there would be no fireworks for me. As life would have it, my water *did* break at the party. Mom and Chris drove me to the hospital, but Mother needed to leave, so I was left alone. The labor needed to be induced. My boy was eager to enter the world. On July 5, I gave birth to another perfect baby boy. I named him Jason Michael. I loved the name Michael, likeness to God.

"So I got me another son." Jim was unable to contain himself. "Where did he get that blonde hair?" he asked teasingly. "Do I need to have a word with the mailman?"

The next day, mother and son were discharged. No more languishing in the hospital. Chris was beaming as she stared at my baby. "He is so cute. Wait till Mom sees him. What do you think she will say?"

"What time will she be back?" My fingers explored the softness of his body. A sweet bud of a nose, a chin in motion as he sucked his bottle, and chubby cheeks that made my heart soar.

The front door flung with explosive force. Mother was home! Without so much as a glance at me or her beautiful baby grandson, she stomped directly into the kitchen, dropping her things on the floor. Chris and I sat frozen.

Doors opened and slammed shut. The teakettle was filled with water, slammed on the stove. Without a word, she entered her bedroom, the TV blasted, the thud from her shoes being thrown could be heard. The peaceful moment Chris and I shared just moments earlier faded, replaced by genuine, intense fear.

"What on earth is going on?" I whispered to Chris. "Did she say anything to you earlier when you called her?"

She chewed on her lip as she answered me softly. "I never got through to her."

We both jumped, gooseflesh rose on our arms at the shrill of the teakettle whistle. To most, it is a pleasant sound, but to the Knight children, it was an alarm. Mom appeared in the hallway, avoiding us again; her jaw set, she turned toward the kitchen. More banging, slamming, stopping with a few curses tossed in for flavor. We sensed a tension unlike any we had ever seen, and we had seen much. This was different. I felt as though we were in physical danger.

My heart was beating out of my chest. Chris looked terrified. My baby was stirring in my arms, as the slamming woke him with a startle. I felt protective of my baby, and without thinking, I asked her when she appeared in the hallway, "Aren't you going to look at your grandson?"

Silence. She was now looking in our direction. The question was repeated. Silence.

"Mom, come see your grandson," Chris requested, her tone so low, it was almost inaudible. I guess she thought that whatever was wrong, seeing this beautiful baby might soften her heart.

She stormed across the room to where we sat. "Why would you let your husband see him before me?" Her words were dripping with anger, with rage. The button had indeed been pushed—she was completely out of control. She continued screaming, walking from room to room and throwing things. She was escalating. Her hands formed fists as she struck at furniture, the wall—whatever was in her way.

"Mom, are you really not going to see your grandchild because the father got to see him first?" Chris said, angry at the injustice. I felt a sense of protection in her voice.

"You got it!" she screamed.

"What difference does that make? He is the father. Do you know how your actions are hurting me? How can you walk right by him? What is wrong with you?" I felt close to tears. She always rejected me, but now, she was rejecting my infant son.

Inches from my face, she screamed words that cut into my soul. "You never cared about me, you're selfish, I wish you weren't my daughter. You don't fit into this family. You Thing." Her words lacked any semblance of rationale. I felt her spit hitting my face. And my sweet Jason began to cry. Not once did her gaze leave my face to look at the flesh and blood in my arms. A new life, only days old, was witnessing an episode of madness. Thank God, he would not recall it.

"Enough!" I screamed.

"I'll tell you when you've had enough." She left, headed into the bedroom. I guess to get some secret stash. Back in the hall moments later, she continued, "You have had enough. I'm the one who has had enough." This was directed at me. Turning to Chris, she said, "You, you little traitor. After all I have done for you." Then anger blended with her internal sadness; her tears formed. She headed into the bathroom. With the door left opened, we heard her running water, the familiar sound to wash down her pills. What was it tonight? Uppers? Downers? Pain killers?

My baby close to my breast, I rose. Chris followed. "Let's get out of here—now," I whispered. Chris gathered the things for the baby without Mother noticing. Our fight-or-flight reaction helped us move stealthily in record time. We ran out to the car while Mother was in the bathroom. Seconds later, we pulled away, leaving Crazy behind.

"Dollie, where are we going?" Chris asked, my son close to her chest. Jamie was with his father, thank God.

"I don't know. I have no idea." My tears formed and spilled. My perfect moment ruined. How many moments that should be treasured, captured on celluloid, shared with family and friends ended like this? Far too many to count.

We had fled many times before. Train trips to nowhere, walks that lasted hours, or simply hiding in the cellar until she fell asleep. This was different. A line had been crossed. My children deserved better. Chris deserved better, and yes, I deserved better as well. Despair filled the car. A new mom, her sister, and a three-day-old baby with no place to go. I was so scared, sad, and hopeless. And yet, I would rather be in the car driving up and down Route 22 than back in that house.

Route 22, a highway dotted with restaurants, gas stations, stores, and motels might provide a safe place, even if just for the night.

"How about that one?" Chris pointed to a two-story motel. The vacancy sign was lit, although it read "acany" due to missing lightbulbs. We crawled through knee-high weeds around the building, only to stop beside broken outdoor furniture.

"It looks terrible. Some of the lights are out, and the paint is peeling. Let's keep looking," I answered, exhaustion setting in. Bringing my sweet baby into Bates Motel was not going to happen.

"How's our baby? Sleeping?" I asked, unable to see his face. Chris was holding him gently. In just three days, she had fallen deeply in love with her nephew.

After what felt like hours, we decided on a place. Was it suitable for a newborn? No. But it would have to do. We were running on empty, and my son was awake and hungry. There would be no joyful grandma this night. No "let me hold him." No innocent baby sleeping in the little basinet I prepared. Would we ever experience normal? What the hell was normal, anyway? All I knew for certain was that this wasn't it. I vowed I would never let her ruin my kids' lives as she had ours.

We spent a few days in motels, and eventually, we stayed at my mother-in-law's. I hated her knowing the family problems, but where else could I go? Chris returned to Mother's house, at least for a while. Mother needed her; therefore, she would do or say anything and make promises to bring her back into her life. With the passage of time, Mother did see her grandson, and she appeared to have feelings for him.

I went back to Jim because that seemed to be the right thing to do. He loved his children. But it didn't last, and we divorced. During our marriage, I obtained my GED, then I went back to nursing school for my LPN. Supporting my boys, with the help of their father, was possible with an education.

After the divorce, the children and I moved to an upstairs apartment, the landlord lived downstairs. A far cry from our beautiful home, on three wooded acres, with four bedrooms, and beautiful privacy that was our family's final home. In our new home, each boy had their own room. I slept on the sofa. Not ideal, but I made it work.

A woman who raised several of her own children was my babysitter. In fact, the reason I moved to this town was because the boys had established a life there. Boy Scouts, friends, and childcare. There was a needed familiarity during such a transition.

12

"So what are you going to do about it?" my older boy challenged me as I entered our home.

"Can I get my coat off?" I asked, thinking I had nothing left to give this day. "What am I supposed to do about what?"

He was on top of me, his face inches away as he cried, "My freckles, that's what? Everyone teases me. I hate them." To a young man, this was a most serious problem indeed. Of course, the fact that tomorrow we would be sitting in the dark because I didn't have enough money for the power bill came second to the melanin crisis.

Working at a school now for the developmentally challenged was difficult. My position was on the wards. This is where residents with multiple anomalies lived. Some had serious seizure disorders, another boy had hydrocephalous, while others needed feeding tubes to survive.

One evening, I heard, "Dollie Sommers, report to the OD office. Dollie Sommers, report to the OD office." Hearing the page was frightening. As a mother, often our first thoughts travel to some tragedy with our children. My boys were with their father for the weekend.

Opening the double door from the wards, I stepped in the hallway that led to the Officer of the Day Office. It was my ex-husband whom I saw first, and beside him my older boy, now about ten. Jamie's expression screamed like a neon sign. Something was wrong, very wrong. Before they spoke a word, I asked, unable to hide the rising panic in my being, "Where is Jason?" The three of us formed a small circle. There were no immediate answers, so I repeated, "Where is Jason?" The delay in Jim's answer and deliverance of the news spoke volumes. With great difficulty, he spoke words that would be a blow to my heart.

"Dollie, Jason is fine. He is with my mother. But your brother Bobby is dead. He hung himself. I am so sorry." I learned later that I released a scream heard throughout the building.

Bobby and I had just reestablished a connection. He was married with children and had fled to Maine. "I want to get as far away as possible from New Jersey. Nothing but bad memories here. I want a life with my family that isn't tainted." Bobby spoke these words long ago. There was no love lost with his wife and our parents: that was certainly understandable.

Back home, alone, in the tiny apartment, I felt a deep melancholy set in. I dreaded the call not yet made to my sister about our brother. Mother never had much to do with him, so no need to worry about her reaction to the news. I dragged the phone into the living room and began to dial. Bobby, with the hot temper, great talent, quick humor, who always sang for me, was gone. He carried with him more answers to the secrets he had just begun to share with me. Secrets about our father's perversions.

Dialing the phone, I tried to organize my thoughts. What words would I use to reveal indiscernible news? One ring. Two rings. Three rings. Four rings. Five rings. "Please, God, don't let her answer." My relationship with God was not really what one might call a relationship. My cries to Him only came of distress. I didn't trust Him or believe in Him to help me. I blamed the actions of humans to taint my impression of a higher being. But that night, I begged Him, if he were there, to help me.

"Hello?" Chris's sweet voice echoed in my ear.

"It's me."

"Hi, how are you? Peaceful here. Mom is working. Are you enjoying your solitude?" She giggled.

A cough ascended in my voice. "Chris, I have some terrible news. Bobby is dead. He hung himself."

Her wails tore into my soul. Unable to speak coherently, she strung words together for me to decipher. "Where? Who called? Why? Are you…sure? Poor Bobby."

"Chris, I don't know any more than what I told you. They were not forthcoming with info. Apparently, he is already buried."

"Why weren't we told?" she asked.

"Don't know. Bobby and Kathy disliked our parents, blaming them for Bobby's troubles to some degree. I guess that is why. Another mystery, Chris."

In a whisper, she said she needed to go. We hung up, both left to deal with our pain. He hung himself. Mother didn't even go to his wedding because she had to work. I know of no mother who would miss her only son's wedding. May God forgive her. He had married on the beach, in a Nehru jacket at sunrise. My memory is intact as to the events. Beautiful. But to Mother, I guess it was not to her liking. He felt that sting of that rejection for the remainder of his life. No one came to his wedding in the family except me and my cousin, Bonnie.

Muscles flinched at the sound of the phone a short while later. I knew who would be on the other end. No fear this time for me. Anger was brewing. I knew it would be our mother.

"Hello?"

Crying, wailing in my ear. "How did this happen? What am I going to do? I can't go through this!" What came next was a flight of ideas. A rambling focused on the impact of this news on *her*. How this would impact *her*. Not his family or his children or his siblings, but it was one more tragedy she could cry about and elicit sympathy. Poor Margaret. Oh, how I hated those words.

Deep within me, something stirred. A volcano of repressed feelings. "How is Bobby's death going to impact you?" I screamed into the phone. I got up and began making tracks in the carpet. "What the hell do you care about Bobby? What have you ever done for him or me or Chris? What about his wife? His children? How are they going to manage?" I started to cry again. So sad that even in death, my brother did not receive attention or love.

The phone was smashed into the cradle. A while later, Chris called. She and Mother had a very similar exchange. She left the house to come visit me. Dad was genuinely upset. "Did you know your brother wrote me a seething letter? Apparently, I was a horrible father." Bobby had shared his sentiments about living with Dad. He did tell me he hated him but never went into explicit details. I knew there were secrets about Dad, me, and him he wasn't ready to share. Now they were as dead as my brother. Dead were so many of our life experiences lay.

Mother was always complaining about her life, her lack of money, and raising children. Chris and I were model children. I ran the house, Chris comforted her nonstop, and Bobby was sent away. Mother had life insurance on all three of her children. She cried the blues about never having money, but for reasons known only to her, she had life insurance on her children. Why?

The three of us never understood how Mother had enough money to pay for insurance on her children. Why did she need insurance? I knew of no other parents who held an insurance policy on their children. I am sure some did, but with a growing list of needs for us, why buy insurance?

The boys were at their father's. Chris came for a visit a few weeks after the death of our brother. Unusually quiet at home, we were able to have a nice, private conversation.

"What do you think Mom did with the insurance money she had on Bobby?" I asked Chris.

"Dollie, I have no idea. I asked her several times, but she just told me it was none of my business. I reminded her that Bobby's widow had three children, young children to raise on her own. But knowing Mother, she would use the excuse that she and Kathy never got along so she could keep the money. I really hope Mother did the right thing, but that is between her and her conscience. We will never know, I guess."

Mother never spoke of our brother again. No more tears, no special memories on his birthday, no stories about him as a child. Nothing. Although I suspect his name came up on special occasions. Those times with her family or friends. Then she would cry and once again; she would be the center of attention. Our mother was a real attention whore. Writing these words, I feel such a sense of loss for her. To live your entire life craving attention, negative attention. Pity. But did she ever receive the positive love and attention she desired and needed as most human beings need? I don't know. What she craved, she drove away. Her attributes overshadowed by her illness. Poor Margaret was the theme. Sadly, if only family could have seen the children behind poor Margaret who screamed for a semblance of normalcy.

Chris and I had no closure with our brother. The little redhead with that fiery temper. Life continued. Bobby was dead. We would never know the secrets he held close to the vest. Truths that might help me understand the *whys* behind his hatred for our father. Those stories he had cautiously been feeding me—just small bites of information. But now we needed to close the chapter that remained unwritten without an ending. It was over. Bobby was gone. No more hearing him sing "Mr. Bojangles," the song he always played and sang just for me. He died in pain. He lived in pain. He caused pain.

13

Years later, on a scholarship, I returned to college to obtain my RN. I received my full salary and tuition from the center where I was employed. I was an LPN, and this allowed me to advance my education by earning my RN. The money allowed me to raise my boys. Although my pay was small, it was enough to make ends meet. Sort of. There were many, many struggles, but somehow, it all worked out. Not only was I on the dean's list, but I made the president's list a few times as well. The coveted Clinical Excellence Award was awarded to me.

"There you are. We just heard you are receiving an award." A student entered the restroom and delivered the news with an authentic smile.

Drying my hands, I answered in disbelief. "My grades were not good enough to win an academic award. You must be mistaken."

"No, not an academic honor, but the Clinical Excellence Award. That is a one big deal. All the professors must agree on the candidate, and, let's face it, that is not an easy task." She paused, put on lipstick, then finished by saying, "I heard this year, you were an easy choice. No real arguments but an easy decision." She blotted her lips, fussed with her hair, then turned. Over her shoulder, she said, "Congratulations, well-deserved."

A deer caught in the headlights had nothing on me as I stood there, mouth open, diligently attempting to disseminate the words spoken. I won the most difficult award of all. My sister was the first person I called.

My parents and my children were there on award night. Afterward, we went to a restaurant Mother wanted. The evening began with my English professor thanking the family members of all the award recipients. He continued to state that without their love and support, these awards would be most difficult to achieve. Chris looked across the table toward me. The message was sent and received. An unseen eye roll cemented the unspoken communication.

Afterward, we all left the hall. We were swallowed up by hordes of laughing, chatting, screaming student and parents. A mad dash to the parking lots had commenced. Our little group was less celebratory. Although, I was in high spirits despite the dark mood of the mother. My boys were as proud of me as boys can be. Truth be known, their goal was to go and eat. That was paramount.

"Dollie, your mother wants to go to that diner on Route 22. She likes it there, and it is closer to her house," Dad spoke. Obviously, he was speaking for Mother. Not at all uncommon, as she always took her side unless she wasn't around. Mother, Chris, and my beautiful boys were in the lead. I could almost picture her subtle smile knowing that she won once again.

"Dad, it's my day, my celebration. I wanted to go to the Clinton House. I told you that when you asked me a week ago." I knew the words stretched out in a childlike whine, but I didn't care. "Damn it, can't something be about me?" I didn't expect or receive an answer that satisfied me. For reasons unknown to any of his children, he loved my mother. She belittled him, yelled at him publicly, and even shared intimate details about him to his children and other members of the family. And yet, he loved her.

"I know, just let it go though, okay, Dollie? Let's keep the peace."

I had no choice. I worked so hard, obtained this award, had other responsibilities as well, but what did Mother want? What would make Mom happy?

We continued to walk across the college campus toward the parking lot. I thought about how much I would miss coming here. I loved school. I excelled scholastically; therefore, my shattered ego received a layer of adhesive that allowed positives accolades to stick. Self-importance took root with each success. Slowly, over time, I began to put the pieces together. I didn't realize that the cementing of the damaged ego would take a lifetime. I took on a "fake it to you make it" position.

At my coaxing, my sister finally moved away from Mother. Already in her mid-thirties, she had a lot of catching up to do. She moved to Virginia without a place to go or a job, but nonetheless, she left the house of our mother. She worked with battered women, made friends, and had her own little apartment. She was finally standing on her own two feet.

As she grew and achieved successes, my mother's hatred of me intensified. After all, in Mom's eyes, I drove Chris away. I loved Chris and saddened to see her locked in a situation where unhappiness was the theme of the day. Finally, her life was beginning. The cost of freedom was great, but it was the right thing to do.

After living upstairs, in a two-family home, I was finally able to afford to rent a house. Yes, a house. I wanted normalcy. The biggest mistake of my life was allowing my son, my older child, to live with his dad. Not because there was anything wrong with his dad, but this act, I am certain, led him to the feeling of abandonment. We had an argument; he said he wanted to live with his father, and I allowed it. But I quickly changed my mind and was told he didn't want to be with me. When one has a damaged ego, that comment was easy to swallow. I was told later that my son did not say that.

Our little home had a side porch, a hedge across the front, a garage, and a big backyard with a lot of green grass and mature trees. And it was just a block from the elementary school. It needed work, but I loved papering, painting, stenciling, cutting grass, and all those things that go into making a house a home.

"Mom, thanks for the bunk beds—they're cool," Jason said. "This room is so much bigger than my old room. I can have kids sleep over now."

"How do you like the wallpaper?" I asked, pleased with the pattern. A really cool plaid with a border of dogs. Very masculine, at least in my opinion. Paper on the upper half, a border, then blue paint.

"It's okay."

"Okay? Is that all?" As quickly as the words were expelled, I realized that for a twelve-year-old, his answer was most appropriate. I started to laugh and wrestled with him. Now at my height, he loved to reach over and run his fingers through my hair to mess it up. He loved this gesture—it made him feel like the adult, and I the child.

Time slid forward deprived of any significant meaning or the anticipated crisis I had experienced from our past. It was Chris's life that turned upside down.

*****

Late one night, the phone rang. There was an absence of contentment in her voice replaced by sharp, unsettled negativity. Without warning, she received the news that her current position, working in a battered women's shelter, was eliminated. Budget cuts forced the shelter to close and put my sister out without a soft place to land.

I was perched on my sofa. Directly across from where I now sat were three windows that formed a bay. Natural light flooded the room during the day. Growing up in a house where there was a total absence of illumination, my thirst for light was insatiable. But tonight, they looked like black eyes.

"So what are you going to do?" I asked.

Over the phone, her voice was soft, sad, and stunned. "Dollie, I don't know. There have been cuts taking place within the organization, and I guess I was on the chopping block. There are no jobs here, as you know. It took me forever to find this one." Her voice was deflated.

Staring into the black void outside, I asked, "Will you be able to stay in Virginia? I know how much you love it there. You have made some great friends." My mind was racing with suggestions and support. "Chris, if you can't stay there, you can always come stay here with us. There is plenty of room."

I could hear the soft sobs. "Thanks. I think moving back may be my only choice."

"Why don't you set a deadline? For example, if you can't find work in a month, you will consider moving back. I am pleased you are not considering going back to Mom's. I know she would open her door to you and be kind, but in the long run, we know what will happen."

"I will take a little time, and thanks for the invite." I hung up, hating to break the connection. My heart hurt for her. She finally made the break and stepped out in faith. Now, after a few years, life determined it was time to return to where it all began.

Six weeks later, she returned to New Jersey to live with us. The upstairs was perfect for her. At the top of the stairs, a pony wall revealed two good-sized rooms on either side. Both quite suitable for her to have a living room and a bedroom.

Shortly after her arrival, Jason hollered as he came home. He and his aunt had taken a ride. They were gone about an hour. "Mom, come here."

"What's that?" Stepping into the hall where he stood, Chris was still on the porch.

He put down his package. "We got a microwave, a refrigerator, and a toilet! Aunt Chris is going to have her own toilet." He thought that was quite funny. "And we had McDonald's and stopped at the Dairy Queen." This was one happy boy. He loved his Aunt Chris. After all, when I said no to something, especially junk food, a little trip up a flight of stairs often brought about a sweet treat hidden from his mom.

Her own toilet, how about that? I mused.

"I am exhausted…and broke. I wasn't going to get so much, but, Dollie, they were having a great sale, right, Jase?" Crossing the room, she steered for the sofa.

"Yeah, she even got…" He fell silent.

"She got what? Fess up, kid," I teased.

"Dunkin Donuts, a dozen. So, Dollie, no need for supper." She and Jase laughed. I joined in. I expected my son to be walking on the ceiling before too long with his sugar high.

Life was good. My boys loved Chris, and she loved them.

****

Driving home from Mother's on one occasion, Jason said to me, "Grandma feels very sad about you and her. She is sad that you don't get along. She told me that she was going to kill herself because you don't treat her nice. What did you do wrong, Mom?"

"Nothing, hon. Grandma has some problems." I was livid. She drew the suicide card—and told my son.

Once home, I placed a call. "How dare you threaten to kill yourself in front of my son! You are not going to see my children now. I warned you repeatedly. How dare you mention suicide to a thirteen-year-old? This is the third such remark. Three strikes, you are out." With effort, I gently placed the phone back. I could just imagine the story Mom's family heard. Through a deluge of tears, the story of her evil daughter blocking her from her grandchild would be replayed. Of course, they sided with her. She omitted the real reason for my decision; of course, there was no apology. She never spoke to me about what she said to my Jason.

She did not see my children for months. I had to protect them. I remembered how it felt to have no one protect us from her.

14

Few things were more daunting than the suggestion Chris made one evening in spring. "Dollie, I've been thinking." She paused, shifting her weight on her sofa. She rose to get what I assumed would be snacks. I loved her little piece of heaven. I loved sitting up there in this cozy space. Curved ceilings, plants, bird houses, all around. Returning to the sofa, she literally plopped on the couch, dropping a bag of chips on the wicker table. "I really want to go back to that orphanage. I guess therapy is causing me to think about things in our past. What do you think?"

My shoulders lifted and dropped. "I guess it would be okay. When do you want to go?"

We agreed that Saturday would be a good day. I was grateful the day was sunny with clear blue skies and moderate temperatures. A perfect day to travel back to hell. The Knight girls were exceptionally quiet, lost in our thoughts that surfaced without provocation.

An hour after we left, we were pulling up in front of the ominous building. When we called to make arrangements, we learned it was no longer an orphanage but a private school. What happened next was right out of a grade-B movie. Turning into the driveway, black clouds rolled in hiding the sun; the wind raged, forcing limbs to drop on our path. Thunder punched the heavens, forcing lightning to crackle in anger. Hail smacked the car as if God were calling out from His heavenly realm, "Go home."

Even with formable warning, we proceeded. A nervous laugh filled the car. "Do you think God might be trying to tell us something?" I asked. Just look at that sky. Let's at least wait. We need to wait until the rain stops." God continued to pelt us as we parked in a spot to the left of the ominous building that housed dark secrets. Chris and I sat silently bonded in fear of what waited for us just beyond the doors.

"Did you see that?" I asked as an intense flash of lightning tore through the blackened skies.

"I never saw lightning going sideways." We both started to laugh, a throaty laugh, shallow and insincere.

Chris was the first to speak after an expanse of silence. "Dollie, did you hear me?"

"Huh?"

"I said the rain is letting up. Let's go in, okay?"

My hand reached for the door handle. "Yeah, I guess. Are you okay?"

Her shrug was her only answer. The walkway was covered with tiny slices of ice, forcing us to move with cautious steps.

"Be careful, Chris. The steps are really slippery." I stood before the same doors that led to abuse many years earlier. I was transferred back in time to a scared little seven-year-old. "Should we knock or just go in?" I asked to avoid the final step.

Chris, who stood just one step below me, suddenly moved past me. Without answering me, she opened the door. A surprising act for my sister. We stepped in and stood silently, taking in the familiar sights and aromas. The chill persisted, even as the door closed behind me. This chill had nothing to do with the temperature but the remembrance of the cold women who still haunted the halls. Feelings of fear, sadness, and loss washed over me as memories flooded my thoughts. I saw a well-dressed woman approach, drawing me back into the present. Her warm smile was in opposition to the icy initial encounter in this gloomy place. I assumed she was the woman I spoke to earlier in the week about our visit.

Lovely and welcoming would describe the manner of the woman who greeted us. After an informal, relaxed exchange, we were given carte blanche to explore. I felt like that little girl again. Scared. We wandered past the church with the ever-present aroma of incense. A little farther down the hall, doors opened on either side, revealing our old dorms that were converted to classrooms.

"Chris, I am having trouble breathing." I paused, frozen in place.

"Why, what's the matter?"

My hands cupped my face. "I was remembering how we were forced to sleep under the covers. It was terrible. I couldn't breathe."

Her voice was void of emotion. "You never told me that."

My chest rose and fell in rapid succession as I attempted to speak. "When the sisters passed by, if they saw our face uncovered, well, we would feel the punishment. It was quick and painful." Tears welled up, not for the adult I was now, standing in a classroom, but for the little girl who once slept in this room.

Like a strobe light, flashes of recollections appeared in my mind. Little girls whimpering. Sounds of wedding bands clinking as they struck the metal beds. Whispering. Doors opening and closing. Noises of unknown origin scurried about. In the present now, I wondered what was occurring in the space that we needed to shield our eyes.

Chris and I moved out into the hall in silence. My sister had shut down. "It looks the same," she commented, passing the large bath area. Sinks, shower stalls, towel racks, and lockers remained. "They never showed our parents the real bathroom we used during the day, the one with rats, mold, and broken plumbing. Sisters of Little Mercy is what they should have been called. There were some sweet ones, but they couldn't dilute the meanness exhibited by some of the others. What the hell makes people act like that? Especially to children." I could now feel her seething anger, like a pressure cooker. She was ready to explode. Conversely, I was a whimpering mess. We had switched identities.

"Does this look familiar to you?" she asked. We had just climbed the stairs, reached the landing, and proceeded upward.

"Not really. I guess this is stupid, but it feels familiar." My words were barely audible. A few minutes later, when we arrived in the gym, I remained void of sensations. No memories or strange feelings.

We both looked around the room. Floor markings in royal blue marked off boundaries for various games. A basketball hoop hung at the far end, bleachers, balls, and the usual array of sport paraphernalia used for children to burn off the fuse of abundant kinetic energy.

Directly in front of us, on the far side of the room, was an opening. I was transported back in time when a seven-year-old needed to use the bathroom. Quickly, I returned to the present, filled with anger at acts heaped upon defenseless children. Without hesitation, I knew what lay beyond and stomped to the site. I was filled with rage.

"Wait for me! What's the hurry?" Chris called out.

The steps were steep, with an unusually high rise made of cement, grayed from time, dirt, and wear. I needed to go back down there. I hoped seeing it as nothing but a bathroom would wash away the thundercloud of what took place there.

"I'll wait here. I have no interest in seeing that smelly place again." I heard her walk across the gym floor.

At the bottom, I noticed the room had been repaired. New sinks, floors, stalls, and a nice yellow paint turned the dismal room into nothing but an ordinary bathroom. The only reminder was the grate in the corner that allowed water to seep out, should there be a flooding situation. All evidence of rodent holes was gone.

Although the steps leading to the rat-infested bathroom triggered remembrance, I wondered why the gym held no such feelings or memories.

"So what do you think?" The kind woman checked on us. "Does it bring back any memories? Were you aware of the reunion for the ladies who lived here last year? It was very nice. A few of the nuns, those in good health, attended. I was told it was lovely. Do you have any questions?" Her question was authentic and benevolent. It was evident; she thought we were two of the hundreds of orphans to pass through this place.

"No, not really. Thank you so much for allowing us to visit." My smile was forced, and I hoped this lovely lady didn't recognize the strain in my words or gestures.

"Oh, I almost forgot to tell you. A few years back, there was a terrible fire here. It started in the gym. They suspected it was lightning, but no one really knows what happened. The gym you saw was rebuilt. It is the only new part of this ancient building. Have a safe journey back. So nice to meet you both." She turned, and we all walked out through the same doors we entered.

The sky was now clear, save for a few dark clouds in the distance. The air was clean and sweet as if the evil had been washed away.

Chris and I were soon back in the car, ready to return home. "The place had the same smell it did when we were here, and it made me sick to my stomach. When I think of what some of those women did to us and the other kids, well, I am furious." She pointed at the thorny bushes. "Remember how we were threatened with those thorns? Evil."

I remembered the story of the thorny crown that pierced Jesus's skull. To a small child, just the suggestion of a similar penance was terrifying. Compared to our last time here, I was no longer that scared child in the back seat, but a mature woman in control of my life. Pulling out and driving away, I verbalized my feelings. "I feel very sad for those two little girls who were abandoned so long ago. What did we do to deserve such abuse? Let's get the hell out of here." I paused before adding, "Whose stupid idea was this, anyway?"

Chris remained silent, lost in her own thoughts. Her body rigid. She was folding like a cheap lawn chair under the weight of her thoughts.

A few weeks after our trip back to the orphanage, I had an opportunity to talk with my friend Helen about the day. Comfortable with my therapist friend, I recanted the circumstances and the side effects of our visit. "You probably should have brought an army of therapists with you." She smiled widely before continuing, "You never should have gone back there without support. Anne, you know from your course work in psychology that memories can trigger feelings, and the feelings you had as a child are quite different than those of a timid child. What if your memory dug up events long since forgotten or deleted?"

I had abandoned the name *Dollie*. In its place, I used my middle name Anne. More professional. Margaret died a long time ago.

Mother, who bore the same name, complained about her name constantly.

"Well, I guess after a few months involved in the therapeutic group, Chris and I felt confident we could handle it. Boy, were we wrong. Chris has been seething just below the surface, but she won't speak of it. All she would say is that she would like to go on a *nun hunt*. Unlike me, she holds her feelings hostage. Lately, my dreams often include water. There are times when I am perched up high, looking down at a thunderous sea. But then, there are times I am perched on a riverbank on soft grass, watching ducks float by. Since our trip, the whirlpool dreams have continued. I am circling in a great vortex, speeding toward the voluminous mouth, wide open and eager to swallow me. Helen, it all feels so real that even when awake, it takes a great time for me to shake of the dread. The symbolism of water dreams can include life, death, change, rebirth, and renewal, to name a few."

"Maybe we should talk more—what do you think? Do you want to come into the office?" That began a relationship born of friendship cultivated into a therapeutic union.

*****

I loved that we lived close to a reservoir. So we would often spend time swimming in the water, boating, if that's what one would call one of those paddleboats, and even flying kites in the park that circumvented the clear lake water.

On this day, kites wiggled in the wind, soaring upward in the air currents. With a twist of the wrist, my Jason would send the tethered object into a different current, forcing the red triangle into a dive, its yellow tail waving above. Just looking upon the face of my special boy and his happiness filled me to the brim with love and joy. Nothing can surpass the love of a parent for their child. Nothing.

"Mom, this is so cool," my man-child exclaimed. He was almost fourteen, going on thirty. He felt he was old enough to make his own decisions, but then again, he would jump up and down about kites. I felt I failed with my older boy. There were times I leaned on him too much, placing adult matters onto a child. With a low sense of self, that made sense. After all, my mother wanted to kill herself because I was so bad—that was the record that played often, especially at select times in my life. Jamie was now in college. I fought hard to insure he would get the education needed.

"Let's go for ice cream afterward, okay?" I smiled. It was a good day, a great day. A memory-maker as I came to classify life's little treats. We hopped into the car and drove away. We pulled into the Dairy Queen parking lot. The place was very crowded with young people jumping up and down pointing at the ice cream selections. It appeared everyone had the same idea on this warm day to indulge in a sweet, cold treat.

Blond hair fell loosely on my beautiful boy's forehead. His body was tanned from the rays of the summer sun. I yearned to tell him how cute he was, but at this age, mothers remain silent.

"Mom, rather than ice cream, do you want to try frozen yogurt?"

My grimaces answered his question. I couldn't even tolerate the smell of the stuff, much less eat it. "Just a small vanilla cone for me. Okay?" I answered, smiling at my beautiful boy. Just the mere glance at my children created a reaction of joy. Pride. Love. Future. Anticipation.

I watched as my son jumped in line. After what appeared to be a very long time, perhaps because it was warm, my ice cream cone was finely delivered.

"Thanks," I commented, noticing the addition of rainbow sprinkles, my favorite.

Jason scooted around the car and got in. "So how is it?" His question was a tad too exploratory. He stared at me as I licked the cone.

My tongue caressed the delicious treat. "Very good."

"Aha!" he yelled, almost causing me to drop my cone. "That's yogurt! I told you you'd like it."

He tricked me.

We both started to laugh.

15

The day dawned with the signs of fall, and Halloween would soon be upon us. Leaves wearing shades of scarlet, gold, and tender brown began their final journey to the warm the earth below. Jason was sent off to school, grumbling all the way. Still in my nightgown, I stumbled up the stairs.

"Morning." My words were as lazy as my body.

"Mmmm," Chris mumbled, watching TV. "Is Jason gone?"

Folding into the rocker, slipper dangling from my foot, I replied, "Yeah, he's gone."

"I must start looking for a car today. My lease is almost up on the Pontiac. Do you want to go with me?" Chris focused on the screen.

"Yeah, what kind of car are you looking for? Do you still want a Honda?" I asked.

"I think so, but I like the VW Bug as well. What do you think?"

"We just need to be back for Jason. Plus, I need to take a rest before work tonight." Just thinking about it made me cringe. I could not understand how some nurses enjoyed the graveyard shift. I felt as if all I did was think about sleep. Not getting enough, when would I get some? Would that be enough sleep? I wandered through life during those days in a mind-numbing perpetual haze.

As a staff nurse at a private psychiatric hospital, all shifts were required. I was presently working the graveyard shift. I hated it. Fatigue was my constant companion. Sleep was in spurts and never enough. Besides, nights were quiet, so the hours crawled.

A few hours later, we left the Honda dealers with several brochures. We chatted on the way home about the different models. Of course, being women, our priorities were the colors and cool features.

Chris entered the leased car, starting the engine. "I loved the one with the sunroof. But I would get it in a red." We discussed various pros and cons about the car, the season and Jason.

Pulling onto our street, we observed a few kids heading home. "I don't want to make a decision until I check out the VW Rabbit. They are really cute. Plus, you get that really cool vase." She teased, knowing I would love the vase.

"Now that's important. I am glad you have your priorities in place," I teased, actually liking the idea of a retro VW Bug. "I can't wait to take a nap."

"Jason will be home by now," she said, turning the steering wheel.

"We're only a few minutes late," I offered. She pulled in the driveway aside the porch.

"The spider web really looks great," she said, climbing the steps. Each Halloween, I took out my yarn. I cut several strands of different lengths, tied them together, then carefully created the greatest spider web. Black pipe cleaners were twisted into the form of a monstrous spider. Jason always loved it.

"Thanks, Chris. As you know, I loved making it. I think I am a child in a grown-up body." My hand reached for the doorknob, turning it. It was locked. We never locked our doors. A pinch of concern stirred in me.

"Let me try." Chris used the key and tugged. She began to call out, "Jason, open up." We waited. Nothing. "I'll go around back and try the back door." She was down the porch steps and heading toward the rear porch that lead into the kitchen.

"I'll keep trying here. Jason, open up!"

Minutes later, Chris opened the front door. There was a calm in her voice when she spoke but an underlying, unspoken statement. "Something is wrong with Jason. He is sleeping on the sofa." Her words scared me, but I guess I thought he was just sick.

The fatigue I felt a mere moment before disappeared like smoke in the wind. From the basement of time, the memory of that day is dim, only fragments of events are recalled. I stepped into our home. Straight ahead of me was the closed door that led to my sister's little apartment. To my left, our living room. In front of me, on my couch, slumped my beautiful boy. He appeared to be asleep. I rushed to his side.

"Jason, wake up!" I called out, touching him. No response. It was at that moment I viewed a small spot of blood on his right temple. I do recall thinking, if this is a stupid Halloween joke, it is not funny.

"Jase!" I called again, touching him. He was unresponsive. He was breathing but unresponsive.

"Oh my God," Chris called. A gun fell onto the floor as I attempted to rouse him.

Despite the obvious, I simply could not grasp what was in front of me. I stepped outside of my own self; the nurse within took over. My fingers circled his wrist, checking for a pulse. I opened his eyes to check his pupils and all those things a nurse would do. Until I said, "Call 911." My brain could not take in what my eyes, my senses were trying to tell me. I felt as if I were melting into a puddle of disbelief, leaving my body, disassociating. My mind struggled for an answer other than the obvious. Everything was fading. The room was spinning. Time stopped. The world stopped rotating. If I spent a week, a month, a lifetime, what I felt in those moments would remain indescribable. The life I knew was about to end. Nothing would ever be the same. It was the shriek of sirens that pulled me from my lifeless state back into the nightmare.

First responders appeared. I don't know if they were let in or just opened the door and entered.

"He is over here."

"What happened? Get the stretcher. He will need to be airlifted."

I was pushed aside, pummeled with questions. I recall little of substance. I wanted to escape, to fade away into oblivion. I must have provided some answers, but I don't really recall. I kept thinking if they would just leave, everything would be okay.

"I don't know. We found him like this. No, I don't know where he got the gun. It is not mine. He's fourteen. He just turned fourteen." I wanted to scream at them to stop asking questions, to leave me alone.

Insanity grabbed me when one of the responders was heard saying, "He is still alive." I will never forget the impact of those words. Words that ripped me from my hopeful place, the safety of my delusions, into a repulsive reality. I hated that man. If Jason died, it would be his fault. I thought, *Of course he is still alive. Get out of my house. You're an idiot.* My period of disconnect from reality was underway. It was that man's fault if my child died.

Folks rushed in and out, questions continued, medical personnel were working on my boy, and commands were shouted. "He needs to be airlifted to the trauma center in Newark." A radio screeched in the background. Whispers by some, while others shouted. Occasionally, I would catch glances cast in my direction. Glances that told the story of what lie ahead. I was comforted by their presence, their acts of care for my son, but I hated them as well. They were making a big deal of everything. My son could not die.

Outside, a man's voice called out, "The copter will be here in a few minutes. They are landing at the school. Let's get him in the ambulance. Move it!" My son was on a stretcher, and men carried him out. Chris and I were alone in the living room, except for two state police officers. One remained with us, and the other was off someplace, I think in Jason's room.

The man who remained with us, and this I do remember, looked at us with deep compassion in his eyes. A young man with a kind heart took my hand as he said, "We'll take you there. It will be quicker. Okay? Where is his father?"

"Work. We're divorced."

The officer stood up. "Do you have his number?"

Once the number was provided, he stepped out onto the porch. I imagine he called him.

So much of that night I don't recall. Thank God, I remember calling my ex-husband as we sped toward the hospital at speeds topping ninety-five. He needed to be told where we would meet him on our way. We stopped to pick him up at a designated place on the highway. He spoke not a word as he stepped into the car—no words were needed. Now sandwiched between Jim and Chris, I reached for his hand, together in agony, silently praying. All previous hurts, arguments, difference faded, as we had one clearly defined objective: our son.

Arriving at the hospital, we were ushered into the ER. Jason was hooked up to several machines. The constant beep indicated a steady heartbeat. The monitors flashed his pulse and blood pressure readings. He was receiving oxygen, and an IV was infusing in his left arm.

"Jason, I am here with Dad and Aunt Chris. We love you." My fingers touched his leg that suddenly folded and rose. "Look, he is moving. Thank God." I remember that feeling as if it were today. My heart soared. He was going to be fine. Just fine.

A nurse, positioned at my son's head, was checking connections, monitors and offered in a soft voice, "That movement is just a reflex reaction." Once again, someone destroyed the image of my son coming home to live out the life God had planned for him. I hated her. I hated anybody who dared verbalize anything I didn't want to hear.

"Please wait outside. The doctor will be right with you," she continued, now looking at us.

Memory fails me completely as to the appearance of this man, the doctor who would speak to us about our child. Although I am absent of the image of this man, his words echoed in my consciousness as if articulated moments ago. "Your son's condition is grave. There are no brain waves. Even if he did survive, he would be confined to a wheelchair, and all his needs would need to be tended to by someone."

I thought, *Okay, that works.* I just wanted my boy.

"There is a room where you can wait over there. Someone will be in shortly to talk with you," he continued as he pointed to a place detached from the ER. Rather than taking the doctor's advice, I fled from the hospital. My pattern of running from painful or fearful situations was in effect. Jim joined me.

"Give me a cigarette," I asked of Jim.

"Dollie, don't start up again. You quit so long ago," he responded.

In the darkened parking lot, we wandered in a daze. I stopped, turning toward him. "I don't give a damn about what might happen to me. Please, just give me a cigarette." He did, and I lit up. Of course, it didn't help—just caused me to cough along with my tears. We went back inside where attempts to guide me into the room failed. If I didn't go into the room, no one could come and tell me my child was dead. Once again, I slipped into an altered state.

Jim and I were in a main area of the intensive care unit. The space was circumvented by small windowed rooms. My boy was in one of those rooms. Monitors hummed, with an occasional alarm signifying a change in vitals. On the far side of this cold, sterile room was my sister. Alone. I walked to her and hugged her. She loved my children as if they were her own.

My sister, who held fast to her emotions, now rode a tidal wave of grief. Her sobs echoed throughout the space. "Dollie, I am so sorry. He can't die. Please, please, God, don't take our Jason away," she chanted. Our sobbing blended like the perfect storm of despair. I was getting the attention while she suffered alone. No more.

"Why don't you two go in there and take a seat?" someone suggested.

Chris, looking as if she were going to fall or faint, drove me to enter the room. I don't recall how long it was before a woman, a minister, entered. She pulled up a chair across from the three of us. She offered the anticipated words of a member of the clergy. Then she said, "I am here to speak to you all about harvesting your son's organs."

I stood up and walked from the room. "You are a bitch," I mumbled. She was talking about harvesting my beautiful boy's organs. I hated her. I simply couldn't talk with her. *Why is everyone so convinced he is going to die? What is that matter with them?* I thought through pitched rage. *My child cannot die!*

Several hours later, my son was pronounced dead on October 16 of a self-inflicted gunshot wound. The world went dark.

When I learned how my older boy was informed and the pain he felt, it was as if I lost both my boys. Jamie, my elder son, was notified by my husband's minister. My son was camping with a group from college. This kindly man took the long drive up to the mountains to inform my son. Jamie told me that the minute he saw Reverend Tiller, he knew something happened to his brother. It was in the middle of the night when the man appeared. If it were one of his parents, the other parent would be the one to tell him, and probably not until the next day. Jamie, like his aunt, held his feelings close to the chest. It wasn't until a long time later I knew what he went through. In a letter, I read of the unrestrained pain that engulfed him when his brother died. He was dragged into a deep depression. My heart ached for Jamie reading his words. His hard shell had been cracked wide open to expose the tender meat inside.

16

The night my son died, I was admitted to the psych ward for observation. My mother placed a few phone calls when we arrived at her house. Health professionals felt I might take my own life. They were correct in their assumption.

The hospital, the admission, and the encounter with the health professionals was like a dream. But I do remember meeting with a psychiatrist. After an introduction, he asked me a few questions. "I am truly sorry about your son. Now I need to ask you a question, and I hope you provide an honest answer. Okay?" he asked.

I was numb, stoic, and empty of hope and life. No answer was offered.

"Anne, your family is concerned about you. Are you thinking about harming yourself?"

No answer.

"Anne, we are trying to help you. Don't you understand? Everyone is worried about you."

I was totally unable to speak because there was nothing left of me or my world. Unless you are unfortunate to survive such a devastating loss, you will never know the darkness that pulls you downward, deeper and deeper.

I heard something behind me. Footsteps moving across the floor. Then a gentle touch on my shoulder. I jumped—to me, the touch felt intrusive, unwanted, and cruel. The touch I yearned for had been stolen.

"Come with me. We'll get you settled in for the night." Dressed in street clothes, this nurse spoke in a gentle whisper. I hated her. I hated everybody. I thought, *Where is the God of love?* Begrudgingly, I stood. I hated this space's harsh lighting. It felt like an inquisition room. I knew in this light, I was exposed for the evil person I must be to have my child taken from me. Mom was correct after all. I am bad. So bad, people threaten self-harm, or actually carry through with the act.

"Sandy," a stoic man addressed the nurse who held my elbow as she attempted to guide me, "I will order something for her to help her sleep, and the pharmacy will bring it up. Keep a close eye, okay?" Code for this one is a suicide risk, an accurate assessment. I thought about the pills I took from Mother's cache.

Ushered into the locked mental health unit, my thoughts remained on my dead child. All I could think about was that my son was dead because of me. Mothers protect their children. Unworthy of living, I felt the world would be a better place without me. My mother's word years ago when she said "You are so bad I want to kill myself" played over and over in my head. Jason, now dead, was the proof. I am bad, really bad.

I was guided to a sofa in the day area.

"Anne, there is a call for you."

I rose, followed a woman, and was handed a phone.

"Anne, it's Allie," The muffled voice on the phone stated in a whisper. It was obvious this good friend from work had been crying. "I am so sorry about Jason." Her words cut into my cloak of numbing protection like a knife through butter. It was true. Jason was dead.

I fainted. Sometime later, I was given a small cup filled with medication.

"Take this, Anne. It will help relax you and help you sleep."

I tilted the cup into my mouth and felt the three pills on my tongue. I attempted to cheek them but was caught. My mouth opened as directed while she provided additional water.

"Anne, please don't do that again. Okay? You are a nurse. You know you need to get some rest. I can't say I have any idea of what you are experiencing, but we all want to walk with you through your pain. Let us help."

Shut up, I thought.

My plan was to store up the pills. I thought about Mother's stash hidden in my clothes. Then, when the opportunity came, I'd take them all. Time to rid the world of the ugliness that was me. The death of my son was my fault, of this I was certain. At least in that moment.

That one night locked away, I fell asleep thanks to medication. Demons and horrific figures filled my dreams. I awoke in a full terror. More meds, more sleep, more nightmares. Of course, in the morning when I awoke, the nightmare continued. My world was void of the light of my special child. I was there for another day and then released.

The details of the funeral, and for a long time after, can only be described as living in a trance, sprinkled with anger, a large dose of guilt. What is more amusing than the giggles of children? I love children. However, those same sounds—that once brought lightness to my heart and joy—now irritated me.

"Chris, what the hell are they laughing about? Jason is dead!" I told her.

Chris just looked at me, her pain searing like hot coals on dry, tender skin. Absent of her own children, she loved my boys. I don't believe anyone could love with an intensity as deep as my sisters for my boys. Tenderhearted, with the capacity to love like no other. She would have gladly given her life for these children, my sons. Barely able to keep it together, my sister was as close to surrendering to the abyss as I was. One look at my baby sister now, I realized she was scarcely capable of willing herself to get out of bed, day after day.

"Chris, come here please." I was in Jason's room. On his pillow was a small stain of blood.

Chris bent over to look. "Dollie, it's on the right side of the pillow."

"It doesn't make sense. He was in the living room, but a pillow in his room has a bloodstain." Fighting back tears, I continued, "Why was the bullet hole on the right when he was left-handed?"

The conversation faded as the image of my son filled every corner of my mind, and new question rose up. I sent for the autopsy reports and made calls to his friends. Somebody might have knowledge that could accommodate a modicum of peace for me.

"Mrs. Sommers?" she spoke in a whisper. When I responded, she continued. There was a nasal quality in her voice, her voice trembling. "I was told you wanted to know about my call with…" Her voice faded. I needed to speak with Jason's girlfriend. Questions were rising about his death. The gun. The blood on the pillow. The lack of a note.

"Thank you for calling me. Yes, please, can you tell me what happened the last time you spoke with Jason?" I really didn't want to inflict any more pain on my son's girlfriend, but I needed to know, so I pressed on. "Please tell me about that call." For a minute, I thought she hung up. She didn't respond. "Hon, are you still there?"

"Yes, I am here." She no longer hid her pain but cried softly. "We were just talking about that stuff, you know?"

No, I didn't know, but didn't care.

"While we were speaking, he heard the signal that another call was coming in. He said, "Hold it, let me check who is calling, it might be Mom." After a few minutes, he returned to the line. Ms. Sommers, his voice was well, he sounded upset. I don't know how to describe it, but he was, I don't know, just not Jason. He said, "I need to go," then hung up. "I was really upset. If the call was of a friend, or please don't get upset, or even if it was you, he would have continued the conversation after he hung up. I don't know who called, but I think that call had something to do with…you know."

Hearing her words, I felt like I was hit in the gut. Another missing puzzle piece. Who called Jason? What did they say? Why was he upset? What could have been so bad to keep him from speaking with this young lady he professed his love to? Jason would certainly tell one of his friends he called them back and continued conversing with a girl. Two people's name came to mind and one of them was Mother's. I already knew she had no filter. I was reminded of stories she told us when we were young. Stories that should never be shared, especially with children.

Chris had moved from my place. The move kept her close to me but far enough away from the emotional shock of a day in October that was etched in our minds. We were at her darling little apartment that was nestled on a hillside. Across the winding road, a beautiful river that cut through the terrain flowed parallel to the country road. A peaceful spot, just perfect for my introverted sister. Somewhere in time, the house was cut into three apartments. Seated at her round maple table, beneath a Tiffany-style lamp, hung by my son. I wanted to talk with her about that phone call with Jason's girlfriend.

Chris's hair was darker now, not as red, and her body plump from a sedentary life. I too had gained weight. "Chris, I have been thinking about what Donna said about Jason's last phone call. We know how, over the years, Mother would speak about suicide to him and often upset him very much. Plus, you know the lies she said about me to the family. Is it possible she was the one who called and said something to upset him?"

Swallowing a sip of iced tea, her response surprised me. "I thought of that already."

"Both boys would be upset with some of the things Grandma said about me, Grandpa, Bobby, and well, a lot of people. Of course, I am certain each time I forbade her from seeing my boys, the world never knew the why, just that Dollie has hurt Mother. Once again. No one protected us from her illness, but I sure as heck was going to protect my boys." Was Mother the one who called that morning? Another one of those missing puzzle pieces.

We both sat in silence, swallowed up in our own secret feelings and fears. Years later, a lawyer friend told me if I wanted, she could pursue obtaining a court order to disclose who called him on the last day of his life. I so wanted to know. But as much as I wanted to know the answer, it was to remain a mystery.

What exactly was I to do with the information? If it were my mother who made a call that resulted in the demise of one of my most cherished gifts, my anger would rise to an unhealthy summit. Anyone who drove my son to commit such an act would forever be hated.

The blood on the pillow. Gunshot wound to the right temple when he was left-handed. A mysterious call, the identity of the caller unknown. Accident? Suicide? Or something else? For my sake, it is best I move past these thoughts and push them back into obscurity. Yet, for the remainder of my life, I will be haunted by the ghosts of uncertainty.

Everything I ever believe in changed the day that beautiful boy left us forever. How many times have I uttered the words "I don't know what I would do if I lost my child." That answer was within reach. Now I knew the answer. Nothing I fathomed compared to the searing pain and loss I felt. Nothing.

I spent months trying to make sense of something that was not logical. Jason was happy, or so I thought. Autopsy reports were reviewed, conversations with his friends took place, a thorough search of his room, even conversations with police and prosecutors, led to more unanswered questions.

Death by gunshot always requires an investigation. The results were mixed, but I really feel they were negligent. I suspected they decided early on and, well, that ended any real investigation. Lack of a note, history of Jason and his friends playing with guns, playing Russian roulette. Was this an accident, self-inflicted, or something else? Questions I feared would never be answered. If anyone wanted to hurt me hurting me children would be the way.

The next six months, life was just a shadow of reality. I developed a love affair with the couch, watching TV as days melted away. My life was not my own. I floated up and under the tidal waves of despair, anger, longing, and guilt. A sea of self-loathing washed over me weighing me down. I was drowning in a whirlpool of hopelessness and helplessness. It got to the point where just making coffee became a challenge of major proportion.

"You have to fight, Anne. I know it's hard, but you are familiar with the story of Job. He lost everything but remained faithful to God," Darlene shared her deeply rooted faith. She had stopped by my home, driven by concern. What I heard was blah, blah, blah. How the hell did she know what I was going through? My God had sentenced me to a living death. My punishment by God, for some sin of omission or commission, was to remain alive so I would forever feel the searing stings of sadness. That was my mind-set in those early months after the death of my Jason. I am bad, so God punished me.

My dear sister suffered deeply. Her life had never really started, so there was no husband or children to comfort her. Much of her life, up until a few years ago, was spent pleasing Mother, and now, just as she was attempting to start over, the young man she loved more than life was gone. At her request, I attended her church. I can't say I was angry at God. In fact, I had brought this all on myself, although I am not certain how. God, for me, was a being of punishment. His love was divvied out freely to those He loved, and I was not on that list. I didn't blame God for Jason's death. He took Jason because I was so bad.

A bold knock on the front door jolted me even though I knew who it was on the other side. I rose, and with a faux smile on my face, I opened the front door, allowing the pastor of Chris's church in. "It is nice to see you again," I said, lying.

I heard Chris on the stairs coming down. As she opened the door to her unit, she offered the man a genuine smile. "Hi, Eddie, come on in."

She ushered him in. He took a seat near the window. Chris and I were perched on the sofa. After we were seated, ignoring the unspoken tension in the air, we spent a few minutes with superficial chatter. A few minutes passed before Chris stood up, saying, "I am going to leave you two alone, okay? We'll talk later, okay, Eddie?"

He rose. "Of course, Chris." Tenderly, he touched her arm just before she exited and headed up the stairs.

"Eddie, are you certain I can't get you something to drink or eat?" I offered, rising. At this stage of my life, that simple suggestion took more energy and commitment than I had to offer. I would have preferred to lie on the couch, speechless, motionless, and lost in self-loathing. He melted into a chair nearest the door. "No, I'm good. Thanks anyway, Anne." He placed his Bible on a table aside the chair. "Your sister told me all about what you are going through. She loves you and doesn't want anything to happen to you. I would like you to tell me what you are feeling. But first, I want to say a little prayer that God will speak to you, ease your pain, provide peace, and show you his love. He does love you. I hope you know that deep in your heart."

My head dropped, but my thoughts were on a God who took my child as a punishment. After all, the words of Mother pricked me: "You are so bad, I am going to kill myself."

He prayed a very beautiful, yet singularly simple, prayer. No elaborate verses instead. He spoke as if he were speaking to his own papa. He expressed his feelings with honesty, humility, and assurance of God's faithfulness.

We talked for an hour. He shared his suicide attempt in his teens and said things to me that somehow allowed a beam of hope into the dark corners of my heart. My pain was still present and would be with me for a long time. But the burden of guilt began to lift. I appreciated his candor and the precious scriptures telling of God's love and forgiveness, but it was his genuine concern for me, like a flower of hope, that caught my attention. Positive thoughts and actions floated into my mind.

"Anne, like me, we are imperfect parents. There is no manual to ensure our children will be safe. But from what I have been told, and from what I observed today, your heart is good. You did your best, and I am certain your son knew. Is that true?"

I felt fluid on my cheekbone as I spoke. "Whenever I asked him if he knew how much I loved him, he would say, 'You are always telling me. How could I not know?' I think it embarrassed him." A parade of images of my son marched across my mind.

It was Chris's footsteps on the stairs that dragged me back to the present and into my new reality. "Hi, guys, is it all right if I come in now?" Her glance in my direction was to explore my present state of mind. I was capable of a smile that she returned.

"It is really so good to see you, Eddie. Thank you so much for coming." She sat down beside me. I could tell she was uncomfortable, not knowing how the visit went or what we spoke about. She was worried I was going to harm myself because of the overpowering guilt I felt. That thought was as close as the next breath of air I would take.

"Eddie, you are the first person who spoke with me since, well, you know, who talked honestly to me." My voice was stronger than it was before.

He smiled. "Well, I would love to take credit, but the truth is I prayed all the way here. I thought I was either going to help or make things worse. Thank God, you are feeling a little better. Anne, keep turning to Him, trust Him, and He will carry you through the dark."

17

I felt the need after many months to seek therapeutic help. One of my professors in college was also a therapist. There was a feeling that went beyond grief, beyond sadness. Guilt? Loss? Was it disappointment? Anger? Unable to capture the feeling and deal with it, I sought the wise counsel of a therapist. Helen was one of my professors in college whom I admired.

Her office was in an old charming building in a historical village a few miles south of me. The first time I used the bathroom, fit with an old claw-footed bathtub, I laughed. Several large goldfish swam about the perimeter This place felt safe. Homey. Perfect to reveal innermost thoughts.

After several sessions, it was on one particular day when, sitting in her office, she said, "If you don't deal with the anger you feel for Jason, you will be stuck."

What the hell was she talking about? Anger at my son? What for? "My anger has always been inward. He did nothing. My job was to protect, and I failed. Not him. What are you talking about? Helen, that's crazy."

"You know the stages of grief. If you skip one, you will never heal, not completely."

Leaving her office, I thought she just didn't understand. I was angry—very angry, but never at my son. I failed him. I walked about in a trance of sorts. I could return to work, but I have no clear memory of life during this period; after all, I was in the mist of despair, unable to see any way out. I accepted this to be my permanent existence. All attempts to block out the images of that terrible period meant I blocked out all memories.

Six months later after I was in therapy, I woke up on a Saturday, a year and a half after Jason's death. From some place, a place so detached to my consciousness, an anger pitched through me. This anomalous feeling was hurled at my son. Anger is an outward expression, a symptom. It is what we reveal to the world, an expression of what we are feeling on the inside. Frustration. Hurt. Betrayal.

After a cup of coffee, some mental gymnastics, a real circus of the mind, I called Chris.

"What's wrong with you today? You are in some mood." Chris spoke harshly on the other end of the phone.

I was perched on the sofa in my new home. A contemporary condo with two ponds, a wooded area off the grassy knoll, and two balconies. Located a short distance from the home I shared with the boys, but far enough away to avoid the happenstance of running into his friends.

"Chris, I don't know. I went to bed last night peaceful and awoke filled to the brim with an uncomfortable anger toward Jason. I don't know what to do. This feeling, so foreign to me, was as uncomfortable as if I were mad at him for dying. But I can't help it. How dare he hurt his family? I gave up so much for him. He had the braces he needed, the contacts he wanted. And let's not forget that damn trampoline. You loved him so much, Chris, as did his dad and brother. Everyone loved him. Now we are left with nothing."

After a long pause, she said, "I have been angry at him for a long time, but didn't want to upset you by expressing it. I do understand."

"I've got to get out of here, go for a ride, and think it out. Perhaps write a letter to him. I don't know what to do."

"Please, drive safely. Call me when you want to talk." The click indicated she hung up without a goodbye.

Not knowing where I was going, I jumped in the car. Before long, I realized I was heading south going down the shore. I parked, grabbed the pad, and exited. The cool air was refreshing, although the beach was empty, unprepared for the onslaught of beachgoers that would soon be here. The summer season would not start for months. I plodded down the beach, found a spot, and flopped in the sand. Notepad in hand, I began to write, and write, and then write some more. Feelings poured onto paper like sand through an hourglass. As I wrote, remorse seeped into my being. God knows, I miss him so. When the writing was completed, the pages were shredded. I walked to the water's edge and released them into the angry, dark sea. She gobbled them up, spit them out, then took them away.

I released my anger. At least, for the moment. Like all stages of grief, he would return. Again, and again.

Back on the beach, I sat still for a long time. Waiting. Waiting for a sign. Waiting for peace. Always waiting.

"Are you all right?" Words spoken in a soft, melodic tone asked by a stranger, a woman. She appeared out of nowhere off my right side.

Looking up at her, my response was deliberate and dishonest. "Yeah, I'm fine."

She squatted down and looked directly into my eyes. "No, you're not." A long pause before she continued, "But, dear, you will be fine. In time, you will be just fine."

Her gaze pierced my heart, and I turned away, trying to regain stability. My gaze fixed on the waves that slapped the sand. When I looked back, she was gone. I rose, looked up the beach, a vast expanse of sand. She disappeared into thin air. Not knowing now or then what to make of the encounter, I believe just when I needed help, divine help, an angel appeared. Her words floated in my heart: "You will be fine, dear."

My therapist was right—that day was a turning point. In time, the pain lessened, but an underlying sadness became my constant companion. A sight. A sound. A memory, and my heart would betray me, and I would fall helpless into the spiral of grief. Life proceeded forward, and with it, occasional happiness, such as my son graduating college or buying my condo. But the best of me, that childlike quality, that love of God's simple gifts, was gone.

That is, until New Year's Eve 2000.

My surviving son James had moved to the city with his fiancée, Grace. They loved Manhattan's energy. On a visit to their apartment on the upper east side, the subject of the 5k run was first raised.

"Mom, we are going to do the Midnight Run around Central Park. Do you want to join us? Rob is coming in too. If you want to join us, you would need to contact the Roadrunners Club and get tickets and your number."

"Yeah, Anne, why don't you come?" Grace jumped in.

I loved my son's fiancé. Grace was bright, spiritual, funny, but her greatest attribute, for me, was she loved my boy, and he loved her. She was blessed to have many siblings. Two brothers and a sister. A lovely family with a lot of energy. I had met Rob on many occasions and grew to love him like a son. He made everyone who encountered him feel special, a gift not often given to the males of the species. Sorry, guys.

Sitting in their little apartment, I began to visualize the night. This was the start of the new millennium: 2000 was just around the corner, and excitement was everywhere. I could sit home or I could be active with my family.

My response was as quick as a hiccup. "I would love it."

New Year's Eve 2000 was exhilarating. The city was alive with anticipation intermingled with an undercurrent of apprehension. The mounting concern regarding computers malfunction was all over the news and all everyone could talk about. Plus, the concern of a terrorist attack at this critical juncture of history. In a few hours, we would bid farewell to a millennium and welcome in a new one.

"So what do you think will happen? Do you think all computers will run amuck?" Rob asked, his words floating in a cloud of moisture.

"No way, it'll be fine. Maybe a glitch or two, but that's all," Grace answered.

The Y2K scare was spoken of in washrooms, boardrooms, and living rooms all around the world. The city's heartbeat was even louder this night as we waited for the birth of a new season, a rebirth. I could have been wearing a diamond tiara and felt perfectly safe. Every corner in Manhattan had massive police presence. I was there for my first 5K run around Central Park with my son, his fiancée, and Rob, Grace's brother. I was so thankful they invited me.

"Look up, the clouds are so low I can't see the top of the buildings. It's so beautiful and magical," I exclaimed. The others were not quite as excited, more eager to begin the run I imagined. But my inner child had come out and, as usual, was in awe at the sight. That night, I was born again. I was in the moment, feeling the cool air on my skin, caught up in the excitement and prepared to run the race of my life after I finished around Central Park.

"Hey, Ms. Sommers, are you ready?" Rob asked.

All around me, people gathered. There was an electricity in the air, like trying to hold on to a bolt of lightning. My gloved fingers were rubbing my arms in the cold. "I guess so."

Sleeping infants cuddled against mother's breast in slings. Their runners' numbers pinned to their snuggies. Then there was Donald Duck, families with strollers, serious runners, and, well, me. A middle-aged woman who was about to embark on a new adventure.

"Mom, we're going to be up in front. We'll meet you at the finish line," Jamie called out as they ran toward the front.

We had been dancing for hours, and there were cameras everywhere. People from every corner of the world were represented. This was a very special night; therefore, coverage of this event was important. High above, helicopter blades cut through the low-floating clouds. The reason we ventured into this great city was upon us.

"Okay, sounds good. They say what you do on New Year's Eve is an indicator of how you will spend the rest of the year. I sure hope so." My long-winded answer lost to the void as my son disappeared in the crowd.

Grace's cheerful manner was a reflection of all the runners who waited for the starting gun. "I am so glad you were able to join us. Good luck. Folks will be providing water as we run, and at the halfway mark, wine. It's ten minutes before we begin, so we better get in our positions." Grace was off to join the real runners, those under the seven-minute mile.

The music continued to play, and folks were dancing all around us. TV cameras in place so they would capture this momentous occasion. Signs posted the starting points for runners of all stages. My little entourage, except for me, went to the true runners' mark. I hit the middle sign. At least I didn't need the old ladies starting point.

Thousands of folks lined up, chatting in the cold. Their words caught in the steam as they spoke. I offered a silent prayer of thanks and thought about my departed son. My relationship with God had changed. I met the God of love. Oh, how my Jason would have loved this. He was a bit of an excitement junkie like his mother.

Then, through the chatter, we heard, "Runners, take your positions." Like noisy children in the playground, the crowd took their positions in line, waiting for the signal. I couldn't have been more excited if I were running in the New York Marathon. My Roadrunners shirt announced the 2000 Midnight Run. And I was part of it. Screams from rockets broke through the night sky, dripping colors to the earth. *Bam!* The run had begun.

Now, as exciting as that sounds, it was several minutes before I even reached the starting point. Thousands of bodies needed to squeeze through the starting gate, which was very narrow.

"Here, take some water," a bystander offered. Others held their hands out to be slapped as I ran around the park. I loved it. "Keep going, number 321!" I felt like a superhero. Of all the people in the world, I was one of just a few thousand who, on this special night, was in a 5K run around Central Park in the greatest city on earth.

About three-quarters of the way around the park, my superhero strength began to fade. Most folks prepare for such an event, but this superhero didn't feel it necessary. As I passed the restrooms, I was convinced I had used up all the oxygen in my lungs. I was winding down like many of the New Year's Eve parties would soon be doing.

"Enough is enough," I spoke into the crisp night air. But just as I was prepared to throw in my running shoes, it was Donald Duck who drove me forward. He was my impetus to keep going. There was no way I was going to allow someone dressed up like Donald Duck, who just scooted past me, to beat me. No way was this superhero going to be outrun by a Disney character.

No way, Mr. Duck! I begged for air, taking in a breath as I rounded the final turn. There it was! In the near distance was the finish line. Alleluia! A figure caught my eye. Someone was jumping in to the race. It was Grace. She waited for me, so I didn't need to run in alone. Together, we passed under the huge clock that was ticking down the time. She finished twice. I finished just once, but I did beat Donald Duck.

My hands were in the air as I passed beneath the finish line. I did it. I did it. In that moment, looking disgusting, skullcap in place, hair falling in my eyes, jacket around my waist, I felt it. Joy. Real joy. It only took eight years for the feeling to return. This was the first day of the rest of my life. I knew I would be okay.

"Your son refused to join you. He said he didn't want anyone to think he was just coming through the gate." I laughed at Grace's words. So typical for my macho son.

As we all walked around the city, I heard a man in a hoodie yell out, "Hey, how'd you do in the race?"

"I won!" I called back. We all laughed.

We had breakfast, talked, laughed, and then it was time to end the night. It was early morning before I arrived home. I was exhausted on a cloud of promise for the future. This was the night I became whole again. Thank God.

18

My life was freshened up like clothes on a clothesline in the warm summer breeze. Stains, ugliness, wrinkles, and odors of the past were behind me. Jamie and Grace were happy as they continued to focus on their talent, their vocation, the writing of scripts. Chris was in her little apartment and working at a group home. Her life was sedentary, but it was *her* life. I knew she was capable of anything she set her mind to, but that ego that drives us was taken from her by a third-grade teacher and a lifetime of living with Mother. She loved her work, was content to some degree but would often confess to feelings of depression and failure.

I loved where I lived. A quaint village with a river running through it. A red mill stood as a sentry to the restored village on the west side of the river. The mill was painted a beautiful red, with a working waterwheel. Thousands have put her image on canvas or captured her on celluloid or via digital media. Before crossing the yellow painted ornate metal bridge, we stopped midway to view the falls. Each summer, a huge event captured the attention of hundreds. Perhaps you have heard of it. The Great American Rubber Ducky Race. Hundreds of rubber ducks are dropped from the side of a rowboat into the water. Their painted numbers on the underbellies hidden in the water as they begin their journey downstream. The bridges, roads, and sidewalk areas are covered with cheering children and adults, many shouting out their number to win. Viewing hundreds of buttery rubber ducks topple over the falls is hysterical. Downstream, a team of men in water weights stood abreast, holding a net to capture the parade. There was even a prize given for the last duck to hit the net.

Although life had settled down, the war with Mother waged on. A silent conflict done in the dark, behind closed doors on the phone, and always my poor sister was caught in the middle. Over and over again, in the middle of the night, the shrill sound of the phone shattered the stillness. I would be jolted out of a sound sleep, wide awake, as anyone would be when a call arrives at that hour.

"Hello?" My yawn forced an exaggeration of the word. I waited. I heard breathing on the other end. "Hello, who's there?" I said with a hint of both fear and anger.

"It's me." Recognizing Mom's voice always stirred fear within me. But at 3:00 a.m., it was intensified.

"What's wrong?" Often with Mom, those were the first words spoken. There was always something wrong. She lived in a constant state of calamity. As stated earlier, the carpenter ants were discussed so frequently, followed by tears. Chris and I would laugh behind her back about them. Everyone laughed at her with her damn carpenter ants.

This particular night, I was awakened from sleep to hear her words—direct, harsh, and cruel. "You are a terrible person, and your son is just like you. Both selfish, unfeeling. Neither of you care about me. I hate you both. I am your mother, and yet, I need help, and neither of you care. Every night I am here alone, thanks to you, Dollie. You coerced your sister to leave me. She was perfectly content with me. You are so evil. Your son is a loser. He will never amount to anything."

Like any mother (except mine), protecting her young was paramount. All the hateful things she heaped on me all my life now was being slung in the direction of my child, my son. I don't recall ever doing anything that pleased her.

"You crazy bitch. You really need help. I cannot stand you. I do not want you to call me *ever* again!" I screamed. I am paraphrasing what I said, but God forgive me, it was hurtful and hateful. My child would not be subjected to the antics of this poor woman who was ill and not being treated as needed. Instead, everyone pretended all was well. Her behavior was always allowed. Therefore, there was no reason to stop.

I would love to write that was the end of it, but it was not. She took to calling me, saying hateful things to get a rise out of me and then she would cry or go silent. Then there were the rambling letters that went no place. She was always, and I mean always, trying to prove her point. Mom had such proclivity to ramble on about some fact that made no sense to anyone but her. I cannot write how shocked and saddened I was when I learned what was behind Mother's actions. The phone messages were recorded. Of course, only my responses were heard, not the words that led up to my outbursts. Later, for the entertainment of family and friends, she would play the recordings. I can only imagine what she told everyone, through tears of course, how her evil daughter attacked her for no reason. Her words were deleted. Even now, all this time later, I can almost hear everyone offering her support. "Poor Margaret. I feel so sorry for you." She didn't need sympathy—she needed help. But she gobbled up those words like a stranded kitten who is offered milk. She needed the same thing that kitten did. Love and acceptance, but she had no idea how to achieve it. Her illness was like a fortress preventing intrusion by acts of genuine love and concern. She called my friends, Helen, and even my pastor to inform them how evil I was.

I always felt different from the rest of my family. Of course, being told "you don't belong in this family" my entire life secured those sentiments. In fact, I would often tease with my sister Chris when we lived at Mother's about it.

"I just know my real parents, my true mother and father, are loving and very, very wealthy. They come from royalty, and when they find me, things will be so different. I think that is why Dad calls me Princess at times—perhaps he knows the truth."

Mom's statements that I was not part of the family were internalized. Her method of informing me that I was different. Not accepted. An outsider.

On one particular day in nursing school, a particular question came to the surface that forced me to question Mother's claim that I was not part of the family. I was sitting in the third level in anatomy class. We were studying the cardiovascular system. Blood types were being addressed. I learned that children must have the blood type of one of their parents. I raised my hand.

"I have A negative, but my parents are both positive," I stated, insistent her statement was incorrect.

"You must be mistaken about your blood type, or your parents, because what you stated is very rare, unless perhaps there is a mutation."

As the students laughed, my insecurities rose to a new height. I know they were not laughing at me but the word *mutation*. But the damage was done. More doubt. More questions.

19

Moving to California was the boldest decision I ever made. It meant leaving behind family, friends, and my home to begin a new life. Many people make such a decision because they are running from something or running to something. But that was not the case with me. I loved my life in rural New Jersey. It was a good life. Life had finally settled into a quiet ordinary existence, something I yearned for. I was active in a church that fostered the congregants to strive to become more like Christ. Both my parents were deceased. My son and his fiancé, Grace, were the catalyst for this move, but certainly not the single factor. They were both screenwriters and had spoken of moving to California, and all it had to offer aroused something within me. It took a few visits to SoCal before I made the decision. I was offered a lucrative job that afforded me the ability to follow my dream.

The move was made in October, and not until this very second did I make the connection. Jason died in October. A sign? A fresh start to start anew. Leaving my sissy behind was incredibly difficult. I made her promise to visit frequently, I would carry all costs. She promised. I knew my Jason was with the Father, but still, my sadness, although irrational, of leaving him behind raised some doubt. Everything, and I mean everything, fell into place. It was ordained. My condo was rented in record time. Despite living 2,300 miles from SoCal, I locked in a condo, on the ocean that was within my price range.

A friend managed to get some men to help pack up the truck. I remember that day as if it was yesterday. My son would be driving the truck, hauling my Lexus to my new home and ready to drive with my son across country, hauling furniture with my Lexus in tow.

My excitement was blended with sadness leaving the only home I'd owned since the divorce. This move was the first relocation not forced on me by some *event*.

We started off, goodbyes were said, tears were spilled, and soon my home would be filled with a stranger, my tenant. To write my son was less than excited about driving 2800 miles in a U-Haul truck with his verbally aggressive mother and a very frightened feline with long sharp claws would be an understatement.

During the trip through Pennsylvania, Ohio, Indiana, and New Mexico, my son would remind me of what happened to Thelma and Louise, usually when my chattering got on his nerves.

"Mom, I just want to stay where they have a gym so I can work out. Okay?"

"Sure, no problem."

Being in the truck for so many hours, he needed to release some of the tension.

Everything I owned, except a large box hidden in my darkened garage, came with me. The container that would remain in Jersey held items of my son Jason. His favorite baseball shirt, the plaque with his name that hung on the wall when he was a little guy. Notes from classmates and other treasured possessions. Leaving it behind ensured it would not be damaged or lost.

That massive box has never been opened and now rests in my walk-in closet. After twenty-six years, I fear the contents are damaged or destroyed by mice or bugs. I know for certain I cannot open the box on my own.

My work with a CA realtor had proven productive, but many leads fell through.

"If you can find me a place on the ocean, I will take you out for a nice meal." I was teasing, of course. With California, real estate being some of the priciest in the country, that was not going to be possible. I was moving to Pacific Palisades into a condo complex I had not seen except over the Internet. I had no idea what I was going to find at the other end as the miles fell away. Yes, it was on the ocean!

It was late afternoon when we finally arrived in Los Angeles. I knew we had arrived in this legendary city when the traffic stalled to a crawl, attempting to circumnavigate past a white pickup truck on the 101. As every person in the planet knows, the traffic on California highways are likened to lengthy parking lots. A snail would have made better time.

"Look, Mom, that guy is using masking tape to hold the truck together."

Working on a broken-down piece of junk wherever it stalls is not all that uncommon.

"Well, get used to it," Jamie stated. "We are going to be here for a while. Nothing is moving, and it's after five."

Harper gave a soft cry. "We'll be there soon, little girl." That was an oxymoron, considering the little girl weighed as much as me. "Let me call the realtor. I hope he can wait and those guys are going to arrive at six to help us move in."

My excitement had faded, while fatigue had dulled my enthusiasm. Instead, all I could see was traffic, buildings, highways, and garbage strewn on the side of the road. As we passed the vehicle, I observed that this poor soul's tailpipe had fell off and was now lying on the highway. It was easy to observe the friendly nature of LA folks. As they passed the stranded group, they offered a one-finger wave of encouragement. This was my first, albeit not my last, stressful moment on the highways of LA. Whatever you have heard about the highways out here is a lie—they are much worse. Pack a lunch, grab some water, and make certain your favorite CDs are in the player because no matter the time, the route, or mileage, you will be sitting behind some fancy car roaring its frustrated supercharged engine.

Attempting to arrive at the condo at the exact same time as our realtor proved to be a challenge. We arrived late afternoon to my new home on Sunset Boulevard; what a thrill for this country girl.

"Jamie, are you going to be able to handle this?" I asked, looking up at the narrow driveway that leads to Edgewater Towers condo complex. There was a gatehouse on the left, with a driveway that had to be forty-five degrees, snaking past four condo buildings. The A and B buildings on the right, C and D on the left with a beautiful, bougainvillea-covered gazebo with tables and chairs up the hill to the right of one of the parking lots. Three steps down from the structure led the guests to a large patio with grass flanking the rear, dropping off in such a fashion that despite the PCH below, all we could see was the grassy expansive yard that appeared to fall off into the Pacific Ocean. I was going to live in 704D—ocean view!

"Park over there. I think that's where the guard said to park," I said.

Jamie steered us along. "Mom, I was in the truck, I heard him. I really don't need supervision. Please, let me do this." There was a tad of irritation in his voice, but understandable. 2,300 miles with his chatterbox mother and a crying cat was more than anyone could tolerate. Driving my Lexus was about as big a vehicle I could handle. So, my child, my son needed to drive solo across the country. He was great.

He pulled into a space that took up several parking spaces, as directed at the gate. Together, we disembarked from the truck. "Oh, I am so stiff. You must be exhausted." I stretched my legs. "Look, there's Todd, I think. I only saw a picture of him." I waved toward the realtor.

We started walking toward the man who was standing near a pathway to the C building. The paperwork was taken care of, keys were provided, and just at that moment—thank you, God—the men arrived to move me in even though we were late.

My son guided the men to the truck. I waited, and together we rode up the elevator. My new life was about to commence. A few hours later, the movers gone, the day bade farewell with the most magnificent sunset over the Pacific. Plopping on the sofa, exhausted from the trip, my promised call to my sister was placed. Windows open to the sounds of the sea slapping the sand—a symphony of nature welcoming me.

"Chris, you wouldn't believe it. The condo is beautiful, all new interior, but you should see the beauty here. I can't believe I am actually living on the ocean, in California."

She responded, "Did you have any trouble? Where is Jamie?"

"You know my son. He's exploring the grounds. There is a hiking trail, two pools, and a workout room. Oh, a tennis court as well. You should have seen Jamie. He was speechless as we walked up the trail a bit, took a seat on the bench, and took in the beauty. Oh, I have a balcony off my bedroom. The temperature here is perfect with a nice breeze. I love it."

My daily view from my new home.

My new home in Edgewater Towers aka ET.

"Dollie, I am so happy for you. Can't wait to see it." I could almost hear her smiling. If I was happy, she was happy. Conversely, if one of us was hurting, the other felt it. Connected deeply by a bond of shared experiences.

This move was blessed. On the last minivacation to California, I received the job offer for a nursing position. The slight drawback was obtaining a California license. A time-consuming feat. But everything fell into place. My home in New Jersey was rented out in record-breaking time to a lovely woman. Even searching for a home, 2800 miles away, was somewhat of a miracle. The search was performed with the help of a CA realtor, lots of multiple listing photos, credit checks, and phone calls. One unit, the one I landed in, I kept rejecting. It looked cold to me in the photos. Several others I thought I wanted would be gone by the time my realtor and I connected. But you cannot change the plans God has for you. My first California home was perfect for me.

The first year in California was like no other in my life. Los Angeles hosted a plethora of cultures, education, languages, housing, and career opportunities. The gap between the haves and have-nots, as the saying goes, was as vast as the earth is to the sun. I loved the opportunity to share my love of God with everyone, as well as any financial or physical attributes of mine that would help others. Everyone, like me, lived in gated communities—even the homeless, it seemed.

Not knowing anyone was extremely difficult in those first few weeks. Not a soul. This drove me to be proactive in my search for companionship. I would stop at Starbucks in Malibu, or the Bu as locals call it, after work. Huge soft sofas flanked the structure, so my skinny vanilla latte could be enjoyed listening to the flopping of water from the fountain in the courtyard. Thirsty for communication, I had conversations with strangers, would talk about anything, and then go home to my beautiful condo—alone.

One night, driving up the coast, there was the most brilliant sunset I ever saw. Orange sky with a brilliant sliver of yellow and orange on the horizon. My car crossed the PCH to park. A man and a woman were obviously in awe of the vision as I was. Attempting to catch my breath, I asked the man, "Did you ever see anything so magnificent?"

"It is certainly beautiful. I wish I had a camera." He brought water to his mouth.

I told the stranger, "I am new to California, so I'm not accustomed to these sights. I moved into Edgewater Towers, and my view is spectacular. Do you live nearby?" I suspect my innocence and excitement loosened my lips. Again. I just told a total stranger too much info.

"I live in Topanga Canyon," he answered with a smile.

Without thinking, I asked, "How do you get there?" I noticed there was no car.

"I walk." He adjusted his worn backpack.

Now that I had nothing to focus on but the man in front of me, I observed his worn and dirty clothes and his hairy face, desperately in need of a trim. That is when I realized this man was one of the many homeless in LA. A very nice man who, like so many others, lives on the streets or beach or in the canyons in tents or boxes. So many broken people who long ago watched their dreams sink like the setting sun.

"You have a nice evening, Miss. Nice talking to you. Tonight, we viewed one of God's miracles." He parted, leaving me alone with my thoughts.

Climbing into my car, I couldn't help but wonder how he ended up homeless. He was decent, and I could tell by the exchange, articulate and educated, but now, his home was hidden up in the hills of Topanga. Later that night, back home, I spoke with my son on the phone. I heard him call out to Grace, "My mother is now making friends with homeless men. Mom, are you crazy?"

He was not the only person I spoke to who expressed the same sentiment. I wasn't crazy, just naïve and lonely. The folks at work stuck to themselves, so I had little conversation with anyone. Whenever I spoke with someone, I either sat on my deck or on the sofa below the window. I loved the sounds outside, especially at night. Did you know there are birds that sing at night?

Several weeks later, on a beautiful Saturday—of course, in SoCal every day was beautiful in west LA—I heard a knock on the door. "I'm Julia. I live down the hall. I wanted to greet you and bring you a little gift." This lady's huge heart pumped for the sole purpose of loving and giving. I liked her instantly.

"Come on in." Internally, I was so excited to meet someone my age, single and just across the hall. I was jumping up and down inside. I showed her my place, and then we sat on the sofa, with the view of my Pacific Ocean over my shoulder.

"Where are you from?" The plant she carried was placed gently on the cocktail table.

"New Jersey. I was offered a sweet job out here. Jamie, my son, drove with me across the country with my belongings. He and his fiancée, Grace, will be moving to California shortly." I filled my lungs with air before I continued. "It is so beautiful here. I guess for you this is an everyday occurrence, but for me, the view, the music of the ocean, and Julia, the aromas…are breathtaking for this Joisey Girl. The only problem is I don't know anyone. I spend my free time talking with strangers on the beach, at Starbucks, and here, in Edgewater Towers, aka ET."

Julia smiled. "Well, first things first. I have a great stylist who is reasonable, and there is a nail salon in Santa Monica you must try. We can go Vivian's in the Palisades. Great clothes with very, very reasonable prices." She knew what was important to women.

I had shopping advice and my first friend in California. There was a gentleness about this lady, a tender demeanor, and a calmness most appealing to this gal from the East Coast. A Jersey Girl would be taught the art of relaxation, sitting still to watch the ocean, spontaneous BBQs, and the lifestyle of SoCal folks. Life does not take planning—it takes living.

Julia stood up. "Listen, we are having a BBQ at the gazebo on Saturday. Want to come?"

Following her lead, I rose. "Sure, what time? What should I bring?"

We walked together toward the door, stopping at the kitchen. "Give me your e-mail address. I will send you more info." I scribbled the info down, handed it to her. It was then I received my first double cheek kiss, California-style.

"I'm in unit 701, so stop by anytime. Have you met Lisa yet? She's from Jersey as well, and she's right next door. She is cool, so you will like her."

I don't think I stopped smiling for ten minutes. I was no longer alone. No longer 2800 miles away from everyone I knew and loved and alone. I had a friend. Of course, the first thing I did was call Chris. She was not quite as excited as I was, but no one ever became as excited as I did over the simplest of things. I do believe this special gift from God saved me from a life of despair. My childlike exhilaration over the simplest of experience drove people crazy. That, and the nonstop questions.

Julia e-mailed me later that evening with info about the BBQ. "Anne. Come on down to the gazebo around seven. Bring whatever meat you want for you and your quest like steaks, chicken, hamburgers, or hot dogs—whatever. And a side dish to share with everyone. There will be about twelve people. So bring enough for everyone to share. Oh, don't forget to bring something to drink…wine is always good." Her e-mail confused me.

When you come from the East Coast, we tighten things up. Dishes are assigned so no duplication. After all, can't have everyone bring a salad. Oh, and what about the silverware, the bottle openers, the charcoal, lighter fluid, plates, tablecloths? That's the Jersey way.

But the evening of the BBQ, there were no duplications. A perfect night. We sat in the gazebo or on the patio just three steps down from the structure. The night was perfect. Everyone was relaxed, laughing and listening to the melody of the ocean, birds, and simple chatter. The night was wrapped in a bouquet of aromas from flowers with names I had not yet learned. I don't think, in my entire life, I ever experienced the peace I felt that night, and so many nights after, in my beautiful California.

For the first time, I felt I had arrived home. I bumped into celebrities—literally. While standing in line at Malibu Yogurt for my sweet, low-fat, sugar-free Carbolite, I was pushed into the man in front of me. A tall, lean man. I was engaged in conversation with the lady behind me, who, after a few minutes, asked me if I knew who was in front of me. My shrug triggered her response. "That's Brad Garrett. He played the brother in *Everybody Loves Raymond*." Of course, as a newbie, I was excited, but after a time, it was no big deal seeing celebs.

I felt normal, although I had no frame of reference. There was a lightness not experienced before. Born again, not just in faith but in life. Perhaps I was awakening to a life of joy, prosperity, self-care, nurturing a very tattered self-esteem.

It was around 8:00 p.m., after a typical long workday, that the phone pulled me away from my favorite pastime. Looking, listening, and feeling all the Pacific Ocean had to offer. The sounds are mesmerizing.

"I am so glad to finally talk with you," I offered, after the caller informed me who she was.

Linda said apologetically, "I am so sorry it took me so long to get in touch with you. I have just been so busy and not feeling well. But I am so happy to be talking with you now. Jeanette went on and on about you."

"As you know, Linda, I met Jeanette just once before I left home. She heard my testimony at church, asked me to go to breakfast with her. With my departure date just days away, I was hesitant, but I listened to that inner voice. We connected instantly. Thank God, I listened to the Holy Spirit and met her. Otherwise, well, life would be very different. I wouldn't have met you, for example." I answered excitedly knowing a new friend, someone who knew my friend from home had just entered my life. Like me, she was a writer.

With my newfound confidence, thanks to Julia's hairstylist Tom in Santa Monica, my voice took on an excited tone. "Let's plan to get together soon. I would love for you to come visit me, if that is okay with you? I love it here at Edgewater Towers, and I think you will enjoy it as well. Then, how about having dinner in the Bu?" I laughed at myself, then apologized for being silly. "That's what the residents in Malibu call it, the Bu."

Linda was quick to respond and sounded eager to meet me. "How about Friday? I could come straight from work?"

We made plans and hung up. She called to me, that beautiful, restless, soft, ever-changing ocean lured me toward her. The moon was rising and spilling her light on the curves of the sea. As usual, I was under her spell. I surrendered, slid open the sliders to step onto my balcony.

20

"I belong to a Christian writers' group." Linda had come over as promised, and we were filling our bellies with pasta. "Would you be interested in joining? They meet at a friend's house in West Hollywood." She twisted her pasta around her fork.

My response came almost before she asked the question. "I would love it!"

Swallowing a bite, she continued: "We have dinner, sing, mingle, and pray for success with our work and our lives."

Inside, I was jumping up and down. Outwardly, I was trying to be cool, calm, and collected.

A few nights later, on a Sunday night, I attended my first writer's group. The host family welcomed me as if I were an old friend, not a stranger from Jersey. Everyone laughed, talked, and ate food outside. Torches illuminated the patio area and glistened on the surface of the small pond. Soon, a guitar-wielding man began to play, and the crowd sang hymns. It was official. I was a writer at a writer's group. Men and women at all levels of success with their craft joined small groups inside. Separated by numerous factors, members, and the newbies. My friend Linda participated in a group with longevity.

A tall, good-looking young man began the prayer. "Father, I thank you for the hospitality of our hosts, the new people who honored us with their presence, and the opportunities to share. I ask this in the name of Jesus." He looked up at the group. "Okay, does anyone want to begin?"

From the corner, a pretty young woman with a silky voice spoke. In a near whisper, like a gentle breeze, she began, "Hi, my name is Joyce. I recently moved from Texas." There was a sadness, a hint of loneliness and possibly insecurity in her voice.

All eyes were on me. "Hi, my name is Anne. I recently moved from New Jersey. I wrote a book and a script. I live in the Pacific Palisades, on the ocean, a real blessing."

A young couple shared about financial concerns. "There is so much competition in a very limited arena. Waitressing is helping with bills, and Mike is doing some freelance work, but the bills are greater than the income. We need your prayers for guidance and direction." The pretty young woman looked at her husband. Their love was obvious as they shared a private moment in a crowded room. His hand rolled across her lap in search of hers. They touched, and smiles lit up their youthful faces.

One man had success with a movie that starred Denzel Washington titled *Deja Vu*. But then again, the majority of writers present were at various stages of their writing careers. Men and women of all ages and social economics talked and laughed about their journey. Never did I even consider writing a script and yet, here I was, with others who had big dreams, moderate hope, and the promise of a future in the movies—God willing.

Time passed rapidly, and before I knew it, we were asked to wrap things up and join the others. I stood, grabbed my purse, and discreetly looked around at the group. One person caught my eye, a beautiful black woman. A pretty lady with a smile that I felt lacked depth. As a woman who learned over my life to be "hypervigilant" as a protective mechanism, I sensed something unsettling about her. Cautiously with purpose, I approached her thoughtfully.

I spoke without hesitation or thought. "You are so beautiful, inside and out."

Her smile did not hide the missing joy in her eyes.

"Thanks." Her voice was as light as a feather. "I'm Joyce."

I gently probed for info that would lift the veil of sorrow I suspected she was wearing. Not certain why I felt compelled to reach out to her.

"Anne, my mother died a few months ago. I miss her so much. We were so close. Starting over without her to support me will be difficult." She talked a little more, then fell silent.

"I am so sorry for your loss." I patted her face as I spoke. "How about it if I fill in for a while?" From that day forward, I was called Mum. I loved it. Lifelong friends were made that night. Doors began to open for me and others as well. Abundant compliments and good cheer offered to me. I embraced them like a cool drink on a hot afternoon. No negativity. A "superstar was born," at least in my heart. Anne, the writer was born.

I met up with Linda after the group meeting. Excited to know how I liked it, she quickly asked, "So what do you think?"

"I loved it. Nursing is my occupation, and I love it, but writing, well, it transports me. Sounds silly?"

I responded, unable to hold back my childish enthusiasm. "No, not at all. You sound like a writer." She paused. "Listen, on Wednesdays, in Studio City, there is another writer's group. They meet in a storefront theater. There are actors and writers, as well as producers all at various stages in their career. The actors act out slices of scripts brought in by the writers in the group. The audience watches and listens. Then we critique the script openly and honestly, providing useful suggestions if needed. It is fun. Are you interested?"

"I would love it. What time do they meet?" We walked together toward the front door.

"Starts around seven-thirty. We could have supper before it starts. There is a great place down the street with the most delish chopped salads. If I am running late, I bring it into the theater and eat it. They meet every other Wednesday, so the next meeting will be next week. I can e-mail you info and directions."

I agreed as the group began to disband. Members called to me as they gathered up their shoes: a rule of the house, no shoes inside. One time, I grabbed the wrong boots. In my car on the way home, I thought to myself, *I am finally experiencing the dream of my youth.* The sunroof opened, a CD in the player, and my heart was light and filled with joy. I had settled into my new life in California. Several times a week, I worked out at LA Fitness that was just across the lawn from my office building. Wine parties with the ladies of ET, walks on the beach, dating, active in a church and just, well, living and laughing. I loved my life.

Some months later, Linda called me. "Listen, I have a friend who has tickets for the opening of a movie. Red carpet and all. Would you be interested in coming? It is during the week though, so you would need to come directly from the office." She took a breath and continued. "It will be at Grauman's Chinese Theatre in Hollywood. I assume you know where that is."

I was still perched on my wrought-iron chair on my little balcony. I so loved the aroma of the unseen flowers drifting up from the gardens below to my little deck. Before her call, I had been thinking how blessed I was, and now, I was being invited to a red-carpet event.

"I would love it. I guess I will see you in Hollywood." As soon as I hung up, in typical female fashion, I went directly to my closet. What does someone wear to a red-carpet event? Finally, a white tuxedo outfit caught my eye. Belted at the waist to flatter with a deep plunged satin collar. It would be perfect.

In the lady's room, I was looking in the mirror and liking what I saw. I smiled. I heard the door open. The manager of my department entered. "Wow, look at you. Something special tonight?" She teased.

Well, actually, I am going to a red-carpet event in Hollywood. It is the premiere of *The Cross*. Have you heard of it?" Once again, inside I was leaping like a child, but outwardly I was acting nonchalant.

"Can't say I have. Well, have a good time." She paused at the door, turned, and added, "I lived in California all my life and have never gone to a red-carpet event. You are here, what, six months? Where is the justice?" she laughed.

So I walked the red carpet that night. Pat Boone was there, so I thought it would be fun to go over to say hello. As I approached him, he greeted me as one would an old friend. "So good to see you. How have you been?" he asked. I stammered, smiled, and turned away. It was so amusing. Linda commented later that perhaps he thought I was Tammy.

For the next eight months, my life consisted of dating, writing groups, and working on Relay for Life with Julia and Lisa, the gal down the hall, another Jersey girl. BBQs under the gazebo that were dripping with bougainvillea, flanked by a view of the Pacific. The only negative was my job. Being what might be called a people person, my contact with others in this job was limited. Chart review for some is exciting and challenging. For me, I missed time spent with direct contact with patients and providers. A good strong company that dealt with provider complaints efficiently. For such a long time, I felt as if I were wandering in the wilderness searching for answers that would never be revealed. Finally, in California, for the first time, I felt stationary in mind, body, and soul.

That was my life for the first eight months is California. But that was destined to change.

Before I left New Jersey, I joined an online dating service for Christians. I met some terrific men. I also met a few liars, cheaters, flamboyant, and materialistic-minded men. One night, I was contacted by a man who was originally from New Jersey. Although, he now lived in Arizona. We continued to exchange e-mails for a while. He sounded solid and nice. He had a long-lasting marriage that ended when his wife died. He had a daughter and a son. There was also a granddaughter. The fact that he was a minister and a college professor was most appealing to me. Spiritual and intelligent. He even had a sense of humor. We exchanged e-mails for a while before he asked if he could call.

"So we finally meet—at least our voices meet," he teased over the phone.

"I like your voice. What is the temperature in Arizona?"

"A balmy ninety-nine degrees. Thank God for a break in the heat."

I laughed. "Make me laugh, and I will follow you anywhere," I said, noticing folks walking their dogs below. There was a breeze that night, and I surmised the sweet aroma that found its way into my being was not coming from flowers. I guessed neighbors below were smoking a doobie.

I liked him. Especially hearing about his family. He spoke more about his childhood family than his wife and children, unless I asked specific questions. Because my childhood was grim, his stories allowed me to venture into his world. At least, that is what I thought in that moment. After a while, we agreed to meet. He would come to LA. We had been talking seriously, so meeting him heightened my anxiety. When you are called The Thing growing up, and your mother said she would kill herself because you were so bad, self-esteem issues were certain. Just the thought of meeting him sent me into simmering anxiety. He would be arriving in a few weeks on a Friday.

A couple of days later, I heard Julia's distinct knock. It was like her personality, light and playful. I led her into my apartment. "So tell me. Who is this professor that is coming to town?" she asked, with a teasing smile and eyebrows that rose to the occasion.

"Come in—have a seat. Do you want a glass of wine? Pinot or Chardonnay?"

She accepted the offer and took a seat. I told her about Robert as we sat drinking our Chardonnay. No emotional component, just elementary facts. Often, my inner voice, the words of Mother, infiltrated my thoughts, holding me hostage so any elements of truth related to my feelings were kept on the shelf. Why would this brilliant man want anything to do with me? That was the lie I told myself at times, but as I developed and grew stronger over the years, the voice was barely audible. Nothing supported Mom's words. But on this day, I surrendered.

A few hours later, after several glasses of wine, she left. But not before she suggested we have a BBQ in the gazebo for Robert as a meet and greet. Her positive attitude about me and the situation gave me an injection of confidence. And with Robert arriving the very next day, it was just what the doctor had ordered.

A final glance in the mirror before I buzzed Robert in. I had gained a few pounds, and of course, that is all I focused on. Five minutes later, a knock on the door. With a smile, I opened the door, allowing him to enter. I was greeted with a quick kiss. "This is some lovely place. Beautiful, in fact. Gated and secure, I like that. The guy at the gatehouse, I think his name was Paul, greeted me with 'Nice to meet you, Professor.' That was nice." He held my hand as I ushered him into the living room, dining area, through the bedroom, and out on to the balcony. Together we stepped onto the tiny space with a massive view.

"Annie, this is amazing. You have got to be so pleased with yourself. You did this on your own, no help from anyone."

I had shared some details of my childhood with this man, including putting myself through college, winning awards in college, and more all without support.

The balcony was small; so being intimate was inevitable. We hugged and kissed and held each other for some time. After a time, as the day was fading, the white stucco façade bore a pink glow from the sunset.

"I don't know about you, Annie, but I am getting a little hungry. Do you want to go get something to eat?"

"That sounds great. Let's go to Malibu. There are several nice places there." I spoke as my body twisted toward the slider. I reached out, grabbed the handle, and pulled. It was locked. Besides being hungry and stuck on the balcony, I really, really needed to go to the bathroom.

"What's up?" he asked, and when I explained, he laughed, then I laughed, but I still needed to use the bathroom, even more now that I was laughing.

Together we leaned over the balcony wall, searching below. We called out to anyone for help, and eventually, someone heard us and called the gatehouse. As the guard unlocked the slider, he glanced at him, then me, then smiled that knowing smirk. We had such fun on that first visit. As an intellectual who spoke primarily with academics, I think my sense of humor was a change he enjoyed. My ability to laugh and make others laugh was a gift from Mom, while Dad provided the gift of a love of nature. On that weekend, we laughed often and with gusto.

"I had a wonderful time. Next time you come to my place, I want to show you White Mountain—of course, with you, we will be climbing it instead of just looking at it." We both laughed knowing it was the truth.

After a few final kisses, he parted. I did not envy him that six-hour trip back to Arizona. Much of the trip is through the desert.

When it was my turn to visit him in Arizona, it was with a good deal of trepidation. I learned the perfect relationship he held with his family was nonexistent. Several times, he was threatened by his daughter not to get involved with someone else so soon. He married, for the second time, after his first wife, his children's mother, had died. It didn't last. There were many times I suggested not moving the relationship forward because I had no intention of getting in the middle of his family problems. He promised me it would be fine. I believed him.

I had boarded the plane to see Robert and was sitting next to a nice-looking businessman.

"Are you going to Phoenix for a vacation or business?" The man fumbled with papers even as he spoke. He looked at me, waiting for an answer.

"Neither. Just visiting someone." I was learning not to provide too much info to a stranger. We judge others by our yardstick. With me, honesty held a lofty place as a result I assumed others were as well. I would soon learn how wrong I was.

Papers were slipped into a brown leather case; its scruffy condition spoke of a good deal of use. "I'm Mike. You are?"

"Anne, nice to meet you. I assume you are traveling on business." I nodded toward the case.

"What type of business?"

"Anne, I was on a trip, but I live in Phoenix. Going home with a very promising contract in that case."

"What type of business are you in, Mike?" I noticed he had beautiful green eyes and a nice smile.

"Actually, my company makes surgical supplies. We are based in Phoenix but have a company in Germany as well. That means I travel a good deal. I guess that is why I am divorced."

I was a little surprised he added that last sentence. "Well, I guess you are eager to get home." Ignoring the divorce comment.

We talked for a while about family, careers, education, trips. Those superficial topics one has with a stranger while being guarded so as not to reveal too much. With me, that took a great deal of effort.

His body twisted slightly toward me. "Would you be interested in, well, maybe having a drink while you are in town?"

"I don't think that would work, but well, thanks anyway." I was taken aback but flattered.

His right hand reached in his jacket, pulling out a small leather holder. "Anne, here, take this just in case you change your mind." I took the business card, smiled, and nodded.

For the remainder of the flight, we fell silent, lost in our own thoughts. From my window, Arizona looked very flat without much greenery. I guess that's desert life.

As our plane touched down, my body tensed. When Robert met me at the airport, he was obviously distracted. I sensed an unspoken concern in his demeaner. A distraction.

"How was your trip?" he asked. Robert was present physically, mentally absent. He was as jumpy as butter on a hot griddle. Unlike the man I had come to know. Passive. Gentle. Patient. His positive nature was soothing, but not that day.

Hours later, at his home, I questioned him. We were in the living room. The sounds of splashing water from the fountain in his yard drifted through the screens. A soothing reminder of home.

"Robert?" Even though he was just a few feet from where I sat, he didn't answer.

Repeating his name, he came back from wherever it was and answered me, "What?" His voice was clipped and harsh.

"What's wrong with you? You have been so distracted all night, yet you keep telling me everything is okay." Growing up as I did, I developed a hypervigilant persona, an exaggerated intensity of behaviors whose purpose is to detect threats. I read people, their emotions, body language as a means of protection from harm. I guess when he realized I was not going to give up, he sat down, hung his head low, and started to talk.

"My daughter is very upset that we are moving too fast. She threatened me not to get married. At least not until she determined *when* we should marry." He never looked up.

I stood up. "Are you kidding me? Robert, that's crazy. Why is she telling her father what he can and cannot do?" When he didn't answer me, I asked, "What did she threaten you with?"

He didn't answer my questions. Right then and there, a huge red flag was waving. There had been previous outbursts and discussions with his daughter, but nothing so serious as to threaten him. He never did tell explain to me exactly what she was going to do if he didn't comply. But his emotional state was fragile. He looked broken. And afraid.

I sat on the bed, exhausted, terribly disappointed, and angry. Although it was a sunny day, my mood turned cloudy. "Robert, I spent a fortune to get here, purchased new clothes, had my hair done, all for this trip. I really wish I was home." In that moment, I thought about that business card in my purse. I wanted to run away, a well-developed pattern born in my youth, a form of escape from real or perceived danger, and unpleasant situations.

His questionable inability to recognize his shattered relationship within his family was a lifelong pattern. Despite being estranged from his son, he recanted story after story that depicted something quite different. Honestly, I think he was just lying to himself about everything. In his mind, he created a perfect world, with perfect people who never existed. Never could exist because we are all flawed.

I shifted to the right, as his weight on the bed was felt. "Let's forget about her." He took my hand, but I pulled away. "Please, let's just enjoy this time together."

That night, I really thought the relationship was over. A strong pull to leave and not look back was felt as I envisioned my beautiful life in California. My night's sleep was disturbed. Deep down, feelings to flee were overwhelming me. In fact, I thought about heading back to LA in the morning.

The next morning, he was still visibly upset. I went outside to take a look in the daylight. There was no grass, just rocks. Some plants and beautiful fountains in both the backyard and in the area in the courtyard off the front and aside the casita. A lovely home indeed.

Stepping inside, he was nowhere to be found. Finally, I went into the bedroom.

"Good morning. I am talking with Colleen. Why don't you come say hello?" he offered. He had her on speaker phone, another weird quirk common in this family.

"Dad, I don't want to talk with her now." Her angry voice was heard on speaker phone.

I squished up my face, shook my head, mouthing no.

He signaled me to pick up the phone and say hello. The red flag was waving, but I opted to ignore. He looked so sad. I felt I needed to rescue him. Anne the fixer. "Colleen, here is Anne. She wants to say hello." He held the phone at arm's length. I reached for it.

Hesitantly, I spoke, "Hi, Colleen, how are you?"

"Anne, get the hell off the phone and shut up. I want to speak with my father." I handed the phone to him, moisture forming in my eyes.

Robert took the phone, saying nothing to her. No mention of her harsh words to the woman he cared for. I fled the room in tears. Her words, spoken with monumental disrespect, startled me. The tears were the result of his failure to act. He never chastised her. Never came to comfort me. Instead, Robert chose to stay on the phone with his daughter. A fair amount of time passed before he finally decided to come join me. When he entered the living room, he smiled at me as if nothing had occurred.

"Robert, I called to change my plane reservations. I am leaving later this evening." I spoke, void of emotion. "I want nothing to do with you or your daughter. She has been allowed to remain in our life while you do nothing. She has sent demanding e-mails. You don't think it's odd that she wanted my social security number? This is not normal behavior." I rose, entered the kitchen area, and grabbed a glass. My mouth was so dry I needed a drink of water. "Why would you sit there as she assaulted without cause and say nothing? Then you spend the next several minutes chatting to her, while I am out here alone?"

In response to my confrontation, he responded, "I can't stop her from saying what she said. She is a grown woman."

I turned to face him. It was profoundly evident: confrontations made him very uncomfortable. Self-protection was his goal. Unable, or unwilling, to contain my rising anger, I answered him. "No, you can't control her. But you should have informed her she was inappropriate. Once again, I might add. Did it occur to you to tell her she needed to apologize to me and then say goodbye and see how I was? If my son ever spoke with you like that—not that he would—I would certainly be disappointed in him. He would be asked to apologize as well. I couldn't make him, but I would certainly tell him about his behavior. Why are you allowing her to direct your life?" I rose, opened the front door, and left. I decided I just needed to be by myself. Over my shoulder, I announced my intentions. "I am going home, back to LA!"

I ambled around the upscale neighborhood. Everywhere I looked, there were houses, stucco with tiled roofs, and an obvious Spanish design. Lawns were carpeted with rocks, cactus, shrubs, and fountains. Flowers, although limited, were orderly, organized, and very attractive in planters or miniscule patches protected with stones. Similar to neighborhoods in LA, the streets snaked through the development instead of the typical grid pattern of many communities. They were naked of vehicles, more than likely sleeping in their garage. I did see a boat in a drive resting on a carrier. I laughed to myself, thinking where in the desert does one take a motorboat.

Back at the house, I entered through the front door. Robert was sitting at a table in the great room. "Where did you go? I was worried about you."

Stepping inside, I began to head for the bedroom, as there was packing to do. "I told you I was going for a walk." I was surprised at the sharpness in my voice.

He rose, went into the guest bedroom, and returned with a piece of paper in his hands. "This is a check for a thousand dollars. If I ever fail to protect you again, you can cash it. I am sorry. You were right. Can we start over?"

As outrageous as that gesture was, it hit home. He was so sincere, I believed him. Unfortunately, there would come a time I would regret that decision. I learned early on that his relationship with his daughter would be a constant interruption in our lives. It would be increasingly difficult to move the relationship forward. On that same weekend, I learned later that his daughter called his pastor and an old girlfriend to talk him out of marrying me. Clearly, she had zero boundaries.

The remainder of my time in Arizona was nice, although meeting his pastor at church the following Sunday was uncomfortable. The minister had called Robert to inform him of the conversation and concerns his daughter expressed to him on a phone call the day before.

From the pulpit, visitors were welcomed warmly. "We always like to celebrate anybody who is visiting with us for the first time. As is our custom, an introduction by whoever brought you today would be wonderful. So do we have any special guests this beautiful Sunday morning?"

Robert had warned me about this custom before church. With emphasis, I informed him I didn't want to stand and be introduced, fearful everyone would see the scarlet letter on my chest. I was certain Robert's daughter had painted a picture of me with a brush of lies and inaccuracies. The room fell silent. When the call went out for anyone who had been missed, Robert stood up. "I am here with a very lovely, special lady. She is a nurse and is kind and very important to me." He spoke with such tenderness, my fears faded like mist on the folds of a hill. He took my hand to assist me as I rose to my feet. I felt secure. Robert continued, "This is Anne, and if I am lucky enough, she will marry me one day."

There were a lot of *oohs* and *ahhs* around the room, whispers, smiling, and inaudible speech. Some folks clapped silently. I shifted my gaze from the congregants to the pastor. A slow warmth climbed up my cheeks as my level of discomfort rose. I couldn't help but wonder what abuse was heaped upon me to this man. One can't defend themselves when one does not know what was said. Suddenly, self-protection kicked in, and I took a seat.

There were other incidents with the daughter. Robert even had the audacity to suggest we marry and not tell his daughter. I was not only furious but questioned his sanity. What power did she have over him? I would learn in time.

We were married a few months later in the same church where he ministered many years before. He was a minister at the young age of twenty-two, with an eighteen-year-old bride. Because it was basically going to be just us, no family members were invited because of the distance. Of course, if desired, they could attend. It would be such an inconvenience for them to come to Iowa just to leave the next day, as we had planned to do. The folks in Iowa were wonderful. There were about fifty folks in attendance, a little postwedding event in the church hall, and a lot of well wishes for this bride.

We spent the day after the wedding visiting the bridges of Madison County before leaving for home.

"Here, these are for you." Fingers were clenched firmly around wild flowers, just like in the movie. Later on, I decided to play the part of Meryl Streep for Robert. In front of the bridge, he popped up, held up his cell phone to take a picture of me. Well, of course, I put my hand in front of my face. After all, this was an encore presentation of *The Bridges of Madison County*. Days later, I learned from one of the locals, I was seated on the Clint Eastwood stool in the movie at the counter in a restaurant where we stopped to eat.

Robert suggested we plan a trip for later, for our honeymoon. Visiting family and friends and taking in some sights was suggested. I agreed. Knowing there were problems with him and his family, I guess I thought I could patch the holes within. An altogether-ridiculous notion, having no concept of exactly what the problems were, or who, if anyone, was the cause of the unrest. Although I had a good idea who was the source of unrest. Ms. Fix-it was on the move.

21

After we were married, we planned our honeymoon. We arrived in New Jersey and went to his daughter's. Apparently, he spoke with her; she softened and suggested we stay overnight. This trip would involve staying with family and friends, and a trip to Niagara Falls after we visited his brother in New Hampshire. He was eager to introduce me, his wife, to family. I suspect, knowing my personality, he felt there might be a chance at restoration within his family.

Robert pushed the button that would announce our arrival. The condo complex was small, at least compared to the village where I had lived. She had an upper unit. I must admit my heart was pounding hearing her footsteps approach. Our last conversation ended poorly, so without any history on this woman, I knew not what to expect. The door opened, and before us stood a very short woman, eyes reddened. There was no effort on her part to hide the fact that she was crying.

Climbing the steps, I wondered if the tears and depression were related to her father's *disobeying* her mandate by marrying me. If I were the reason, this would be a very long night.

Once upstairs, she went into the living space, and we followed. She collapsed into a chair. Robert and I manipulated our way around the coffee table and seated ourselves.

"What would you like to drink?" I barely heard what she said. Robert asked for just a glass of water, and I echoed his request. As she passed, she spoke to no one but into the space in front of her. "I have some snacks for you." This woman who attacked me not all that long ago, like a bird of prey, now stood before me like a wounded sparrow. She was lost and broken.

Leaning toward Robert, I asked, "Robert, you need to ask her what is wrong. You're her dad."

A few minutes later, she returned with drinks and crackers and cheese. Avoiding our eyes, she placed the items on the table, returned to her chair, sat down, and continued to weep—oblivious to our presence.

Robert leaned in, grabbed some nuts, exclaimed how delicious they were and, to my utter amazement, ignored the proverbial elephant in the room. "So, Colleen, where do you want to have supper tonight—my treat?"

Her head was bowed low, and she just shrugged.

"How about that place we went to the last time I was here. Remember? What was the name of that place? They had great seafood."

I looked deranged as I attempted to speak without words to Robert. My head bobbed, I mouthed words, and I looked from him to his daughter.

Nothing. He just pressed on about the food. The weather. California. How could he not speak to the situation? His daughter was in pain. That was my first encounter with what I learned was a lifelong pattern of avoidance.

When Robert commented about the piano, asking questions about her ability to play, her response was filled with condemnation. Suggestive of an absent father who knew little about her life as a child. She glared at him. The tension was horrific.

Unable to stand this nonsense for a minute longer, I rose and announced that I was going for a walk. "Listen, you two need some time together to talk—without me."

"You don't need to go, Anne." Her words were muffled. "We don't talk in this family." Robert insisted that I stay. I learned later I would be the buffer in all unpleasantness. As stated, he bolted from any confrontations; therefore, he would pass his discomfort on to me, if I were available.

Once outside, I let out a sigh of relief. I wanted to get away from the dark cloud of emotional fragility inside those four walls.

As I navigated the unfamiliar neighborhood, I yearned for my home and my life in California. Life was simple and beautiful. People made sense. I feared this family was far too intense, too convoluted for my gentle spirit. I had lived through difficulty in childhood, and I was unwilling to revisit that neglected neighborhood of dysfunction.

There was not much to see in this neighborhood, unlike the area where my condo was located. Trees and ponds, quaint towns and rivers, and wildlife turn a walk into pure joy. After forty-five minutes, I returned to her unit. In my mind, that was enough time to allow the daughter and father to discuss, at least open the door, to whatever trouble lay behind her depression. If it were me, I wasn't certain how that would be handled. Climbing the stairs, I picked up on the silence. The antithesis of my vision appeared. These two were in the exact same position when I left. Nothing had changed. She was still crying, and Robert still appeared oblivious. What was going on here? Did he not see her crying?

"Anne, you should have stayed. I told you we wouldn't talk." She glared at her father.

I so wanted to be somewhere else. The dynamics were so intense. Colleen cried and looked downward, and Robert stood and walked me into the room. His voice was so casual, it was uncanny, as he asked, "So did you have a nice walk?" He looked in the direction of his daughter. "Anne loves to walk. Didn't I tell you that? In fact, she would often be walking when I would call her from Arizona. She would tell me what celebrity house she was passing. Once it was Joan Crawford, another time Tom Cruise, and even Steven Spielberg. She so enjoyed walking in Beverly Hills. Right, Anne?"

I shook my head. Did he really think she cared?

Several minutes passed as we all sat in silence. Robert snacked on the food as I studied my nails. His daughter sat still and glared at her father while crying softly. Why? I knew now—the problem was deeper than marrying me.

I walked over to where she sat. As I moved forward, I couldn't help but wonder what her response would be if I hugged her. After all, her actions could be at least partially about her father marrying me. But I chanced it. I let my guard down as I sat down beside her. I reached my arms around her trembling body and held her. She held on for a lengthy period—in fact, I was a tad uncomfortable. This was the hug of a small child, not a woman her age. Apparently, she needed to be recognized. After a long time, she smiled, stood up, and said she was going to bed. She ignored her dad even when he told her good night.

"I am exhausted. Robert, why didn't you talk with her? Didn't you see her crying and you kept talking about dinner or nuts?" Inside me, something was stirring—the truth that I had made a huge mistake.

"I don't know."

"That is a child's answer. She is your daughter," I whispered as we passed her door to our room.

He sounded annoyed. "I didn't know what to say."

"Why not just ask her what's wrong? She's your daughter."

"I don't know." He was a prisoner of his fear of conflict. "Thank you for being so kind to her. I think she likes you."

In that moment, I didn't care if she liked or didn't like me. All I wanted was to go to bed and put this day far behind me.

Most couples honeymoon alone. This should be a time of exploration. Discovery of the nuances of each other. Connecting with each other to become one to share love and joy of a union made before God. Instead, I was entangled in a long-standing tumult within the family. I knew it wasn't about me, not really. I was just the target for transferred anger by his daughter.

We washed up, prepared for bed, and carefully avoided the other's touch. When he reached over to kiss me, in return, he received an absentminded brush on the cheek. In the dim light flowing into the room from a streetlight, I lay there asking myself the question: *who was this man?*

*****

Then I awoke the next morning to his voice.

"Good morning!" he stated, almost singing. "Did you know you snore? The windows were rattling and woke everyone in the building." Sitting on the bed, he lowered his voice. "Colleen is in a wonderful mood. She is much better. Guess what? She put the picture we gave her on the counter."

For me, *good* morning is a contradiction of words. All I could muster was "okay."

We own our emotions. They are not the result of others; therefore, I would decide on this day to be happy. That is, as soon as I could shake off the ghost of sleep.

My smiling husband began to leave while I remained in bed. "Listen, I'll take my shower and let you sleep a little longer, but don't forget, we have plans for today. Colleen needs to leave for work soon, so maybe you will be able to see her before she goes."

"Sounds good," I said.

Twenty minutes later, I was up, in my nightgown, sitting at the kitchen across from Robert. His daughter was in her room. I assumed she was getting dressed.

I was at the stove making coffee as Robert and I discussed the day ahead of us. A few minutes of idle chatter was broken with the entrance of his daughter. Her smile was disarming but pleasant, especially after the night before. In fact, when she entered the kitchen and walked directly toward me, I was unprepared for what happened next. Her arms went around my waist, her head leaning in. The hug was firm and was again uncharacteristically long-lasting. She needed love and acceptance. And…

"Good morning, lovely daughter. Feeling better today?" my husband asked.

She released her grasp of my midline and turned to face him. "Yeah," she answered. "I need to finish getting ready for work. I really hate that you have to leave."

It was as if a button were pushed that illuminated her world. The change in her mood was uncanny and unnerving. Last night, she snarled at him, he made her skin crawl, she admonished him, and he pretended everything was just fine. We hung out at her house because we still needed to meet his son. Phone calls to Kevin went unanswered. He lived alone in the house he shared with his wife and daughter. They were getting a divorce, so she had rented an apartment with her daughter. Originally, they moved in with Colleen, but something had happened—a quarrel—and she left with her daughter.

Robert entered the living room where I was watching a home improvement show. "He still won't answer the phone, and I know he is there. I guess that's it." He released an exaggerated breath.

"Sit here," I said. I pulled my feet up beneath me, a very bad habit. "Listen, why don't you just go over to his house? Knock on the door and hopefully, he will let you in. You need to fix the problems in your family. Don't you think?" I was at it again, Ms. Fix-it to the rescue.

"What if he doesn't answer the door?" he asked.

"Well, then, we leave, but it is worth a try."

Later that night, we drove to his son's house. He slid the car up to the curb. "Ready?" he asked.

"Robert, I never met him. So I think it's best if you go in and I wait in the car. This is a family matter. I doubt if he would open up with a stranger in the room. If things go well, then let me know, and I will go in."

"No, I want you to come with me," he vehemently responded.

"Robert, it is not about what you want but what you want to accomplish." I shifted in my seat. I was getting annoyed. My honeymoon spent sitting in a car, going for walks all for his family. Now he doesn't want to address his family problems.

I suspect he knew I was not about to give in. I am like that when I think I am right about something. I stand firm.

"I guess you're right." His voice low. He was waving the white flag of defeat. He opened the door and walked up to the front door. He was there for quite a few minutes before the door opened, and he was invited in.

As I sat in the car, alone, I thought about this so-called honeymoon. In the dark, feeling stupid, I wondered if there was an encore presentation going on with his son. Was he talking about the motor home, the sailboat, and the great nuts at his daughter's, or was he having a meaningful conversation? Eventually, I was called in.

"Hello, Anne." I was greeted by his son as I entered. His son remained in a chair as I took a seat on the sofa, across from where Robert sat. Once more, not unlike the climate at his daughter's, the tension was like guitar strings wound too tight. I knew something was going to give. The tension needed to be released, but the question was when.

When I get nervous, I start to talk even more than normal. I don't think I came up for air for five minutes. I sensed from body language both men were relieved. My chatter took the burden off them. I think I covered everything in my life for the past few years, plus, I asked a million nonsensible questions.

"So you are a psychologist. That must be interesting." He nodded but remained silent. "How long have you lived here? What's the dog's name? Have you used the motor home lately?" My questions summoned up the occasional nod.

The visit was brief. Conversation, superficial. In my judgment, this man appeared very depressed. There was an absence of life in his eyes. I took a few pictures of him for Robert, and later, when I zoomed in, there was something very wrong. It was as if he were missing a spirit. A shell of a man.

"Anne, you can come back anytime, but without him," Kevin teased, nodding toward his father. "Did Dad tell you he has Asperger's?"

"Kevin, don't be ridiculous. Let's not start that again." Robert was visibly irritated. "Anne, are you ready?" He was heading for the door. It was clear Robert wanted to make a quick departure. Lurking in the silence was the undercurrent of a brewing confrontation. Therefore, leaving was the route to travel if he wanted to avoid an accidental dispute with his son.

Even as a nurse, I was unfamiliar with the diagnosis. Kevin was a psychologist, so my assumption was that it was a mental disorder. Immediately, I felt a constriction in my chest. It felt tight like a boa constrictor was forcing the air from my lungs. Two children both with depression. Now, another disorder, but this time, the illness was born in my new husband. Why did his son tell me such a thing, especially on our first meeting? Was it to cause problems between his father and me? To get even with him about some sins from the past?

In the car, to release the constriction, I called on my close friend, my coping mechanism: humor. "Robert, have you ever considered giving up teaching and becoming a honeymoon planner? These past few days have been, well, what's the word? *Unique*—that's it, unique and entirely unlike anything I have heard or read about the perfect honeymoon."

My head rolled back onto the headrest. My body felt heavy and clumsy. The events of the past two days combined with the absence of a good night's rest weighed heavy on my spirit and physicality. I continued, hoping that to do so would bring about what I yearned for: an escape from my reality. "Why would anyone desire a long, boring trip to Italy? Nothing there but people who don't speak English, and old buildings. But I cannot even imagine the horror of spending day after day lying on some beach on an island in the Pacific. No drama, just the annoying sounds of waves rolling on the shore. Nothing can compare to the excitement of spending the night watching someone cry, or the thrill of sitting in a darkened car—alone. Now, that is what I call entertainment."

My efforts to reduce the tenuous moods experienced by the two of us was unsuccessful. The roadblock to inner peace were the last words spoken to me by my married firstborn. They lingered in my thoughts. *"Did my father tell you he has Asperger's?"* With all that has happened and what I have discovered, I was fearful of what lay in wait.

I knew Robert needed comforting—after all, it was obvious that the time spent with his son did little to dissolve the dissension between them. I thought about words to console him, but they caught in my throat, my mouth too dry to speak. Besides, who would comfort me?

As soon as I got back to Colleen's, I headed for Robert's laptop. I typed the word *Asperger's* into a search engine. Within seconds, several links appeared. I began to read the characteristics. "It is a form of autism, a high-functioning autism. Characteristics can be difficulty in expressing emotions, mental shutdown response to conflicting demands, and multitasking, low understanding of the reciprocal rules of conversation, relationship difficulties, and so much more." For the second night, I was robbed of peaceful rest as a caravan of images patrolled my thoughts, taking with them the elusive peace I sought. For the second night, tenderness, closeness, and connectedness were absent. What had I married into? Friends told me to wait, but no, I didn't listen. I ignored red flags, the feeling in my gut that signals me when something is not right.

We left his daughter's and traveled up to meet his brother's family, and then our plan was to go to Niagara Falls. A real honeymoon destination. I began to feel as if all was well with the world as the distance between the odd events we left behind faded away with each mile. We took a plane, rented a car, and traveled to his brother's in Massachusetts. I enjoyed meeting them and felt peaceful once again.

Niagara Falls was beautiful. I loved it, but not the "maiden of the mist" boat ride. Oh, now the ride was great, but when you have hair that tends to curl with the moisture, I looked like a chrysanthemum. Robert was kind and attentive and willing to do anything I wanted. He climbed under the falls because I wanted to.

"You are not really going up those steps, are you?" I asked. The spray created a dangerous wet surface, and even I dared not to venture forth. But Robert did to impress me. I am certain. I was impressed as he was pummeled with water as he climbed. I watched from below as he climbed, struggling with each step to maintain balance as the water smacked him and the others relentlessly. Daredevil Annie was, I am embarrassed to admit, scared. I have this love-hate relationship with water. I love her, but I know she can cause havoc. Plus, most of my nightmares since childhood were about water ever since the death of my young friend.

"I am so proud of you!" I screamed to be heard above the thunder of the cascading torrent of water that slammed down the falls. He smiled, proud of himself. For the first time in days, we hugged each other with passion, entirely free of uncertainty. It was exciting, thunderous, and provocative, not unlike the falls.

"Are you ready?" Robert asked tenderly, taking my hand. He smiled a smile that spoke of a man in love. He squeezed my hand tightly to secure my steps.

The remainder of our time was pleasant. We visited friends of mine in New Jersey, and then the four of us ventured down to Cape May. Marianne and Al took us sailing, then out to dinner in a restaurant overlooking the marina. Pennsylvania and the Poconos were to be our final destinations before heading home. Of course, home was still in question. Would we be living in Arizona or California? That was yet to be determined. On the way to the village where I lived many years ago with my children's father, we stopped along the highway at a hippie shop. I captured the visit with a picture of Professor Robert standing in front of a multicolored van, one used by the owners. I was a faux hippie. Donning love beads was the length of my hippie movement. No drugs for me, or communal living—just multicolored beads hanging low on my chest.

An explosion of dust flew in the air as I pulled the car to a stop in front of an A-frame house. Strangers lived there now in the place I once called home. The road was gravel and dirt insulated from the rest of the world. A tiny pond rested in the comfort of tall grass across the road from our former home. I had a clear view from the driver's seat.

"This is where Jim and I lived." After a long pause, as the memories of hikes, swimming, and sleigh riding played in the theater of my mind, I continued, "We loved it here with all the natural beauty. My husband would come home from a crazy workday, shed his clothes in the open, and he and my son jumped naked into the pond. Their pale little man butts bobbing up and down as they played together. Such a nice memory." My voice trailed off, carried away on a fading memory.

"I can't believe you lived here. You said there is a home for the criminally insane just up the road. Crazy."

The car lurched forward, slipping on the gravel. "Let me show you the rest of the property." Back on the road we just traveled, I made a right and began the slow drive upward. At the midpoint, I slowed down to a crawl. Off to the right, the great pond slept partially obscured by wild growth of weeds, trees, and unkempt grasses. I pulled into a little flat grassy area, stopped, and got out. The pond was awakened suddenly from her sleep by a beaver busy at work slapping his tail as he prepared a new home. High above, birds suddenly swooped downward, focused on their prey. Hand in hand, we walked.

"This is really nice but so deserted. You really liked it here?" he asked. The question annoyed me a bit—it was like he was insulting something I loved.

After a while, we headed home, but not before stopping at a farm where good friends lived. Life was so simple in those parts. Everything centered on just living, surviving, and pig roasts, bailing hay, and breeding. Simplicity took an effort to avoid the traps of their counterparts in other areas of the country. Material possessions, money, and fame were not the object at the center of their being.

"Oh, it is so good to be home. Tonight, we sleep in our own bed," Robert stated, stepping into the house. We entered his home through the garage that led to a small alcove. A wall of cabinets hung directly above a beautiful granite counter. Keys were tossed down, and lights were switched on as we both entered the great room through the open-concept kitchen. Nothing but the best for Robert. The home was lovely, warm with two large fountains in the back and front open areas. But I was in love with nature and the joy of discovery, and this place lacked both.

Robert's legs elevated with the flip of a switch on his recliner. I was at the other end of the sectional that had a built-in chaise. We talked about the plan to go to the Grand Canyon, but first, a necessary trip to Tennessee. Robert was asked to speak at an event for his great aunt who had a reputation for her work as a lay minister. Travels to Jerusalem whereupon many antiquities were purchased sent to the United States and displayed in a Christian college. The artifacts were to be on display for a few weeks at this location, and Robert would provide a historical background for those in attendance. Staying at Robert's home was nice, but I missed the beauty of California.

A few weeks later, the day prior to our trip to Tennessee, Robert spent the day working on his PowerPoint. He grappled with the content, agonizing over each slide. This day, his mind was filled with the approaching deadline. As for me, I liked the sounds of deadlines as they go speeding by.

I touched his back as he sat facing his computer. "So how's it going? You have been at this for days. I thought you were going to show me around?"

Silence.

"Robert, I asked you a question."

Silence.

"Hey, I am talking to you. You're being rude. And selfish. Is everything going to be about you and your family?" Unable to conceal my annoyance, my words were sharp and cutting like a knife.

He turned. "What?" It was clear he had been oblivious to my presence, lost in his head, his world, a secret place no one was allowed entrance. That day, I met Asperger's.

"You've been working on this for days. I read what you have written, and it's informative."

His face was toward me, but I suspected his thoughts were elsewhere.

"What happened with your promise to show me the area? We leave tomorrow, but for the past several days, I have been alone."

There was a change in his countenance. His face grew dark—a storm was brewing. He stared through me. His voice was terse when he spoke, like a teacher scolding a child. "Give me an hour or two. Then we can go get something to eat." He turned. Once again, pulled into the images on the computer screen.

"I guess I will go for a walk," I stated, my question left unanswered.

In the weeks since our marriage, Robert's very unusual quirks surfaced. Anytime we were driving, he'd read every sign we passed—out loud. Then he would have periods where he would zone out, leaving the world behind as he did this night. In fact, it occurred the night before we were to leave for Tennessee.

It was 8:00 p.m., and the sun would be down soon. I walked for at least an hour. It was cooler now as I ambled around corners, passing houses that were all similar in shape and material, except for one or two differences. I stopped and sat on a bench along a path that ran parallel to a drainage ditch. Unfortunately, I got lost. The houses, although lovely, all looked similar. In the distance, I heard the all-too-familiar howls of coyotes. I am terrified of these animals. I was teased in California because my fear outweighed the actual danger of physical harm.

Eventually, I found my way back to Robert's beautiful house on Tránsito Pacífico. I opened the curved gate that led me into the interior courtyard, passing the casita, circumventing a sleeping fountain toward the entrance. "What the?" I observed the house had fallen into complete darkness, except for a faint glow from nightlights. Robert loved his nightlights.

Thank God, the door was unlocked. I entered and stumbled forward, searching for a light switch. The living room was illuminated. As I approached the hallway leading to the bedroom, I saw the faint light shining beneath the door. Even in the dim light, I could see his form. He was sound asleep in bed.

I hit the switch, and the form moved. "Robert, what are you doing?" I asked. "Why are you in bed while I was still out? I got lost, but I guess you weren't concerned."

He looked at me as if I were a being from another planet. The truth was he completely forgot he was married and that I was out wandering alone. His focus was on the presentation. That is Asperger's at its finest. Any memory of me disappeared like smoke up a chimney. I imagine the reason many notable men, brilliant in their careers, can accomplish their objectives is because, unlike most of society, they have a filter that blocks out anything and everybody. Tunnel vision. A mind free of distractions, including a new bride.

"I, uh, was tired. Who? What?" This was his response. It was clear he was attempting to make sense of something that made no sense to him, at least in this minute. He had forgotten me, his marriage—everything but that presentation. It took several minutes for Robert to return, and it was a struggle. Once he did, he offered, "Let me get dressed, and we will get something to eat. I'm sorry."

My appetite faded, replaced by a fear that was roaring down to consume me. "Robert, I am not hungry. I just want to go to bed. I'll sleep in the guest bedroom."

He rose quickly from bed, came toward me, and grabbed me tenderly. "Come on, honey, let's go. How about we go to that place with the great ice cream?" His focus was now on his growling tummy. Whatever he was, he was kind and loving. Always trying to please. He didn't have a mean bone in his body.

"Okay, are you sure?"

Within minutes, we were in the car heading up the highway toward his favorite fast-food establishment. I decided not to question him about earlier events.

Later that night, the house in total darkness, I awoke. In the dim light cast from one of his many nightlights, I observed the empty space where Robert slept. I threw back the covers and rose to investigate. Walking toward the living space of the house, I felt a sense of dread. I began to think the worst. Feeling my way along the hall, I reached the open area that led to the great room. At the kitchen table he sat, only the light from the computer shown on his face. I had no idea what to make of it all. I knew I was sad, scared, and stuck. He was lost in a world I would never be allowed to enter. It was 3:00 a.m., and his obsession had taken over. Without saying a word, I went back to bed. Sleep was lost in a myriad of images.

Once, I said to this dear man, "I would love to be inside your head, even for a brief time."

He responded, "Trust me, you wouldn't want to be inside my head." I didn't push him to explain. Instinctually, I knew he was correct.

I began to do extensive research on his condition. He had a lot of quirks, but his fixation on areas of special interests became somewhat difficult to endure. There were times when we would spend hours and hours at Best Buy talking about or buying computers. Then there was the repetitive reading of signs. Every trip, and that is not an exaggeration, every trip to the store, a day trip, anywhere, he read EVERY sign we passed. This was a symptom of Asperger's disorder. I would ask him if he read signs aloud when he was alone, and of course he didn't, so he could control it. He monitored and reported the weather statistics all day: a stimulation for him; for me, not so much. As boring as the actions were for others, for him, an object of desire.

We were in LA, having moved permanently from Arizona, when I broached the subject. Watching the news one night, I interrupted, "Robert, I found out some interesting facts about Asperger's." I plopped onto the sofa next to where he sat, focused on the news, another of his fixations. I took the controller, turning down the volume. "You are in a very elite group of men. Albert Einstein, Bill Gates, Sir Isaac Newton, and even Mozart all have Asperger's. There is a lengthy list of some of the most intelligent, talented, and famous men with the disorder."

He denied having Asperger's until, after a good deal of research, I identified several famous, intelligent, well-known people with the same disorder. Instantly, he was okay with his diagnosis. I was not. His account of his life, his family, and finances were all part of his false history. I read a book and shared it with Robert. I helped him learn how to communicate with others, speak from the heart to his family, and control his urges to read signs by pointing out that he doesn't do it when alone in the car or if he were with his colleagues.

Robert and I shared so many fun events the first year of marriage. We traveled to numerous missions in California. Robert flew a biplane up the coast—a gift from my beautiful sister. I used the money gift from Chris for a ride in the plane. We were happy entertaining, walking on the beach, joining a small group from church, hiking, boating.

Colleen and I were getting along very well after that first physical encounter. She had come to visit us, and it went well. In fact, she appeared to be drawing very close to me. We spoke daily, usually I was the one to call her. I felt she needed a motherly influence in her life now. Therefore, when she called one afternoon to speak with me, I was not surprised.

"Does your dad know about Kevin?" I asked after she informed me he was very depressed and entered a mental health facility. I recalled his lifeless eyes, an indicator of a serious problem. Colleen shared some extremely disturbing information about her brother that alarmed me. Plus, her feelings regarding the situation with her brother were, well, disconnected and extremely disturbing. It appeared to me there was no love lost between the siblings.

She continued to speak with me even when I informed her that her dad was back from the grocery store. I was becoming more uncomfortable as the call progressed, and all I wanted to do was disconnect. "Listen, I better go take care of your dad," I said, desperate to escape from this very dysfunctional conversation.

"We have to do this again. I mean, have a nice long talk." Her response was jubilant.

My response was a lie. "Sure, let's talk again soon." I was shaking when I hung up. She told me things that disturbed me deeply about her brother, her lack of concern about him.

Even Robert, who glossed things over, stated his son had a history of depression, and even had a few suicide attempts over the years. I couldn't believe the words she had just spoken about her brother, and with such a casual manner. I was sickened. The last thing I wanted was to ever have another conversation such as this.

The only major, consistent problem we had—or that I had—was his family. I didn't understand the hot-cold relationship with his daughter and what I perceived as an abnormal fixation on the daughter's part with her father. Contact with his son was nonexistent during that first year. The only contact his son had with his dad was when he wrote this in an e-mail: "Change your password." That was it. No explanation. I learned later from him the reason he sent that cryptic note was because he heard his sister and someone else reading personal e-mails from Robert's AOL account. She had his password. Every private message I exchanged with my husband was read by his daughter. I felt so violated.

Something was off within this family. Trust me, I am an expert in these matters. But it was widespread. Facts were obscured or canceled out completely. I suspected lies became realities and truths became obscure. At times, I felt I was losing my mind. Robert or his daughter would say something that simply had no roots in truth, but they held on to it. Robert's stories about his life with his wife and children were in direct opposition with stories told by other family members.

He was about nine months into the marriage when Robert received a saddening call. It came in the bedroom where I was asleep.

"Annie, I just found out that Kevin and Cheryl are getting a divorce." His voice trembled as he spoke. This man, who had no contact with his son, still held a strong love in his heart.

Rubbing away sleep, I asked, "What happened?"

"I don't know. Nobody said anything to me about problems. Apparently, his wife and daughter are staying with Colleen." This family held back pertinent facts about their lives. And I often wondered why.

Leaning on my elbow, trying to focus my eyes, I offered, "Hon, I am so sorry. This really bothers you, doesn't it?"

"Yeah, I married them. Everyone I marry gets divorced." I think he was attempting to minimize his discomfort.

I asked what he wanted to do and suggested to call him to show he cares.

"I'll send an e-mail." He rose and left the room. I rolled over and thought about the recent news. Once again, something as major as this was not discussed with Robert. I could understand his son's silence, but why didn't his daughter mention it to her father? Too many secrets.

"Hon, I think a phone call might be better. What do you think?" I knew his answer before he spoke it. Direct contact might lead to confrontation, and that was worse than death for this man.

His son never responded to his outreach, or mine, for that matter. Colleen was evasive. Although we learned he was very depressed. On one of the last telephone calls I had with my stepdaughter, she told me her brother hated their father. She even admitted Kevin felt the relationship between father and daughter was abnormal.

"There's a restraining order against him, and he was looking at guns on the Internet," Colleen told me. My stomach literally hurt at the thought.

Late that same day, I spoke with Robert. "I am really concerned about what's happening. Don't you think it's odd that nothing is said until your family is in the middle of a crisis? The divorce, the depression, and we hear nothing. Being spoon-fed now about something so major is worrisome."

We were informed Kevin was in the grips of depression. Robert and I were both on edge. Initially, Robert was far more concerned than I. Robert had always been uncomfortable in sensitive situations. I continued to help him with communication skills so he could be an effective communicator with family.

The day was a perfect SoCal day. Warm, no humidity, sun melting on our skin as we walked the path that snaked through the sand in Santa Monica.

"So did you get all your work finished?" I asked. Robert still taught at the university, but it was all virtual now. If he could connect to the Internet, he could teach anywhere.

He held my hand tightly. I was his security blanket. "No, I have a few more PowerPoints to go through. Do you want to sit with me later?" I enjoyed reviewing his students' presentations.

"Sure. Let's finish after supper, okay? Do you want to eat out or go home?"

There were benches along the path, and he sat on the one closest to us. The blending of children's laughter, seagulls singing, waves crawling across the sand, and flip-flops slipping swiftly across the sandy pathway delivered peace to the soul. I wanted to stay there forever. This was why Robert left Arizona behind: for times like these. Although, losing his beautiful home to the bank was heartbreaking. Robert was just one of thousands who lost their property during the 2008 financial crisis.

"Have you heard anything from your son?"

"Nothing."

"What happened with you two? Did you have an argument?" I asked, knowing his answer would be ambiguous.

He released a sigh. "I think it was because of my discarding something of his mother's after she died. Some papers he wanted."

"What papers"? I asked. He didn't answer. I learned later he wanted his mother's journal. I was informed Robert threw it away, although I don't think that was the truth. I was informed about the content from someone who came into Robert's life long after his wife had died.

We sat for a time, lost in our own thoughts.

Back home, we parked in the garage and rode the elevator to the sixth floor. I could hear the phone ringing as Robert unlocked the door. Robert headed for the bathroom, and I grabbed the phone. It was Robert's daughter. God forgive me, but all I could think was another day would be ruined by Wright family problems.

She began by telling me that Robert's son called her for help. He was checking in to a mental health facility. Apparently, she resisted at first but then complied. Her voice lacked empathy, as she reported the details like a radio announcer. Detached.

"I couldn't hold back. As he was checking in to the hospital, I told him what I thought of him. I was screaming at him. I couldn't help it. I was just so angry," Her tone, terse. Trying to make sense of this family was like trying to hold the wind in my hand. Who screams at someone who is so depressed, he is voluntarily checking himself into a hospital?

"Well, keep us up to speed about what's going on, okay? Robert's e-mails have gone unanswered. I must admit I am saddened for him. To be that depressed must be terrible. To lose all hope…"

"He's always depressed. Whatever." She reminded me of someone. Mother.

Robert entered the room. I mouthed it was his daughter on the phone.

"Thanks, Colleen, talk soon, or just send Dad an e-mail. That would be fine." I slammed the phone a little too hard.

Robert was a gentleman, unable to handle the emotional weight of the details about his son. He would collapse like a flower in the pouring rain if forced to face the unpleasantries of the present situation. Besides, he was blinded by some secret code, a code to protect and cover the flaws of his daughter. Therefore, I made the decision to hold back information from him. He did not know that his daughter advised me of a restraining order taken out against Kevin, or that he had done a Google search for shotguns. He would never hear from my lips that his son hated him. What purpose would be served by providing him with this information? Besides, it was highly probable he would no doubt block it out of his mind in a millisecond. So

I carried the weight alone. Additionally, was the information even accurate?

One day a few weeks later, I had learned that Robert's son was soon to be released. He was going to stay with his daughter, if she would allow it, and then he was heading for California. If he truly hated his father, attempted to purchase a weapon on the Internet, and feared enough by family to have a restraining order against him, I was plagued with one question: were we in any real danger?

So, on a typical, beautiful SoCal morning, I went to visit my former neighbor and friend, Julia. We sipped wine, laughed, and got caught up. She was concerned about what I told her and made me promise to be careful. She was aware of my husband's family problems. Arriving home early afternoon, I went directly to the small area, off the great room, assigned as Robert's office.

"Hi there, how are you?" I asked, my voice happy and relaxed. I seated myself in a hand-carved chair made by his dad. One of Robert's treasures. Not looking up at me, he responded, "Okay." His response felt like a slap or a bucket of ice water being tossed on my sizzling good mood.

"It was so nice to see Julia again. We talked about some of the BBQs we had here. Remember when that mouse joined us, not at all fearful of our presence? It walked around our feet, completely at ease, searching for a handout. All the women were skittish, hopping on chairs, diving for the steps. You guys just laughed at us. Remember? We had a nice visit. In fact, she suggested we go walking later. I think I'll go. Can't remember my last walk. It will be really nice."

Without warning, his chair swiveled around, his face crimson as he screamed, "Sorry if I can't be happy about your partying, but I am trying to save my son."

Without warning, the floodgates opened, and my thoughts poured out. "Do you have any idea how much you just hurt me? Did you forget how many times I reached out to him because you couldn't? How about the e-mails I sent, encouraging him and your daughter. By the way I called a friend in New Jersey who is a therapist to seek advice to help him. Did you forget I suggested he come here and stay when released? Oh, and what did you do? Nothing. Leave it to Anne, she'll fix it. Nonstop intrusions into our life. Problems dumped on me. Who worked diligently to save your home? Me. Who helped you to learn how to communicate with Kevin? Karen? Others? Me. Forgive me if I needed to escape your family problems."

I stormed out, heartbroken and angry. Not wanting to slip into the dark place of self-effacing behavior, I went and sat on the bluff, overlooking the ocean. Surrounded by flowers and greenery, my view of the surfers below was perfect. I asked myself and God, *Why am I the one person people dump on*? I simply cannot be the blame for everything that happens. In my opinion, I had done far more than Robert, who would hide in his cocoon of denial and avoidance protected by his wife.

Entering the house, he was on his feet and greeted me. "I am really sorry for what I said. You didn't deserve it. You have done a lot more than me for my son. If I wasn't for you and your help, I would probably never have been able to talk with him."

Even though Robert doesn't have a mean bone in his body, that doesn't mean he hasn't hurt me. Nothing was intentional—mostly self-protective and avoidance of conflict. I couldn't help wondering what or who caused him to attack me as he did earlier. I had my suspicions there was a phone call, like so many phone calls in our marriage, that lit the fuse. It was easier to unleash his anger and confusion on me than the woman on the other end of the phone.

"You really hurt me, Robert." I sighed, taking a seat across from him.

He hugged me and left to return a short time later with a lovely bouquet of roses. "Let's go to Duke's. Okay?" I smiled. He sure knew the right things to say and do. I knew he was saddened he hurt me. How can anyone turn down flowers, the ocean, and great food?

A few days later, we learned his son was discharged. He was at Colleen's, temporarily. She made it clear his stay would be brief. Unfortunately, Colleen was no longer speaking or writing me. After my episode with Robert, I realized that I needed to step back from the situation. I was not his son's mother; in fact, I barely knew him. All I knew was there was a plethora of stories, each describing a very different person. As Robert's wife, I needed to remove myself from the family drama and allow Robert to father his son. I sent Colleen an e-mail explaining why I was stepping back, but not the actual event that led to the decision. From what I was told later, she interpreted that note as an act of abandoning her. So she did what most people do with her disorder: she abandoned me first. She had the same disorder as my mother. Another person with borderline personality. Those inflicted, life is black or white. They love you or hate you; no gray areas. I had fallen off the pedestal. That e-mail was the end of any relationship with Colleen…forevermore. She never called to discuss it, but her actions were all too familiar. She went silent.

I had spent the afternoon in Glendale on an interview for a position I desired. Step 1 in a three-step process. I was pleased it was over, as I arrived back home and parked in my condo-assigned parking space in the garage. Content and peaceful but eager to shake off the dust from the interview. The beautiful late-day weather called to me. A few strides across the driveway, I stood at the top of the steps that descended beneath a heavy-laden trellis dripping bougainvillea, like melting strawberry ice cream over a cone.

"Hi, I am sorry. I didn't see anyone here," I said, stepping into the gazebo. All the beautiful glass tables had men, women, and children. Bademjan and Tahdigin filled beautiful bowls. Foods of flavor from Iran. His hair was black, his smile sincere. "No problem. My name is Ashtad, and these people are my family." I was introduced and brought in to meet everyone in this place. I didn't want to interfere. I was just going to sit here for a few minutes.

"My dear, today you are family. Come, eat something with us," an elderly woman said, approaching us. "You look like you could use the company."

Thirty minutes later, after wonderful conversation with various members of the group, I actually felt like family. Their generosity, their stories about the situation in Iran, their journey to America, and their inability to return to their motherland provided a comprehensive understanding and acceptance of their culture. Even the discussion about faith was authentic, with all listening to each other for a better understanding.

"So, if I am family, what's my new family name?"

They laughed and said, "Haghighi."

"Uh-oh. I can't even pronounce it. Now I am really in trouble. Thank you so much for accepting a stranger into your family, even if only for a few minutes. I guess I should let my husband know I am back. I am certain I will be seeing you about the grounds. Don't you just love coming up here or going down on the grass and looking at the action below on the beach?" I loved the diversity in California. Meeting people from different background, culture, and religions. We all want the same thing. Love. Family. Friendship. Peace. Joy.

We hugged, and I parted, taking a short walk up the hiking trail, savoring the ocean below from a bench on a bluff before heading back down. Stepping into the elevator, I so desired to go back out, but I needed to let Robert know I was back and provide an update.

Stepping into the condo, Robert called out to me. Robert seated at his desk near the bank of windows. I flung my purse on the kitchen counter as I passed. "I got an e-mail from Kevin. Colleen doesn't want him to stay with her any longer, so he asked if he could come here." This was a first actual communication initiated by his son. His tone said more than the words he spoke. He was pleased.

"Oh my gosh! I can't believe it!" My mind was racing as fast as my heart. "Did you answer him yet? You said it was okay, didn't you?" I asked, wanting to bite my tongue. There I go again, a lifetime habit of jumping into the pool without checking the water. I was torn between wanting to help this man and genuine fear. Most folks would think it over, weigh the pros and cons, then decide with their head and heart. Not me. My heart takes the lead.

All I could think about was that this depressed man had a restraining order against him in New Jersey. The addition of his Internet search for a shotgun, combined with his intense dislike for his father, created a frightening scenario. And he was on his way, on his way to our front door.

Colleen had provided very little information on his mind-set while he was staying with her. Despite our pleas, she remained silent. I asked often in e-mails, as did Robert, but she communicated in her usual fashion: silence. A myriad of scenarios played in my head. None had a "happy ever after."

I called friends when Robert wasn't around to express my concerns. A few friend suggested that perhaps some information was inaccurate, an exaggeration. As stated, I never heard so much diversification in stories as with this family. False memories?

"After breakfast, let's take a ride to Rancho Palos Verdes. Kevin will be here soon, and we don't know how long he will be staying or what's going to happen. Let's take advantage of alone time."

Grabbing some healthy snacks like nuts, raisins, apples—and chocolate cookies for Robert, I tossed them into our little carrier. I was startled when arms circled my body. "You know I love you, don't you?"

Fingers moved slowly around my waist, stirring me to giggle. "Stop it. You goofy guy. I can be ready in ten minutes, okay. Are you ready? I just need to finish our little snack box. Do you want me to bring water for you? Oh, make up a couple of food bags for the homeless. There is peanut butter in the pantry. I got some last night. And if you are willing to surrender a few cookies, we can bag them as well. You need to pick a few Bible verses for the bags."

Robert loved to make homemade bread. We would rarely leave the house without a few paper bags filled with food for the body and spirit for our homeless friends. Smiles, many toothless, brought us such joy. Our most important objective: to inform these dear people that the bread was homemade "just for you," as the note read.

A few minutes later, from the hallway, I called out, "Are you ready?" I was eager to escape, at least for a few hours. He had returned to his perch in his huge leather swivel chair at his desk. I saw the glow of the computer as it came to life. "Yeah, let me check my e-mail. I'm missing some students' assignments." Minutes passed. I was wearing jeans, a stripped top, and a baseball hat with lettering that read *Pacific Palisades*. "I'm ready."

"We can eat lunch down there. I got an e-mail from Colleen." He was still at the computer.

From the kitchen, I called out, "What did she say?" A fluttering in my chest always occurred just hearing her name. So many trips were ruined by some problem that I just wanted to go. I set up Robert's ringer on the phone. Special rings for Colleen and Kevin. Kevin was an antique car; Colleen's was an alarm.

"She wrote that when she woke up this morning. Kevin was gone. She didn't know where he was going because they didn't talk."

I entered his office. "How long will it take him to get here? What is he driving? Did you mention his e-mail to you that he was coming to California?"

Standing up, facing me, he smiled. "At least a week, I would imagine. He's driving his Alfa Romeo. It is not in very good shape, so I hope he will be okay."

I started biting the inside of my cheek. The clock was ticking. Wheels of logic and reason kept spinning, searching for answers to all the unanswerable questions racing through my head. A few hours later, we were seated on benches overlooking the ocean. The calm from this place filled me like an aphrodisiac. There is nothing so serene as the beauty of the ocean, the thrill of viewing waves as they collide with the palisades. High above, pelicans floated like kites without a string. Unseen currents carried them upward, and just as abruptly, they dove deep into the azure blue liquid.

I rose, aiming my binoculars to an area off to the right where others were pointing. "Robert, look, a whale!" Men and women formed a human wall, standing shoulder to shoulder, binoculars raised high, fingers pointing far off to the left. "Robert, do you see it? Wait, there it goes." I was on my feet, but Robert remained seated. Clearly, the man was lost in the hope of seeing his son. I know he hoped there would be resolution to their estrangement.

"I'm getting hungry. Let's go get something to eat," he asked, suddenly on his feet. This man was always hungry, especially for fast food.

"Okay, but let's come back, okay? Please. I don't want to leave yet." I realized I was whining like a child, begging to stay out just ten minutes longer. I was reluctant to let go of this day.

He grabbed my hand. "Of course. But first, food."

"Robert, let's go to that cute place we passed on the way here—the one with the brightly covered outdoor tablecloths and umbrellas. It was so cute, and we can see the ocean if we sit outdoors."

Pulling out of the spot, he started to laugh. "Heaven forbid, you don't see the ocean—you would go into withdrawal."

Seated, I took a bite of my chopped salad. Robert was making love to his burger. The sound of an antique car horn sounded. It was Robert's cell phone; the tone indicated it was his son.

Swallowing, he answered, "Hello, Kevin. Where are you?" He paused. "On your way to New Orleans, really? Well, just let me know where you are so we can be ready for you, son. Please, be careful. How is the car holding up?" A lengthy silence as he held the phone to his ear. With Robert, all attempts to read his facial expression failed—he was a closed book. Today was no exception. My research indicated a commonality with persons with Asperger's. Before clicking the phone off, his final words were spoken, surprisingly with a great deal of emotion. "See you soon. I love you, son." After reading up on Asperger's, I attempted to help him communicate, especially with his family. When he first learned about Kevin's depression, he called him and started asking questions about the motorhome! He prattled on without a single question to his son.

"Robert, what did he say? What's up?" I could almost hear the bubble bursting. The day was over; a dark cloud descended.

"He thinks he will be here by Saturday. That's nine days. We can set up the air mattress. Only nine days, and my son will be here." Robert ventured off to his special place that he alone could visit. I was left behind. Conversation was null and void during these moments. I felt utterly alone.

Later, as we drove home, my mind drifted. Nine days. What would happen in nine days? Kevin was arriving two days before I was to start a new job. The wheels were turning, bringing uncertainty into my world.

22

On Saturday, another typical Southern California day greeted us. Sunny with a gentle breeze off the ocean kept the humidity low, bringing with it a briny aroma.

"I need to run out. Want to go with me?" Robert didn't hear me; his eyes mesmerized by the computer screen. "Robert, did you hear me?"

"What?" There it was again, that tone I knew so well. The man was annoyed. I entered his world, that special place, a place I will never belong. I repeated the question. His eyes, the window into his soul, were now focused on me, my words. Robert was returning, leaving his world of images, unusual thoughts, and security behind. "Sure. Give me a few minutes to wrap up my work. Okay?" He was almost back, but he had one foot with me, in California, and the other, well, I don't know. His schoolwork was finished, so I was uncertain what work he was focused on. I had learned just to give him the time he needed.

Later that day, everything was prepared and set up for Kevin's arrival. There was a little specialty bakery in Santa Monica I loved, so I went there to purchase diabetic treats for Robert's son, who was a diabetic. After grocery shopping, I suggested we take a little walk on the beach. I felt the need to speak with him about my concerns, based on what his daughter told me a few months back when we were still speaking.

"Hon, do you think we have something to be concerned about with Kevin's arrival? I mean, he is depressed, and you and he have not had a good father-son relationship. Remember all those things your daughter told us?" I decided a few weeks back I needed to inform Robert what Colleen said about restraining orders and weapons.

Of course, he wasn't at all bothered by what Colleen told us. Robert had not even owned up to the obvious fact that there were problems between the two men. In many ways, he reminded me of my own father. These men created a world of perfection in their minds. Ignore. Ignore. And then, ignore again anything that was unpleasant. Of course, that does not bring about resolution but lifelong, unmet needs and unspoken hurt.

As we walked slowly along the bike path that cut through the sand like a snake, fingers opened, and our hands dropped. Gingerly, I remained beside but moved about four feet away. "What on earth are you doing?" he asked, concerned.

I smiled. "Just in case your son is coming to get you, I don't want to be hit." My attempt at humor failed.

"Not funny." An anticipated response. The sound of a car horn emanated from Robert's phone alerted us that it was his son. We stopped and took a seat on a cement bench created to ward off the homeless. "Hi, son. Where are you?" As he spoke, I watched the seagulls, wishing I could fly away, get caught in the wind, and be light and free. I walked a short distance, allowing Robert his privacy but also to escape. A dark cloud suddenly covered the sun, and goose flesh rose on my arms. I was chilled to the bone.

"Kevin said he is about two hours away. I think we better get back." There was that look, the absence of presence in his eyes. I could see and feel more than ever that Robert was drifting away into his own peculiar world. As I have learned from past experiences, this was not the time to ask questions. We left the beach and drove up the coast. We slid into our parking space in the garage, rode the elevator up, and entered our condo in silence.

"Does your son like meatloaf? Let's eat out in the gazebo. Do you think he will find us okay? Should we tell them at the gate he is coming? Do you think he will be okay sleeping in the open area?" I fired questions with machine-gun speed. I just needed to fill the silence. My anxiety was bubbling over and pouring out of my mouth. It didn't matter—my husband was absent and probably didn't hear me.

Should I hug him or ask if it is okay first? Maybe I should hide in the bedroom and allow Robert and son a few private moments. I ran scenarios through my head as I often do in my attempt to control my environment.

The sun was low in the sky over the horizon when the gatehouse called. Turning to Robert, I announced, "He's here." Robert was present again but perhaps cautious about seeing his son, although he didn't verbalize it to me. In New Jersey, there was still a distance between them, an invisible barrier. Up until that visit, he was estranged from his dad. So why did he travel across the country after being discharged from the hospital in a beat-up car?

At the sound of the bell, Robert headed for the door. "Hello, son. Come on in."

Joining the men, I asked the younger if I could give him a hug. "Sure, but I might be sort of smelly driving in the sun all day with the top down."

I hugged him, aware of his odor and sunburned face and peeling nose. He was a tad uncomfortable—at least that is what his body spoke to me. Hugging did not come naturally to some, and this man acted as if I had assaulted him, his body tensed. I felt sad for him, unable to receive the warmth of human touch.

As anticipated, eating outside overlooking the ocean surrounded by drapes of pink relaxed the trio. Robert's son shared the same communication pattern as his daughter. There was none. Silence blanketed the space. I learned unless a question broke through the wall of silence, only then would he speak. If not, it just dangled in the air until it faded away like cotton candy in the wind.

The silence was broken when his son said, without provocation, "This meatloaf is good, and I don't like meatloaf."

"Thanks, Kevin. Your dad didn't tell me you didn't like meatloaf," I teased, feigning annoyance.

That remark hit its target, even though unintended. He looked square at his dad, stating matter-of-factly, "My father knows very little about me, Anne. I am not his favorite child."

No response from Robert. The cold war between these men created a hostile environment. Surrounded by beauty, and yet, there was an element bent on destruction. Communication is the key. And yet, here we were, two bright men unable to express their hurt or needs, unable to slice through to their truths.

Sometime later, back indoors, we were all seated in the living space. *Pawn Stars* was on, one of Robert's favorite shows. While the men relaxed, I took a few candid pictures with my cell phone. Kevin was on a small sleeper sofa, Robert in his recliner, and I on the sofa. Once taken, I reviewed the shots, and I observed Kevin's lifeless eyes. I felt this man had already checked out. My fear faded, and my empathy grew. This was depression, not a situational sadness but much deeper, chronic. My heart hurt for him. I knew this disorder very well, an unwelcome intruder in my family. It robs the carrier of life.

I did most of the talking and asked questions, mindful of his discomfort at times. The younger man even teased with me about his dad—it was fun bantering.

When Kevin took the trash out, I looked to Robert. "I really think you should spend time alone with him. After all, it has been a very long time. He didn't drive twenty-five hundred miles to see *me*." My comment was said with a little force. I knew Robert would want me along because I am more comfortable when dealing with *feeling stuff*, as he called it. Besides, he hated confrontation and there was a powerful likelihood that could occur.

Robert rose when he heard a thump at the door. His son was carrying a large, beautiful, refurbished toolbox. It looked more like an elegant jewelry case. Different-sized drawers, with a center, deep well. The top flipped up to reveal a lined drawer. The oak finish was as smooth as rose petals. Communication had begun in the form of a gift. But as happy as I was to see Robert's face, I knew what the meaning of this gift could be.

Setting it down on the fireplace hearth, he said, "This is for you, Dad."

"Kevin, thank you. It is beautiful." Robert's heart was showing. He rose, hugged his son, and said softly, "I love you, son." I wondered if these men had ever hugged before or expressed their feelings verbally.

Robert had begun to talk with his son from his heart, but it still didn't come naturally. He was delighted commenting on the beauty of the gift and explaining how difficult it was to bring such a large item in his tiny sports car. Robert was visibly pleased. I, on the other hand, felt swelling panic. Giving things away is one of the signs a person is considering suicide.

The next few days, at Robert's insistence, I went with the two men. But when they spoke about going to the San Diego Zoo, I spoke up. "Hey, guys, I'm going to pass." I sat on the sofa, legs under me. "I have a good deal of paperwork that needs to be completed before I start my job on Monday. Besides, you two need some alone time." Robert insisted I go, but I was just as insistent, and if my ability to judge body language was still functioning, I sensed Kevin was pleased.

Sad to say, I was pleased to be alone. I took a walk alone, completed the required paperwork, tidied the house, and took a nice, long, bubble bath. My little felines were ever so pleased to have my full attention.

Around seven-thirty that evening, the phone rang. I thought it might be a friend in the neighborhood suggesting I come over for a glass of wine. Everyone knew I was home alone today. Hearing the deep tones of my husband's voice, I must admit I was surprised. "Where are you?"

I could barely hear him. He spoke in a whisper, "We are about a half hour from home."

My heart sank. "Why are you coming home so early? I didn't expect you for hours." I hoped he didn't hear the disappointment in my voice. I needed some more alone time. The past several months in this first year of marriage had delivered a trunk full of problems to my door. There was still some paperwork that needed to be completed.

"I'll tell you later. Do you need anything?" he asked cryptically.

"No, I'm good. Drive carefully."

As predicted, the men arrived home a little after eight.

"Did you all have a good time?" Awkward questions presented at an awkward time. Just one look at these men indicated something was off.

Kevin avoided my eyes and went straight to his bed. We had set up an air mattress, a gift from Chris. It even had a blowup headboard. We had several decorative screens that were placed in such a manner to provide privacy, almost a little room in the great room. Kevin was such a private, introverted man. For him not to have a private space to go would be very difficult.

Robert entered the living room, signaling me with his head toward the bedroom. I rose and followed him.

"Robert, what's wrong?" I sensed what he was about to say would change everything.

"He was very quiet on the way home. Then suddenly, he said that he traveled across the country to say goodbye." He sat on the bed.

"Oh my God. Oh, dear God. What did you say?"

"Nothing." Even though I should have been shocked at his response, in this family, it was the norm.

Without a word, I left the room where I entered the great room. "Kevin, may I speak with you?" No response. I entered the area where the younger man lay. I felt what he had in his heart was so private and plagued with pain that only a confidante would suffice. Was this the right approach? I had no idea, but I had no choice. Logic had been replaced by emotions pulling me forward.

"Kevin, may I talk with you?" He didn't answer. I sat on the bed and spoke from my heart. He was offered promises of support and hope. Shared trials and stories of survival, successes, and the return of real joy. Without knowing the problems, all I could do was a feeble attempt to shine a light in the darkest of corners for this man. When he spoke, I was saddened by his words, and those words will remain between this man and me. I asked him if I could pray for him. I interpreted his silence as agreement and prayed. He remained silent. I kissed his cheek, stood up, and went to leave.

"Anne, I am just so tired of being depressed." He rolled over with a blanket tucked around him. He looked like a little lost child in the dim light.

Not sure when it was that I finally fell asleep, but it was near morning, as evidenced by the hint of a sunrise. I felt the bed sink. "Anne, wake up."

My eyes flung open. "What? What's wrong?" I had difficulty acclimating myself.

Two words: "He's gone."

"What time is it?"

"Only six-thirty. I never heard him leave. He could have left anytime during the night but, well, how could he without us hearing him?"

I got up, walked out of the room, looked at the place where he and I spoke less than twelve hours earlier. He was gone. Where? What can be done? My mind raced. I was so scared and sad. Several hours later, I prayed and then placed a call to my friend in New Jersey. Explaining the events to her, I felt a rise in me, a feeling of helplessness. A few minutes later, I hung up. Robert had joined me. He stood over me, waiting.

"As expected, there is nothing to be done. We can't call the police because he is a grown man and can do what he wants. We don't even know where he went. They can't stop him and say, 'Are you planning on killing yourself?' All he would need to say is no."

The next few days were agony.

Monday was my first day in my new position as a quality improvement specialist. It was impossible to sleep restfully the night before, as a plethora of images and scenarios played out in my thoughts. The endings, the same. Kevin is gone. Raised as we were, I became an expert at pretending.

The next day at work, I pretended to be happy and confident or, in this case, prepared. Pretending to be happy and interested in the work when all I could think about was the inevitable.

"Anne, listen, why don't you get comfortable in here? You can familiarize yourself with the contract, and later, we can talk. Write down any questions you have. Here you go." She placed a huge binder in front of me, smiled, and turned to leave. "We are very pleased you decided to join us, Anne." The door was closed, and I was alone, finally. I released a sigh of relief. I pulled my phone from my purse.

Attempting to focus on the scope of work was a challenge of gigantic proportions. I would stare at a page, read a sentence or two, drift off, then pull myself back. Every word that entered my mind disappeared instantly. It was futile. I just wanted to go home. My first day of work and my focus was traveling down a highway, somewhere in California in an Alfa Romeo. At least I hoped that to be true.

We waited. And waited some more for the phone call. Praying for a dead phone, not a dead son. Unable to concentrate at work, I was surprised I was able to function at all. Of course, I could not explain the why that I am certain was obvious to all. My ability to pretend everything was all right failed. I smiled, but it was one of those smiles you give when your picture is being taken. Insincere, forced, and fading.

A few days later, arriving home, my husband greeted me with, "He's coming back. He called this afternoon to ask if it would be okay." Robert was as relieved as I was. "He said something you said to him gave him hope."

My smile could have been recorded on the Richter scale. "When is he coming?"

"Tomorrow. He was up in Santa Barbara. He sounded good, Anne."

"We have a slight problem—remember?"

Jamie and Grace were scheduled to arrive in a few days. As lovely as our home was, space was at a premium. It was my son's birthday, and these plans for their visit were made awhile ago. Robert and I came up with a few scenarios for sleeping arrangements. It was me who came up with what was a perfect solution. Robert still had the house in Arizona. I took his hand and sat him at the table.

"Why don't you and Kevin go to Arizona? There is so much more room in your house, and you could have father-son time, and Jamie and Grace could stay here. Then, on the weekend, you guys come back. We celebrate Jamie's birthday, and Kevin could meet them. They leave the next day, so all would be well and Kevin could come back here." I was smiling at my own brilliance.

"No, I want to stay here with you. Maybe my son could stay in a motel for a couple of days." He was adamant. A man so quiet and passive was now loud and assertive. Was it because he felt safe with me that he allowed himself to freely exhibit the frustration he felt? Frustration is derived when we try to control life.

"Come on, Robert. He is depressed and, well, even though he likes me, I'm a stranger. He needs you. And as you know, I'm a chatterbox, and he is so quiet, like your daughter. This is the best solution for everyone. He would have his own room at your place, his own TV, and you could continue to build your relationship. Isn't that what you want?"

"That is not what I want. I don't want to be away from you." Fear was talking now. Fear of confrontation. He had no problem confronting me without hesitation. I was safe, not reactive like others in his life.

Kicking off my shoes, I thought, *No mention of my new job.* Once again, my husband's family story was being played out. We had been married less than a year. I had faced a myriad of difficulties. I grabbed the comfy recliner. He sat on the sofa. My first day on the job. Nice. "Robert, I am thrilled your son is feeling a little hopeful and very thankful to God for this gift. But with me starting my job, it would be good for me. Kevin is still very fragile, and we need to reduce his stress. Sleeping in the great room with no privacy must be awful for him. He is so private. Robert, are you listening?" My voice had a catch as I spoke.

"I heard you." He shifted his gaze from the TV to me.

"Well, what do you think? When was the last time you guys have been alone? Just the two of you?"

"I am guessing it's been, well, never. Don't you think it's time? What he needs, I can't give him. He needs family. A father." I observed the familiar look on Robert's face. That look that he was uncomfortable with the conversation and would soon have the vague facial expression I was all too familiar with. "Robert, please, listen to me. There is so much more room there, he is familiar with the house. He can be by himself or talk, he will have the option. Here, there is no place for him to go." Robert rose and stood by the side of the chair I was seated in.

"Annie, I don't know. What will we talk about?" Robert was likened to a small child as he asked me. I felt like his mother in that moment. Folks with Asperger's can have a great deal of difficulty with communication. He was a brilliant teacher, but that is not communication. Communication is the giving and receiving of information, both verbal and nonverbal.

I felt compassion for this man who loved his son but had no idea how to connect with him on an intimate level. I knew Kevin felt the same. A family lacking communication skills. Small talk for Robert was nonexistent before he met me. They were quiet. Or superficial. It appeared to me and others that they had no idea what or why they felt as they did.

"Talk about how he is feeling. Ask if you can help. Talk from your heart. I know you love him. How about starting there?" I pulled the side arm up, my legs elevated.

"Okay, I'll go." Conversation over. Back to TV. The news. Always the news. I hated the news, especially when it was the same reports repeated during the day.

A few days later, Kevin returned. His face bore no outward signs of tension. I think I even caught a glimpse of a smile. In fact, we teased with each other quite a bit. It was fun. I felt hopeful.

The next day, while I was at work, they left for Arizona. I felt relieved. Concerned. Pleased. Hopeful. Alive. Perhaps this was the beginning of something positive. I was looking forward to my son's visit with Grace. I thought it would be great for Kevin to meet them, have a nice birthday out, and then work on his forward momentum plan. We would help with advice and suggestions. I even lined up a possible place for him to stay. He verbalized he liked Santa Monica. We had a friend who owned a few apartments there. The light was shining in the recent dark corners, at least in my idealistic mind.

As predictable as the setting sun each day, I received a nightly call from Arizona. Notably an absence in intonation in his voice with each call. Tonight was no different. My idea of how this trip to Arizona would play out had gone up in a puff of smoke. It was like pulling teeth to obtain information. I received an overabundance of *okays* or *fines* or *I don't know* to my general questions. Therefore, my sense of stability with these men, strangers in many ways, was uncertain. Although he remained primarily silent, his absence of dialogue screamed of his discomfort. He was miserable. Why? As much as I wanted to know, a huge part of me was content to be in the dark.

I needed to focus on me, my career. I had done all I could in the moment and offered the promise to help his son, if needed.

On a Thursday, the phone was screaming as I entered. The tone of Robert on the other end was atypical. There was a pleasant lilt as he spoke. "Listen, I am coming home tomorrow. I miss my wife." What he wasn't saying was, *without you, there is no substance, no connection, just empty spaces where love and commitment should be.* I suspect the void for both men was impenetrable. At least when I was around, I was occasionally able to uncork the bottle where secrets, fears, and misunderstandings slept. One such breakthrough was when Robert told his son a few days earlier "I love you." Kevin's response was "I love you too."

Later that night in bed, Robert cried with joy. But they soon fell back into the lifelong pattern of holding in of emotions. Or much worse, not having recognizable, identifiable feelings about anything of substance. I was an outsider, looking in, but from my viewpoint, there was nothing sustainable with these men. Too much time had passed, too little open dialogue, too much hurt, disappointment, betrayal.

"Robert, that is not a good idea. You only have a few more days until you both can return. Leaving him alone now, a man who is depressed, without a car, is not wise. Robert, he is suicidal. The worst thing you can do is leave him alone." I was upset, and my words were sharp, but I didn't care.

"I told him I would pay for a rental car. Then, in a couple of days, he can drive back."

I continued to try to reason with him, but he had his mind set. "Robert, please think it over. I hope you will reconsider and stay. He should not be left alone." Robert continued to say he and Kevin spoke, and it was fine with his son. He tried to assure me there was nothing to be concerned about. I didn't believe a word he said. He wanted to come home. Period. He was uncomfortable—perhaps they were both uncomfortable. I would never have suggested this trip if I had any inclination it would end like this.

By the time I arrived home the next day, he was already there. I was very upset with his decision. We wrote Kevin and called, but he had, once again, gone silent. The only responses we heard from Kevin over the next few days were limited and informational. In an e-mail, Robert was told he had lost Internet connection. Now he had no TV or computer. And he refused to get a car. He was alone without distractions. The stage was set. The curtain was about to rise, the drama was about to be played out on the large screen of our lives. Robert and I prayed each night about him. I am more of a realist than my husband. Some people live in the world they desire and block out the dark areas. Perhaps that's why there are so many variations of accounts of his past. The stories are based on false memories.

His sister had contacted her father to tell him that we *must* get her brother to contact her *right now*. Pushing someone in his condition to do anything is unwise. There was an urgency in her request. We told her neither of us had any contact of substance with Kevin but informed him to get in touch with her. Our approach was less urgent but more: "Give your sister a call if you get an opportunity. She said she needs to talk with you." Kevin told me Colleen didn't talk with him but went to bed when he was there. The lack of compassion he felt sealed her fate; he would not contact her.

Having just arrived at work, I had one of my feelings. As stated earlier, I honor them as if they were a special gift from God. Sitting in my little space, in the moderate-sized office on the sixth floor, I grabbed the phone. Time to act. The phone rang five times before I heard Robert's voice.

"Robert, call that psychiatrist the church recommended. We need to be proactive. I am really concerned about your son. I want to be as prepared as possible when he returns." I heard the panic in my voice that was reaching up into my gut. I began to believe there would be no return. He was alone with his thoughts. Facing a divorce. Possibly feeling abandoned by his dad, a man who loved him but just lacked what was needed to connect.

"Okay, I will call and set something up for later in the week." He agreed over the phone. I sensed he was just placating me, but I didn't care.

"No. Today. Trust me on this. We are not prepared to help him." The gal in the cube perpendicular to mine looked up. I feared she had heard more than my desired intent.

He surrendered. "Okay, I'll let you know how I make out."

Just as I was hanging up, I heard him mutter something, but I couldn't catch it. Even if I did, he would have denied it anyway, especially if it were negative.

Minutes later, my desk phone rang. "He can see us at five. I explained everything, so he is willing to stay late. He is located on Pico Boulevard."

Entering my boss's office, I felt moisture form in my palms. My employment was brief, and here I was requesting an early leave. "Excuse me, Ron, but may I speak with you?"

He smiled, and I entered, seating myself in a leather chair across from him. There were photos of happy faces, his family, I assumed.

"What's up, Anne?"

"I, uh, *we* have a bit of a problem at home. I would rather not discuss it, but I do need to leave a little early today. Around three-thirty?"

"No problem. I hope it is nothing too serious." His voice was tender with concern.

I rose and said thank you and went back to my little corner, anxiously watching the clock.

23

"Anne, it's me." I knew what Robert was about to say. My feelings were alerting me that something was wrong. He need not say another word. I knew the message he was about to deliver. His voice spoke volumes. "The state police are here. Kevin is dead. He hung himself in my garage." His voice was steady—as if he were giving me the weather report. Or reciting a dissertation in school. Robert had shut down.

Through tears, I spoke, "Hon, I am so terribly sorry. I'll be right home." I felt nauseated. I couldn't stop thinking, *Dear God, please fix it.* I gathered my belongings, stopped back into Ron's office, provided a quick overview through a steady deluge of tears, and left. I probably shouldn't have driven, but no one lived near me. Plus, I wanted to be alone.

"Anne, wait." One of the dear women in the office ran out into the parking garage. "I can take you home. Ron doesn't want you to drive like this."

My foot on the gas, I thanked her and pulled out of the lot onto Glendale Avenue. I had an hour drive ahead of me. I would be alone. I had regret. Anger. Loss. Sadness. And my companion from childhood: guilt. Over and over, I thought about what I should have done, or not done, to prevent this from occurring. I was responsible. I failed him.

To be blessed with special friends is a true gift from God. Those exceptional people who love you even when you are unlovable or when your life has just changed trajectory.

Driving on the 405 at seventy-five miles per hour, I called one of those individuals. "Lynne, he's dead," I cried. "I don't know all the details yet, but I am on my way home now." Lynne offered words of comfort and concern. "Robert's daughter is calling through. This can't be good. I'll call you later. Prayers please." I knew I didn't have to ask her to pray, but I felt some comfort in the knowledge I would soon have an avalanche of prayers pouring down on my wounded heart.

Hearing Colleen's voice, all I felt for her was sadness. I offered up sincere words of comfort and love. Despite her change in feelings for me, at a time like this, everything melts away. "Colleen, I am so sorry. I don't know what to say. I will help your dad and do anything that is needed." My newly falling tears were for this woman who just lost her brother. To my surprise, her voice was void of emotion or distress; in fact, she sounded calm, controlled, and matter-of-fact. I thought, *She must know, right?*

"You need to have the coroner call me. He is not to talk with my father. Dad will just mess everything up. When you get home, call me and give the name and info about the coroner. Do you hear me?" An order from the sister of a man who just took his life.

My eyes dried up. Instead, I felt a wave of disbelief. "What!" My only thoughts in this moment were for Robert, his son, and his daughter. Up until this moment, it was also a deep sadness for this woman.

"I don't want Dad involved. There is too much to deal with, and we will take care of it." To me, in that moment, it felt as if she were barking out orders, focused on a task, not the loss of her brother. Was this her way of dealing with the loss? Was it uniquely hers alone to carry and process? Or something else? For me, as well as those closest to me, we dealt openly with our feelings. This lack of expression, or at least expression in a way considered the norm, was foreign to me. If you're happy, you laugh—sad, you cry. But to remain mute was foreign.

The communication rug was once again pulled from beneath me. I thought to myself as I drove the last few miles, *Perhaps the only method of communicating would be determined to go silent.*

I made it home in record time, and on the California highways, that is a feat indeed. Entering our beautiful home, I was in fear of what lay in wait. State troopers stood stoically next to a dry-eyed Robert.

After an introduction, and an expression of sympathy, the tallest man with the steel blue eyes commented, "I can't believe your husband, ma'am. He has held it together."

If he only knew. Robert shut down. He retreated into that distant place deep in the cavern of his brain filled with images of signs, computers, and God knows what else. A place where denial lives. No admission for anything painful, ugly, and especially anything confrontational. There were only two times he cried.

Robert remained dry-eyed until I approached to embrace him. Only then did he allow denied emotions to surface like rain off a leaf in a storm. He would not cry again. Ever. At least about his son. There were a few times his eyes glistened, but he always seemed ashamed.

I remember when he went with me to the cemetery where my boy was laid to rest. As he did tonight, when I fell down weeping, he too was able to feel pain, my pain. On that day, his emotions—emotions I suspect held in for a very long time—were released.

"Well, now that you are home now, ma'am, we will leave you alone. Once more, sir, and you too, ma'am, we are terribly sorry. Tonight was a part of our jobs we officers hate, delivering the news of a death, especially that of a suicide." Both the troopers extended a hand as they began to exit. "Take loving care of him, miss."

A nightmare was born.

I learned that Colleen had the audacity to call Robert's neighbor in Phoenix. She insisted they go over to Robert's house and get certain items then send to New Jersey. I could hear boundaries shattering. They did not comply. I called the coroner and others to obtain info into the events of Kevin's death. I was told Kevin hung himself in the garage. The garage door was open about a foot. The determination was he did that so his body would be found. No note. Although, apparently, it was on his computer.

Not only was there the grief to deal with, but the controlling absence of emotions or facts provided from Robert's daughter. My family was annoyed that I was shocked by the behavior when it had been a common thread used to weave discord and disharmony. There was to be a memorial handled by his wife and daughter in New Jersey without any real input from Robert. Although his daughter-in-law did request Robert to speak and offered us suggestions as to where to stay, she was dealing with the death of her husband and father to their child. Even though a divorce was pending, there were still feelings for this man she had spent most of her life. Robert's daughter made no gesture to invite us to stay with her when we returned to New Jersey. I felt like a hungry sparrow in winter being fed nothing but tidbits.

One night, at the computer, I searched Robert's e-mail. We had each other's passwords, and often, he would elicit me to check his e-mail in the event there was communication from one of his students. Especially if he was caught up in his other stronghold, the news.

"I really wish I had some more information about the memorial service for Kevin. I am really feeling frustrated. Airline tickets need to be purchased, and we need a place to stay. Dealing with noncommunicative folks is, well, ridiculous. You're his dad, and yet, you have little input." I paused, waiting for the comforting and anticipatory glow from the computer. "I can't imagine what his daughter is going through. My heart hurts for her." I paused, clicked a few strokes on the keyboard, and waited for the familiar, "You've got mail."

"Robert, there is an e-mail from your daughter, but it reads as if it were meant for someone else. I think you are going to need to read this. It makes no sense to me whatsoever."

"Would you read it to me, please?" Robert pleaded.

I read phrases such as "now they can blame us for what happened" and "they can stay in CA with their friends." So odd. I suspected I know the truth about this e-mail but without facts. I can't fabricate stories. It stems back to my last conversation with his daughter. Without facts, I need to let the unusual content of the note remain a mystery. Although when questioned, the answer was more far-fetched than the e-mail.

The pendulum had shifted again. She appeared to be in the dislike phase of her relationship with her father. I have seen and heard this shift many times in the past. I didn't understand because Robert was constant in his behavior.

This woman sought what she already had: the love of her father. But it didn't seem to be enough, or perhaps she didn't feel love. At times, she so reminded me of my mother. Both women seeking what was in their reach, except they didn't know how to get it. Personality disorders, I have been told by a psychiatrist friend, are the most difficult to treat. I loved this woman at first. I loved my mother. But that does not mean they were not to be made accountable for their acts. In fact, that is the greatest gift you can give them. Yet, mental illness remains in the closet. Is taboo.

I went with Robert to Phoenix to collect his son's belongings and take care of loose ends. No one else offered, stating it would be too difficult. Being me, I offered to drive when we reached the Phoenix area because I didn't want him to drive into the garage where his son's body hung just a few days earlier. As the door opened, I vomited in my mouth as I saw the spot where his son's body hung. It opened up the wounds of my brother's final hour.

"He really kept everything neat. I think he did so, knowing the house was to be sold." Robert offered. He was in the guest bedroom where his son slept. "Here is his computer." He called out. I was in the bathroom attempting to compose myself. I returned to the guest bedroom.

"I need to send this ASAP to his wife. There are things in it that's needed for his memorial."

"Robert, give it to me. Let me check it out to make certain there is nothing in it that would upset his wife or daughter." There were things that disturbed me greatly. My stomach turned. The secrets were revealed to me and will die with me. I deleted them. The note to his wife went unread.

*****

Jamie and Grace arrived, slightly altering the climate in our home. For me, there was an element of suggested normalcy. Saddened to hear about Kevin; they were very kind and loving to Robert. I know they were uncomfortable feeling intrusive during this sensitive period. Neither Robert nor I felt that way. In fact, I was pleased. The trip was partially for business, so they were out a good deal. They are screenwriters and would come to LA for a visit and take a meeting.

I rose to greet them. Hugs all around. "So how was your day?" Robert was lost in the world of his computer. Not certain he was aware they entered.

"Great," my son answered, dropping his stuff on the counter and kicking off his sneakers. "We had a good meeting today on the Paramount lot, and later tonight, we go to Malibu to speak with someone about the script—the one you don't like too much. But first, a swim. Are you coming?" His question was directed at Grace who had gone in to say hello to Robert.

"No, I think I will run on the beach a bit—maybe the hot tub when I get back."

Robert joined us. "What do you guys want to do about dinner?"

"Nothing, Robert. We will grab something while we are out."

"How about eating before you go, would that work? I would love to visit with you." Robert asked. I was surprised at his request, but I suspect he too needed normalcy. Not the drama we have been living with for so long.

A conversation with them regarding their day lightened the tension. A mother always feels at peace when their children are doing well. Jamie would go to the pool downstairs, and Grace would take her daily run. Normalcy. Of course, concern for Robert's son was the unspoken unease. We all agreed to allow Robert to orchestrate conversation about his son. There was no conversation.

"Just look at that sunset," I said to the group, standing at the bank of windows. An orange sky created the illusion of an amber ocean. An orb of orange melting into the amber sea. "God is at it again. This is just for you, guys."

"Oh, Grace, another sunset. Quick, let's look," my son teased. "Robert, do you know how many sunset pictures Mom sends to everyone? Every day, every night—sunset pictures."

Sitting at the round slate-top dining table, he got up. "Well, she is right. It is beautiful. You know your mother. Sunsets. Babies. Flowers. Puppies. Oceans. Annie responds as if she is seeing them all for the first time. That is really a gift to get that much pleasure out of the simple things. No one will ever tell her to stop and smell the roses." Robert's response was "right on."

He slipped his arm around my waist. I know he felt comfortable with me. Safe. Loved. Secure.

"Can you imagine how she would be if she saw puppies playing in the flowers as the sun set?"

The room erupted in laughter. I was always being teased like this, but it was okay because it was true. As I turned to face my son, whose gaze was focused on the scene outside, I was remembering him with his curly red hair. Now there was an absence of auburn, and even the "dreaded" freckles had gone the way of maturity. "So where do you want to go for dinner tomorrow? Your birthday, so your choice. Although I was thinking of an encore, a lovely meal at the fine-dining place you took me. Do you remember?"

"Yeah, I remember. It wasn't that bad," he rebutted, knowing what was coming.

With emphasis, I asked, "Grace, did he ever tell you about the night he treated me to a wonderful meal?" Grace looked from me to him, smiling. I turned to my son, "You remember that fancy Mexican restaurant in Malibu? It was a fast-food place that served only Mexican, and I hate Mexican food. Outside, there was a massive statue of a man wearing a sombrero that lit up the night. We sat on stools around a table that was so high off the ground, I needed a stepladder to be seated. But the pièce de résistance was the outdoor toilet. I climbed down the ladder to leave the table, then felt my way around back to the unlit toilet. We could never repeat the elegance of that night."

Everyone laughed. Even though it was not quite the laughter released during a joyful time, we were still able to catch a glimpse of lightness in this darkest of times.

"As much as I love to relive that special moment with my mother, how about Duke's?" my son suggested. Hawaiian cuisine and décor, including massive surfboards hanging on the wall, and the icing on the proverbial cake, it was right on the ocean. Heaven forbid I go without seeing my ocean.

"Perfect!" I answered. "Good food, ocean view, and well, a lively, happy atmosphere."

This was to be the night Robert's son would meet my family. Jamie and Grace are intelligent, funny and bright, interesting people. Kevin would have felt at ease, even with his shy manner. Robert was the one who insisted we move forward with our plans.

On Saturday, we all went out to eat for my son's birthday celebration at Duke's. On this rare occasion, I felt as if I looked hot in an outfit that complemented my figure. My self-assurance level was elevated, perhaps a nine on an assurance scale. Hawaiian influence gave the eyes a place to rest as we waited to be seated. Long surfboards were on display, photos of famous surfers, including Arnold Schwarzenegger donning a black speedo. On this night, our little group was personally entertained by a hula dancer. They performed for my son and for Robert and me. After all, it was my son's birthday, and we were newlyweds. It was a fun night, including having a stranger, a nice-looking man, grab my arm to usher me forward. Of course, when he realized I was not his wife, we both laughed. The wife, well, not so much.

At the conclusion of our meal, after cake was served, candles were lit and a traditional "Happy Birthday" sung. It was the hula dancers where Robert rested his eyes. Out came his phone. Ready, aim, shoot.

Nudging Robert, I whispered, "No pictures of me, Jamie, or this place, but hula dancers? Oh yes." He pushed me so he could get a better picture.

"Are you ready to go?" my son asked. The entourage rose, and everyone was feeling great. After all, great food, Chardonnay, and the ocean topped off with hula dancers—what more could we ask for?

Out in front as we waited for the valet to get our car, I suggested a family photo. An elderly couple stopped in front of us.

"Would you like me to take your picture?" Her smile was authentic.

"That would be wonderful, thank you." I handed her my phone, explaining the functionality.

The woman offered to take our picture. We positioned ourselves in front of the fountain that was surrounded by tropical vegetation. Monstera deliciosa, elephant leaves, and purposely positioned ginger plants created an outdoor tropical garden oasis. There was a gentle breeze that lifted and carried the aromas, a potpourri of island pleasure.

"Okay, are you ready? Say olive oil!" the woman suggested in a drill sergeant delivery. We all giggled at her suggestion. The picture looked great. This night, despite the death of Robert's son, offered us a respite. Horrific events of the past week, as well as the emotional events that lay in wait for us in the weeks to come momentarily took a back seat. I thanked God silently as we drove the short distance to our home.

When my family returned home, back to New Jersey, I felt a terrible absence of normalcy, as if the world went from technicolor to black and white. Beauty remained just a gaze away, but the magic was gone. I saw it, but I couldn't feel. I think the absence of free-flowing conversations, honest dialogue, blended with a healthy dose of humor, forced me to deal with the loss and my feelings of guilt. I didn't save Kevin. I failed.

It was Robert's daughter-in-law who contacted us. Despite all she was dealing with, the loss of her husband and a teenage daughter who would forever need to deal with the events of the past week, she thought about Robert.

"I can send you some information about places to stay that shouldn't be too much money, and car services. After the memorial service, I am going to have a little something at my house, just for family and a few neighbors." She also invited my son, Grace, and a friend who offered to come to support Robert, but primarily me. It was she who provided the details about the memorial service, not the daughter. Robert always spoke of his daughter-in-law as if she and his daughter were very close. I guess, therefore, I felt distrust. I was wrong about her; I am sorry to admit. Once again, perceptions were skewed. Robert saw what he wanted to see. It was a fact his daughter-in-law and his daughter had a relationship, but it was not as Robert described. They were friendly, and I assumed, cared about each other. Robert always spoke as if Kevin's wife and Robert's daughter were connected at the hip.

At my computer, I began making a to-do list: call airlines about special circumstances, tickets, order flowers, car services, and of course, a place to stay. His daughter had not invited her father to come to her home, despite a second bedroom. As stated, for reasons known only to her, she locked her father out of her life…again. Once again, I suspect I know the why, but it is only supposition.

"Robert, I am ordering the spray now. Do you want to see the selection?" I asked, computer open on my lap, still in my nightgown regardless of the hour.

Yet again, he was lost in thought, gazed fixed on the screen.

"Robert?" My voice was slightly louder.

"I hear you!" he snapped. "Don't bark at me."

Biting the inside of my cheek, I swallowed hard before repeating, "So what do you think? Do you want to look at the sprays for your son?"

"Pick one out."

"There is one I really like. Let me show you." Carrying my computer, I walked to where he sat and seated myself on the overstuffed arm of his massive leather chair. Pointing to the far-right corner, I said, "Look, I thought these would be really nice. Yellow produces a warming effect and is said to arouse cheery mood. Besides, it is one of my favorite colors. What do you think? Because of the color, it offers up hope and the promise we will see him again."

"Very nice. But I want to add a banner. It should read, 'We love you, son.'"

"Robert, I'm not his mother. I really don't feel comfortable having that on the banner. Do you think that is appropriate? Do you? I mean, I barely knew him. He was your son, not mine."

"You are my wife. I don't care. You treated him like a son, and my relationship was better with him because of you." He was adamant, so I surrendered. His sentiments were thoughtful. Most importantly, this is what he wanted, and it offered him comfort. Back at the sofa, I selected the flowers, the wording for the banner, and put it on my credit card. I then made arrangements for a car and motel. They no longer offer special rates for air travel due to a death, so I had to pay the highest price because of the last-minute purchase. I paid for it all.

A few days later, we were in New Jersey. Our exhaustion, both physical and emotional, felt like a crushing weight that just walking was a strain. We picked up the car and checked into the motel. Within minutes, we were both asleep in bed.

The service was the following day. My son, Grace, and my friend Lynne were there. Their presence showed their love and concern for me. Such a soothing, comforting, and yet simple gesture spoke volumes on this day. Uninvited remembrances of the night my boy died crept into my thoughts. I needed to be strong because my husband needed me.

We arrived at the church, parking our rented vehicle in a slot in the rear. Robert was approached by some colleagues from his days at the university. Their offers of sympathy provided Robert with comfort—he had such a fondness and connection with these people who were a part of his life and career for a long time. The smile was weak on the aged man who approached Robert. Beside him, a tiny, expressionless woman who approached her old friend with trepidation. In the end, what words can one offer to a father whose son died in such a tragic manner?

Robert smiled seeing these people from his past. There was a connection with these people, a piece of his history, I would never have.

"Thank you so much for coming. It means so much to us." There it was again, the pronoun *us*. Is it possible thinking of me as Kevin's mother was comforting him? A few minutes of introductions, catching up, and reliving stories from an era long passed allowed Robert to detach from the here and now.

I heard him offer, "Wait until you see *our* granddaughter. She is not a little girl any longer but a beautiful young woman."

"Will you excuse me?" I smiled at the small entourage and walked toward my family and friend on the walkway. Robert continued to chat with the man; the woman, I learned later, was the chair of the religion department.

"Mom, who are those people Robert is speaking to?"

"Jamie, they're colleagues of Robert. Their attendance pleases him. I am so delighted they could make it."

"How are you doing?" Lynne, a dear friend, asked. Her voice, low and dripping with concern. She knew almost as much about my life as my sister did. So she was familiar with the family dynamics; in fact, her attendance was, for me, just in case. Acutely aware of the dynamics with Colleen, her feelings regarding Kevin, her lightning-quick changes in mood. She was there to make certain I was safe.

My shoulders rose and dropped. Robert approached from behind, so I was startled. He took my hand. "I guess we should go in."

We entered the space and there, off to the side, stood Colleen. A few folks approached her, hugs were exchanged, words were spoken, and they moved on. I watched as Robert went toward his only daughter, his only living child, who stood there, arms at her side. No hug for her father. No words exchanged. In my entire life, I will never forget that tragic scene. I was furious.

Lynne and I were about twenty feet away. "Oh my God, did you see that?" I asked Lynne.

"Unbelievable." She shook her head back and forth. "Who does that?"

My jaw tightened, and moisture filled my eyes as the emotions heightened. "How could she do that to him at this dreadful time in front of everyone? She broke his heart—again."

He moved on. I knew I needed to go to her. As his wife, it was my responsibility to play the part. Folks were close enough to hear me, so I said, "Colleen, I am so sorry. I am here for you if you need me." My arms encircled her small frame, but her arms remained by her sides. My hug tighter, I thought I could break through the veneer, the stoic stance, and reach a person, a hurting person. Nothing. I even said, "Colleen, stop it. Hug me. You are acting like a brat." That is what I would have said to my child, so I hoped it would be effective. She did, but there was an absence of emotion. A stone statue holds no warmth.

The nightmare continued inside the church. Roberts's first wife's sister and Kevin's aunt sat in a pew. My inclination was to offer support and sympathy. "Hello, my name is Anne, Robert's wife. I cannot tell you how sorry I am." No response. "I have heard so much about your family and your sister Mary. I feel as if I know her."

"I hope you didn't hear anything negative." There it was, that chill again. For the second time this day, my efforts to comfort were greeted with disdain. I didn't even know this lady. She spent the past few days with Colleen. God knows what she told her about me. Remember, the only thing I did was send her an innocuous e-mail stating I felt I needed to step back from family concerns I knew nothing about. All my efforts to love, express concern and comfort for Robert's daughter meant nothing to this woman lost in her mental health disorder. Sad. She reminded me of the woman who gave me life and hated me. Her reasons locked away in the corners of her illness. Her delusions.

Kevin's suicide was the fourth in my world. My brother, cousin, son, and now stepson. On this day, I was on the brink of …

In church, every family member was on the right. Robert and my family, on the left. Talk about awkward, unkind treatment. Poor Robert. A handful of family members spoke, including Robert. Observing this man's struggle brought tears to my eyes for him, and suddenly, for me. The image, a sense of my Jason, suddenly were as real as if he were there.

"Kevin brought me a beautiful, refurbished, lined, antique toolbox. How my son was able to transport something so big, in his Alpha, I will never know. But I will treasure it always." Even though he was speaking about his own son, it was obvious to me that there had been a disconnect for sometime. This man who made his living teaching, excelled as his craft, was as awkward as the occasional student during their dissertation.

"We loved our son and will miss him terribly," he concluded, stepping down from the pulpit.

"Are you okay?" Grace asked me discreetly as she gently rubbed my back. I pulled myself together. This day was not about me but Robert and his family.

The tribute was very nice. I felt as if I were allowed a view into the man I didn't know. A man who married the love of his life, held his baby daughter in his arms, and cared for brain-injured patients. A man who lived with depression, self-doubt, disconnected with his father, and oh so alone, as he told me that night in California.

Colleen was next. Upon completion of her memories of her brother, she took a few steps to return to her seat. Suddenly, she fell down the steps. No one moved, not those folks closest to her. The only person on their feet was me. Not even Robert moved. The actions of this family made no sense to me. Once she managed to get up, she returned to her seat. I saw her lie down on the bench, her head in the lap of her aunt. An act of a small child, not a middle-aged woman. There was much that disturbed me with this family. But the secrets would remain secrets, and for that I am grateful.

"Are you ready?" my husband addressed our little group.

Someone whispered, "More than ready." We rose, began to exit, but not before Robert thanked the minister. I joined my little group.

"I can't wait to get out of here. What we witnessed today was not limited to grief." As I walked with my family, I began to ruminate as I have done before when dealing with this family. Something deeper, uglier, and diabolically opposed to anything I wanted to deal with. This was a very painful day, the loss of a troubled man. His young, beautiful daughter left to deal with things that no one her age should have to deal with—made worse by the actions of one person. Like a marble on the floor, my thoughts rolled from question to question. Why the treatment of Robert, this man's father? Where was the hatred coming from, and why directed at me? My tendency to obsess had begun. She had a love-hate relationship with him, even though he did nothing to stir it up.

Prior to leaving California, the decision had been made. Post the service, I was not going to go back to his son's home. I was thankful for the invitation, but I was not part of this family, and the events of the day only cemented my stand. Robert would spend time with his daughter; perhaps away from me. There might be a shared grief that would dilute some of the hostile feelings.

When someone does something they perceive as wrong, hurtful, and socially unacceptable, they somehow place their feelings onto another. Is that what was happening here? The small group of attendees had begun to dissipate, leaving through a door to the parking lot. I stood with my little group waiting for Robert. "Did you notice the banner I ordered for our flowers was missing? And placed almost completely out of sight. I wonder who could have done that," I asked, but the question was rhetorical. Who else would have ripped that banner off? Only one person, filled with rage, would have done such an insensitive act. I was informed by the florist when I called that the spray was delivered with the banner intact.

Robert joined us. "He is such a nice man." He nodded toward the minister. "I told him how beautiful I thought the message was, especially when he lost his child not all that long ago. Everything was very nice. So are we ready to go?" He hooked his arm through mine.

My group looked at me then walked away. They knew what I was about to tell Robert. "Listen, I am not going. I don't understand what happened here today, or why we were treated as we were, but I barely know these folks, and I am choosing not to put myself in a position where I would be hurt or embarrassed." Despite my firm delivery, he continued to argue his case. He lost.

As we walked toward the exit, he asked, "I want you to come. What am I going to tell everyone?"

I stopped and pulled him toward a private spot just inside the door. He looked sad, but distinguished with his newly trimmed beard, white shirt, and dark-blue suit. "Robert, anyone with eyes would understand why I am not there. My presence might cause a flare-up."

"What can I say to them, though? I don't want to go alone."

My grief for my son was rising to the surface. I felt like I had one foot in the present and one in the past. I was sad, but desperate, to flee from this day. All I could say was, "Tell them I think it is best if I stay back so you can be with your family. And, if needed, I am missing my son. I really don't think anyone will care. I only know three people, and except for your daughter, my relationship has never had the opportunity to develop. Robert, I need this. I'll see you in a little time, back at the hotel."

We walked toward the car. Most folks were gone except for his direct family who remained inside. "You will need to drop me off."

"Of course," I answered. I could feel the weight of the day fade as sunlight bathed over my skin. An aroma, unfamiliar to me, albeit extremely pleasant, was an offering of hope. In the car, my family waited patiently.

We went for lunch, and for the first time, I felt safe. Robert joined us. Conversation was lighthearted even as we spoke of the events of the day. Upon completion, we delivered Robert to the former home of his son.

Robert exited the car in front of the small house and slowly walked up the sidewalk.

"Come on, let's go. I don't want to run into anyone." My words spoken in haste to my son. I could still see Robert in the rearview mirror amble up the walkway. Then he was gone.

"Mom, you do know we all came today for Robert, but to protect you, just in case. From what happened, I am glad we did. Boundaries mean nothing to her, and I didn't want all that hatred turned on you. What the hell is going on, anyway? I felt like I had fallen down the rabbit hole." I shrugged.

As we drove away, my mind raced. How does one explain the unexplainable? Mental illness not only grips the impacted person, but everyone who meets them. Why is it that the focus on mental health issues are still kept in the dark? Families ignore it. Or hide it. Or run from it. Anything but address it. As with any disorder, it needs to be treated.

All of us needed to get as far away as possible from the events of the day.

My phone rang. On the screen, the word *Robert*. We had just dropped him off less than twenty minutes ago, "It's Robert. This can't be good." I answered the call. "Robert, what's the matter?" I would like to say I couldn't believe what he was saying. However, I have learned nothing was beyond comprehension within this family. I thought the craziness of my family was gone. I would relax, enjoy; yet here I was again.

"Anne, what's the matter?" Lynne asked after I hung up. All eyes were focused on me. Jamie pulled the car off the road.

"Well, apparently, there was a huge verbal confrontation. His daughter screamed at him in front of everyone. I don't know what was said, but he was so upset he left and began walking away. How could this happen? He must be heartbroken and embarrassed." I could hear boundaries breaking over the phone. When I am frightened, I want to run—that feeling was gripping me now. Jamie turned the car around, throwing a few curses into the air.

We approached the block where his son's home was, and there stood Robert and Kevin's wife at the corner. I couldn't even look at her. At that time, I thought she and Colleen were alike, but I learned later, and was reminded, that she was the one who offered to help us with our travel plans. She was hurting, had a child to deal with, a house full of company, and yet, she left them to stay with him.

He entered the car. Out of respect, no questions were asked. What he needed now was to be with his wife who would take care of him. The circle of support was formed. Robert informed me later he was not completely surprised by the events. I was a newcomer into this family; the history, behaviors were still foreign to me except what I saw, experienced, and heard.

Much later, back at our room, we both collapsed into bed. This day was difficult enough without the added burden of acts of hate heaped upon us.

"Robert, I am so sorry about, well, everything. I am exhausted." I literally fell into the bed fully clothed. Oh, how I needed to sleep. "Do you think I could sleep in my clothes?" Not exactly a question but more of a description of the depth of my fatigue. "Since I met you, I have missed more sleep than in my entire life."

Robert, already in bed, reached for his cell phone. I knew who it was by the ring; after all, it was me who had set up the different tones for his family members. This was my idea, developed when his son began to contact us; we didn't want to miss his call.

Robert answered his cell and mouthed it was his daughter. "Now! You want me to come there now? I don't think that is a good idea. I am tired and already in bed." I was tossed a smile his way of saying he was taking a stand. It appeared to me there were demands being made of Robert, demands he struggled to understand and resolve. He remained on the phone, visibly upset as she persisted. He mouthed that Colleen didn't want me to come with him. I knew he didn't want to go without me. I was his buffer. Plus, he was exhausted, sad, and I heard a hint of anger.

With anyone else, there would not have been a problem. A daughter wanting to see her father alone on a day such as this. The death of her brother—she needed him. But recalling her behavior before her brother died, after he died, her behavior all afternoon, screaming at him, ignoring his aching arms for this night, her demands went unmet.

Here it was again. The cycle of "I love you. I hate you." Now, I love you. Under it all, embedded deep within her being, I suspect I was an obstacle in her path. My feelings in that moment were both of compassion and anger. Whatever drove this woman came from a giant need to feel loved. Was it possible, that likened to my mother, her personality disorder drove her actions? The same actions were in direct opposition of meeting the desires of her heart.

Escape was the impetus that pulled or pushed me out of bed. Gosh, it was so comfortable, and I was so tired. Robert, still holding the phone, looked up at me as I got out of bed. "Excuse me for a minute, but I'm getting ready for bed. Let's order some wine. Okay? I am going to shower and get ready for bed. Then we can have a nice glass of wine and hopefully relax. I really don't think it will help much, but let's give it a try. Okay?"

Sitting on the side of the bed, phone in hand, head bowed low. A broken man. A conflicted man. A lost man. A hurting man.

"Listen, Colleen, I've got to go. Let me call you in the morning. Okay. What? We are going to spend the day with Anne's son and daughter-in-law. They invited us." He was being matter-of-fact, but I am certain that is not how the comment was received. "Colleen, I don't have the energy for this. I am…"

That is all I heard before I went into the shower. As I allowed the cool water to bathe me into a tranquil state, I thought about what as transpiring in the next room. Our children need love, support, discipline, to be held accountable for their actions. What he is doing now, he should have been doing long ago. She abused us, ignored us, did not offer us a place to stay. Now at this hour, she wants her father to come to her. Really? But if this is what he has done, the behavior rests on his shoulders as well. To insist he come without me is such an insult. If he did, that would have been the end. This person has caused me a great deal of pain.

When I reentered the bedroom, Robert was lying in bed, phone on the nightstand, staring up at the ceiling. I felt so much better. The shower brought new life into a very tired body and spirit. Instead of getting to the bed, I circled it and sat next to my husband. I felt the best approach would be to ask an open-ended question. "So why do you think your daughter wanted you to come to her place now?" When he didn't answer, I probed deeper, as if this man who was unable to connect with his emotions would suddenly expose his deepest thoughts. "Hon, do you want to talk about anything at all?"

"No, I just want to get ready for bed." He lifted the phone off the cradle. "Hello, yes, this is room 505." He ordered some wine and staggered to the bathroom. He was a broken man, but in a few minutes, he would bury those emotions deep within, never to be felt again. That is how he *didn't* deal with issues. The key: don't acknowledge. Unless, like a pressure cooker, without warning, the lid blows, damaging everything that once was your life.

The door closed behind him, followed by the sounds of a shower.

Lying on my back, staring at the ceiling, I thought about Robert's son. The secrets he shared with me. The beautiful stories shared by those he cared for in his position, the absence of concern by some members of his family, and mostly, how his death meant little to some. A life wasted. I prayed not.

That was a very long night. As predicted, the wine failed to induce sleep or reduce angst. Instead, I lay awake thinking about the events of the past few weeks. Once again, the wheels of logic and reason kept spinning—searching for resolution, searching for missing pieces.

24

Forgetting to close the drapes the previous night allowed a sliver of sunlight to settle on my face. For the slightest of moments, I forgot where I was. Attempting to focus and navigate the empty room helped pull me into the present. Robert's suit on the chair, my black dress rested in the closet, and the one rose stolen from the spray had already begun to wither on the dresser. I didn't think it possible to feel more fatigued in the morning than I did the night before, but I did. It reminded me of that feeling I had when I was pregnant. A deep sadness rose up within me remembering the events of the previous day. Thank God the phone rang, and I heard my son's voice.

He suggested that we drive over to the coast and spend time with them. I was thrilled.

Robert was not in the room. A chronic early riser, plus his lust for breakfast, was the impetus needed to leave and venture out to locate the dining room. Married now, just under a year, he learned early on not to awaken me.

Sitting in bed, applying makeup, I heard something at the door. "Good morning, sunshine. I got you some coffee and a muffin. Is that okay?" A different man from the one I kissed good night just a few short hours ago entered our room.

"Good, thanks. I need my coffee. Did you sleep?" I asked, sipping on the mocha sweetness.

"Not really. How is the muffin?" That was my Robert. Focus on pleasure and push ugliness into the recesses of your mind. I guess that is the right thing to do when you can do nothing else.

We watched TV, caught catnaps, and talked about anything but the proverbial elephant in the room.

"I have some really exciting news," I offered, shifting my weight on the bed. "Jamie called while you were out. He and Grace invited us to spend the afternoon with them at the beach. Afterward, they want to take us out for an anniversary dinner." Robert and I had not even been married a year, and yet, I had faced a suicide, a foreclosure of Robert's home, my husband's financial situation, numerous family problems. My family was giving, thankful, and fun. When Jamie and Grace visited us, and borrowed my car, it was returned clean with a full tank of gas. When Colleen came out, after using Robert's car, with hands on the hips, she let Robert know she needed to fill the tank. Behavior of an entitled woman. The stories I have been told is she always received what she wanted, not what she deserved. It was easier to surrender than dare to deal with temper tantrums. Lack of parental control fostered a sense of complacence.

Late afternoon, as the sun moved westward, Robert and I sat together on the soft sand. In the surf, Jamie and Grace maintained balance on their boards as they conquered the waves that would deliver them to shore. My family was out surfing, enjoying life. Warmth from the sun on my skin and the sweet breeze lifted me from the ugliness that had become my life of late. Robert was quiet, but there was no tension in his face or actions. He had retreated to his secret world. And for now, that was just fine. Twilight would soon be upon us, a time for surrender. A time to say goodbye to the day with the promise of a new day filled with hope.

Grace wore her two-piece suit, and Jamie's was red. I loved watching them as they approached us. Their joyful feelings showed on their faces in the form of bright smiles. After they toweled off, we ate in Asbury Park and joked about speedos. A welcome release, like the valve on that pressure cooker. It felt so good to surrender to the joy within, even though for days, the muck of foul words, actions, and death held us captive.

We actually laughed a lot at dinner. Laughter that bordered on hysteria.

Back at the hotel, we packed and set the alarm. Our flight was, thanks to Robert, early in the morning.

Arriving back in LA felt wonderful, although fatigue, tension, and loss joined us on our trip. Emotional overload caused me to be short-tempered, a state in which I felt most uncomfortable.

For me, loving comes easy. What I witnessed, especially those past few days, were as foreign to me as cursing at God. Is it not a gift we give ourselves to extend a hand of love to those whose hearts are empty? Hate, at least for me, takes such energy to destroy the giver and the receiver. Love is like gently drifting along with the current in a stream; conversely, hatred means extending energy to paddle against the current. As I have been told, I am unrealistic and idealistic. I don't see it that way.

In LA, our luggage was retrieved, as was our car. We were home in thirty-five minutes.

"Hi, Paul." We greeted the guard at the gatehouse.

"Professor, I am so sorry about your son. He seemed so nice when he was here." Later, Paul confided to me in private that he too viewed the sadness in Robert's son's eyes.

We rode the elevator in silence, too tired to speak. Once inside, we both dropped our bags and parted. He to the living room, me to our bedroom.

This day was our one-year anniversary.

"I need to try to sleep," I told him.

"I made arrangements for us to go to Ruth's Steakhouse for our anniversary. Take a nap. I want you to feel better for later." That was Robert, so thoughtful. This man was like a kaleidoscope, always changing and unpredictable.

The truth of the matter was all I wanted to do was stay home. The past four days were overflowing with grief, anger, horrific fighting, false assumptions, sleepless nights, and hours sitting at the airport for our flight. Then, six hours in the air. My eyes felt as if there was sand in them; there was a poverty of sustainable thought, and just beneath the surface, there was an unexplainable fear. I assumed this was all the result of persistent stress. Sinking into our wonderful bed was a bit of heaven. Home. Through the open window, the sounds of surf, seagulls, laughter, chatter, and the breeze slapping our drapes on the wall lulled me to sleep.

The next few months were not without trials. Robert would call me during my work hours with the latest demand. "She wants me to come back to New Jersey right now," he moaned.

"Robert, I am at work. She's your daughter. Why are you calling me?"

I suspect because of his discomfort with confrontation, if I objected, which I did, he could blame me, and he would be off the hook. This is just speculation on my part, but relevant past behaviors are often evidence of future performance.

*****

We continued to see the psychiatrist we called before Kevin died. His office was in Beverly Hills in a typical high rise. As with most office buildings in LA, the basement parking was so costly, you needed to sell a kidney to pay for an hour.

We rode the elevator to the fifth floor, walked down a short hall, and entered the plain outer waiting office. Robert grabbed an archaeology magazine and took a seat.

I hit the switch on the wall beside the door. A light in the therapist's office would indicate the arrival of the next patient. As is the case, after our session, we would exit through another door. God forbid someone would see us leaving the office of a therapist. Oh, how I wish my words would drive into the hearts of people to help those suffering from a mental illness and bring it into the light.

The inner office door opened. "Hi, come on in." We followed him. His height dwarfed us both. My usual perch was on the sofa facing the massive windows. The view was powerful. Hills and houses dotted the landscape, and of course, the ever-abundant flowers sprinkled an array of hues.

"How are you doing?" he asked Robert sympathetically.

"I am okay. I don't know what I would do without her." He gestured toward me.

The doctor smiled in my direction. "Not surprised. Anne is a real caregiver. Sometimes I wish she would take better care of herself, right, Anne?"

"I guess. We are on different ends of the spectrum with a certain situation that I felt we needed to discuss with you." The kindly man nodded as he tilted, a nonverbal method of communication that suggested he was listening. "Robert and I had planned a trip to Italy many months ago. Italy has always been my dream vacation. Robert has been several times to do research. But with the death of Kevin, and all that transpired over the past few months, I'm really not in the right frame of mind to go any longer. Robert is okay with it."

Robert remained silent.

Dr. Miller rotated his chair, facing me straight on. "Do you want my opinion?"

I nodded.

"I think you should go. It would do you both good to step back and get away. You have had a very difficult first year of marriage."

"I am also concerned that if we let some people know we are going, there will be problems. Perhaps actions that would prohibit us from leaving, therefore, costing us a lot of money."

"From what you both have told me, I would suggest you not say a word. If there is a problem, you can be reached by phone. Go away and have a real honeymoon."

"See, I told you." Robert had a sweet smile on this face.

"*Grande, andiamo canguro*," I responded in my best *Italian for Dummies* fashion.

Both men laughed. Robert stated after he stopped laughing, "Great, let's go Kangeroo."

I joined the men in laughter. It was settled. We were going to Italy! The corners of my mouth turned up, no longer held captive by the actions of others.

25

We landed in Florence, Italy, in the late afternoon. A lifelong dream was now a reality.

"I can't stop smiling. This is so surreal." My words spoken between gasps. We climbed the steep uneven steps to our hotel, dragging our luggage behind us. Could it be we were about to start anew? A fresh start and journey of exploration into the other was about to begin.

Our hotel was quaint, many shades of Italy in hues of Naples Yellow, Paolo Vernonese Green, and Valentino Red. Our room had doors that opened onto an outdoor garden, a magical place. Antique statues, wrought-iron tables with matching chairs, planters stuffed with multicolored flowers. Vines climbed, stretching their offshoots across the salmon-colored stucco and not wanting to stop; they wiggled across up and over the tiled roof.

"Fantastico!" I said, stepping into the space.

After a little snuggling, we headed out in search of a restaurant. As we walked the winding, cobblestone streets, toward the piazza, all cares floated away. Aromas of baked goods teased our senses, the dimly lit streets created unique shadows, music; beautiful Italian music floated in the air. Life was perfect. Hand in hand we strolled.

"How about this place?" Robert asked, stopping to check the menu. I was handicapped. A few weeks of Italian for beginners on tape hardly allowed me to maneuver without Robert. His ability to speak Spanish helped because apparently the languages have enough similarity to allow him to make our needs known.

"I love it. Let's go in." Inside, brash laughter, chatter in Italian, and waiters hustled as wine glasses clinked.

A good-looking young man approached our table. *"Buon amore, hai una sedia fresca?"*

I said, flashing a flirty smile. I hoped I didn't just tell him he was a pumpkin or something worse.

He responded, *"Che cosa posso ottenere tu? Vorresti un bicchiere di vino?"*

My cheeks flushed with embarrassment. What did he say?

"Una bottiglia di vino della casa per favore, bianco," Robert responded. The handsome Italian smiled and departed. I got a little wink, the one offered to tourists who can't speak the language. A wink is universal.

"I ordered the house wine. Okay?" Robert spared me the embarrassment of telling me that I said "you have a cool chair" to the waiter until later that night. We both had a good laugh and agreed he would do the ordering in the future.

"Perfect." I smiled at the man across from me. He was kind, loving, and considerate this night. I was in Italy, thousands of miles away from things and people that brought sadness into my life. Two glasses, a bottle, and a match to light our candle were delivered. The candle cast a romantic glow, illuminating my spirit even more. I smiled at the waiter and replied, *"Grazie, donna."*

Robert laughed. "You just said, 'Thank you, woman.'"

I was a tad embarrassed in front of my handsome waiter. He smiled, winked, and offered, "Are you ready to order? May I recommend the Veal Saltimbocca, or if you are interested in fish, we have the Chilean Sea Bass with Broccoli Rabe. Very popular."

He spoke English!

"I want spaghetti and meatballs," Robert stated. I knew that would be his choice. Not much of an adventurer.

Leaning on the table, contemplating my decision, I finally said, "Let me try the Chilean Sea Bass. Is it really fresh?" By the look on our server's face, it was clear I insulted him.

"Naturalmente, serviamo solo cibo fresco."

"Wonderful, that is what I'll have. *Grazie!*" I was certain I thanked him appropriately. He turned and left.

Robert poured us each a lovely, ample glass of wine.

"*Salute!*" We clinked glasses and sipped. He reached across the table. He took my hand in his.

"We are really in Italy. I am so happy." Warmth rose in my cheeks.

"Are you happy?" Robert would ask questions, knowing the answer. He liked to hear me voice my feelings if they were positive.

He leaned on his hands, smiled, and glowed. It was going to be a very good night for us both.

After eating, we strolled around the marketplace. Vendor stands dotted the streets selling beautiful leather jackets and purses, jewelry, scarves, and handmade items to entice the rich travelers. We held hands and smiled as we made our way back to the room. I closed the door, but not before the DO NOT DISTURB sign was placed on the knob.

I awoke to a sweet breeze, sunshine, and singing birds. Robert opened the French doors leading to the courtyard—an ornate, gothic fountain splashed onto the terrazzo tiles. My senses were embraced by the combination of moisture, floral essence, and aging stone.

"Good morning, sunshine. I got you some coffee and a roll. I met the rest of our group at breakfast, but I knew you wanted to sleep in. We need to meet at nine to begin the tour of Florence." He handed the food to me, as I was still in bed. Florence was magical. Our guides were educated and obviously in love with their work. We visited the cathedral, the Palazzo Vecchio, and my favorite, the Ponte Vecchio. I never much cared for history, but when you experience it and everything we see is explained, it brings a new interest.

Tired and content, our little group met for dinner at an intimate family Italian restaurant. We had seven courses! The meal was more like a performance, each entrée brought with its own entertainment. The flaming meat was the highlight. Well, that and the wine, lots and lots of vino. Laughter that derives from some place so deep within us all that the experience is pure joy.

We traveled next to Voltera and a few more villages in Tuscany, but it was Cinque Terra that captured my heart. It is a portion of the rugged coast off the Italian Riviera dotted with orange, pink, yellow, and blue dwellings nestled in the hillside. There are several villages along the coast only accessible by train and boat. Of course, the hiking is exhilarating.

But hours later, I was hiking alone along the cliffs on a path so Robert could do some work. Below me, aqua water beat the sides of tidal pools, pouring in and out of caves as gulls screamed above.

On the top was a rock, a place to sit and reflect. I prayed, thanking God for this experience. In the quiet moment, surrounded by beauty, I thought how wonderful this trip had been. No distractions. Just a newly married couple getting to know one another. With just a few days remaining, the weather turned colder with drizzle. Unfortunately, my asthma was triggered.

Back in our room, I said, "Hon, I think I will stay back tonight. Walking in the rain, feeling as I do, just for dinner is not worth getting sick. I can take a nice hot steamy bath, go to bed, and rest."

"Are you sure?" Robert asked, looking out the window. The view was of a winding cobblestoned street, with balconies hosting an array of flowers in clay pots of all sizes. I knew what he was thinking *I need food.*

"Positive. Listen to me. I feel like a musical instrument with this wheezing."

He turned away from the window. "Should I stay here with you?"

"No, of course not. With any luck, I will sleep."

"Can I bring you back something?" he asked.

"No, I am okay. Maybe a roll?"

A sweet kiss on the cheek, and he was out the door. Tonight, the restaurant was a bit of a hike, our guide, Tommasso, had informed us earlier. Robert never was much of a walker, unlike his hyperactive wife.

I felt much better after my steamy bath. In Italy, taking a bath can be a bit of a challenge. Ours was small and had a raised area, so relaxing was not really a possibility. Oh, and the hairdryers are vacuum hoses extended from the wall blowing warm air.

I donned my nightgown and got into bed, covering up in the nice linens and puffy quilt. Sleep enveloped me, sweet sleep, a place of silent discovery. I heard the door unlock. In the dimmed light, I saw Robert enter. He was damp and carrying something in his hand.

"How are you feeling—any better?" He placed the bag on the dresser.

"Much. I am so glad I stayed back. I feel relaxed and rested." I pulled the pillow up behind my back. "I am sorry, though, that there will be no more delightful whistle when I breathe. What's that?" I asked as I gazed at the bag resting on the dresser. I was hungrier than I thought I would be, so I sure hoped there were a few buttered rolls waiting for me.

He shook off his jacket and walked with a cautious gait to the dresser. Clearly, this was a very tired man. His clothes glistened from the rainwater. When he returned, he folded like a wet dishcloth onto the bed. I shifted with his weight. We both laughed as we almost slid onto the floor. As I righted myself, in front of me was a complete five-course meal. Enough food for two people.

"Robert, how sweet. You didn't have to do this." My eyes met his, and there was love exchanged. I will never forget the kindness of his actions that October night in Italy.

"I love you. When are you going to accept it? It makes me happy to do things for you. Eat up."

Shifting my weight back to a seated position, pillows fluffed behind my back, I broke a piece from the roll. "How far was the restaurant?"

He started laughing. "Well, let's just say when I asked the waiter about the fish, he said, *'Oui, le poisson est frais.'*"

"Oh, no!" We were both laughing now.

"Every dog and cat trailed me through the poorly lit streets following the aroma of the food. And with all the twists and turns, it is fair to report I got lost more than a few times. What an experience." There was not an ounce of regret or complaint in his voice. He was just reporting his experience.

My eyes welled up with love for this man. His kindness heightened my feelings for him.

After I finished my five-course dinner, Robert reentered the bedroom. The steam from his shower followed him. There was a sense of safety, protection, and love I never felt before. Once again, the DO NOT DISTURB sign swung on the doorknob. At least, I think that is what it said.

All those sleepless nights were made up for in Italy. I slept with the angels, as the saying goes. On the following morning, I awoke with the aroma of coffee in the air. On this particular day, there was a variety of Italian breakfast pastries. Delicious fruit-filled pastries dusted with light powdered sugar sleeping on their surface.

"Now I know I am in heaven. Hon, these are so yummy. I can't imagine they are good for the diet, but who cares. In heaven, weight doesn't matter. Right? Did you sleep okay after…well, you know?" My smile was devious and flirty.

"I dreamt about my son last night. I even dreamt about your son, and I've never met him."

"What did you dream about?" Before he answered, I offered him a treat. "Here, join me. Try a delicious pastry, sweetie." This was comfort food indeed, and I sensed he needed to be comforted.

"No thanks—just coffee. I had something earlier."

Pushing aside the delicious treats, I asked him, "What's the matter? Hon, let's talk. Okay?" In my entire life, I believe I have never tasted such a perfect blend of tartness, sweetness, and buttery mastery as in this first bite.

Sitting beside me on the bed, he began to speak. "I dreamt he was missing, and I couldn't find him. Then a young boy appeared beside me and said, 'I am Jason. I am here to help you look for him. I am good at finding lost things, ask Mom. He was so sweet and loving, like you.'" After a long pause, he said, "I miss my son."

Together, two parents, members of the club no parent desires to join, remained still in our shared heartache. My son's image appeared in my thoughts. His face dirty from the dust in the woods from riding his dirt bike. He was my man-child. My arms ached with an emptiness only parents who have lost a child recognize.

"Hon, what can I do for you?" I asked, taking his hand. His wounds were fresh, even if he hid them with a protective dressing of repudiation.

He didn't answer. His fingers tightened around mine as if to say, *stay close to me, that's all I need.* Then he loosened his grip, stood up, and announced, "I am going to go down and check the posted schedule for today. That will give you some time to finish up your breakfast and shower." By the time he returned, I was dressed. "You look pretty today. I told you they would have hair dryers here. I like your blonde hair."

I smiled as I saw my reflection in front of the mirror. "Sir, I agree. No humidity, and I have straight, silky hair." Of course, my newly acquired little pouch I now carried in my midsection was unwanted. Too much of everything on this trip. Wine. Gelato. Pasta. Bread. Even all the walking didn't counteract the huge intake of carbs.

"Okay, I am ready. Taking the subway in Rome should be a memorable experience." We closed the door securely behind us and stepped out into the maze of hallways.

"Hi, buddy," Robert's partner greeted him. Even though most of us were coupled, in addition, we had one other person, our buddy, we needed to keep track of. A great idea. She was a nurse like me. This extra step to secure all members of the tour were accounted for was beneficial on a few occasions.

Our trip ended in Rome. Today's activities were to be your typical tourist-type events. Starting with the Colosseum. Robert's previous time in Rome was primarily to do research. He was granted permission to go into the catacombs in the Vatican to examine documents. What an honor. Admittedly, on those trips, he saw little of the city except where study needs took him. This time, he was just Robert the tourist, not a prominent professor fixated on research. He could become so intense when he was focused on work.

"Hi, buddy. Where's Scott?" he questioned his new friend. She nodded her head, indicating the direction of her husband.

The group assembled in the breakfast room. Our guide, Tomasso, greeted his small band of excited Americans. "*Buongiorno. Siamo pronti per Roma e il Colosseo.*"

In the lead, we headed deep into the subway system into Rome. One really doesn't want to get lost in a country where you don't speak the language. Rome was a city where the past and present converge, that pulsated with Romans at work or at play. Everywhere we looked, our vision was fed beauty, history, and life. Motor scooters darted around cars and buses, and pedestrians sprinted across the congested avenues. It was perfectly imperfect. It was magic. A place where feeling alive is commonplace. If only this feeling would persist, covering me like a shield from anything ugly back home.

Looking into the Colosseum was disturbing, a place of silent discovery. Rich with history and interest, but the lives lost there—it forced me to look deep inside in an attempt to understand what happened there so long ago.

Then we were off to the Vatican. The beauty, the history, the religious significance of this country was like none other. One feels connected to the history of the faith of the Catholic Church and Christianity. It is the home to the pope. We walked where beloved men of God walked. Everywhere one looked, there was beauty in its art, statuary, coins, and tapestries. The basilica took my breath away, and ceilings of gold told stories of the history of the Roman Catholic Church. Photography was limited to prevent damaging the art. Miles of corridor weave throughout the many spaces with over two thousand years of history.

*****

Our trip was drawing to a close. Tomorrow, we would leave for home. A long journey. I will forever be haunted and courted by this experience. I carry with me heightened awareness that I shall never revisit the joy, security, and love I experienced on that trip. All thanks to Robert.

Back in LA, our trip became a beautiful, treasured memory. Renewed with hope and love and promise of a rich tomorrow, I felt contented, safe, and filled with peace.

The holiday season was approaching. Our new friends from California joined us for Thanksgiving. Our plans were to travel back to New Jersey for the Christmas season. I delighted at the prospect of spending the holidays with my family. Envisioning Christmas Eve service surrounded by loved ones was one of pure joy.

We arrived in Newark, New Jersey, late that evening. Instantly assaulted by a typical winter blast of bitter cold, compounded by a bone-chilling light drizzle. As in Italy, the weather triggered my asthma, especially as a blast of wind slammed into us while we crossed the street to the parking lot. I was thankful our driver was dealing with the luggage as he led us to his waiting town car.

"So where are we going tonight?" our driver asked with gusto. The holiday season was upon us, moods were a tad more cheerful, people were more gracious, except for anyone daring out on Christmas Eve for that last-minute gift.

"Annandale, straight down seventy-eight. Are you familiar with the area?"

"Absolutely. Listen, there's water back there, some candy, and well, that's it." He laughed. "Where are your traveling from?"

"Los Angeles," Robert responded.

The driver looked over his shoulder. "Man, are you kidding me? Why are you here in the lousy weather?"

We learned our driver's name was Dominick, born in Sicily, who came to the United States when he was four years old. He continued to provide us with vital information for the duration of the trip. We enjoyed his banter, especially when he spoke of his children and wife.

"Welcome home." He pulled in front of my sister's apartment.

We didn't even need to knock. The door flew open, and there stood Chris.

"Merry Christmas, brother-in-law." She hugged Robert and kissed him on the cheek. "Hi, sissy. I am so glad to have you home. I have been so excited and I guess a little afraid something would prevent you from coming." The bond we shared was like none other. What a beautiful reception Robert received from my family.

We nibbled on some food and chatted a little longer, but soon the fatigue monster hit us, and we succumbed. We headed off to the bedroom, and she volunteered to sleep in the TV room.

Chris and I were so close. If she hurt, I hurt. When I was happy, so was she. Growing up as we did, we derived our strength from the other. We parented each other because there was no one there for us.

26

Christmas Eve was sunny and frosty. No snow, though.

"I hate getting back into the car for another drive. Should we call a limo?" I asked with levity.

"Sure, Dollie. On you, of course." Chris laughed. I wanted to have sissy chat time but that was not possible. Not with Robert there. I would have time before we left for home. We had a secret world with secret, unspoken language. Messages exchanged with a look, cough or, even a laugh would send a message. Message always received.

My sister's little yellow VW beetle was cute but a tad crowded with three adults. The engine started, and we were on our way. I was wearing my Cheshire cat grin. At each toll on the parkway, I wished the toll collector a Merry Christmas.

"Your sister talks to everyone," my husband volunteered, his voice tender and playful.

"Yeah, I know. But she almost always offers a smile and adds something kind."

"That's what I love about her. I remember once, when confronted in VON's Supermarket by an incredibly unattractive, obese, short gal, absent of several teeth, Anne stopped directly in front of her. I knew what was coming next, but for the life of me, I couldn't imagine how she was going to dig up a compliment. Then my little genius here started laughing. Looking directly at this woman, she said, 'Do you know you have the greatest laugh I have ever heard? I wish you could can it and sell it. You made me giggle. Thank you. Keep laughing, the world needs it.' The woman beamed. She was so happy."

"I never lie. We can always find something in our fellow humans to praise. Remember, we are going to be celebrating the master creator soon," I answered, a tad uncomfortable with the praise.

We pulled up in front of the two-story Victorian shore home. White clapboards, blue shutters, and the welcoming massive front door drew guests forward. My Jamie and Grace lived on the second floor. Due to the age, the steps were steep and challenging.

Summer is when Ocean Grove comes alive. A blend of folks from New York, Joisey, and Pennsylvania flock to this beautiful Victorian town. Homes with deeply pitched roofs, large wrap-around porches, elegant gingerbread embellishments hung from roofline. Pops of colors appeared from well-tended gardens. Men with rounded tummies that fell onto their swimming trunks. Couples hoisting surfboards, coolers, and chairs make the familiar flip-flop noise as they passed aimed for the white sand and blue sea. Children yelling in that high pitch reserved for kids. Up and down the street, folks sat on porches, guitars strummed, gardens groomed, Frisbees take flight, and of course, burgers are dressed in cheese, ketchup, and pickles wearing a double bun hat. This is Ocean Grove. In the evening, the town comes alive. Music from the entertainment at the Great Auditorium spills out onto the streets.

"Hey, guys, look up there! The Carriage House has rope garland on the porch railing. With the lights, it is so beautiful. Oh, and can you see all the trees in every window?" My gaze was transfixed. The others, not so much.

Ocean Grove also well-known for Tent City. Each summer, the town hosts famous religious ministers to preach for Sunday service in the massive building. The structure is octagonal in shape, built from aged timber, and boasts of the natural air-conditioning of the 1800s. Performers are subject to the familiar humidity of New Jersey in the summertime. The building was exactly as it was when built, no upgrades.

"Let Chris go first. Are you okay, hon?" My voiced dripped with concern.

Chris had difficulty climbing the aged, narrow stairs with the high risers. She suffered for years with arthritis, enduring hip surgery at an early age. Robert had some difficulty as well. The rise was higher than usual, throwing stepping off. Reaching the top, I knocked. Internally, I heard, "Come on in." It was Grace's cheerful, welcoming voice.

We entered and stepped down three steps into the living space. Unpretentious elegance. Small but massive in its welcoming aura.

"Hi, Anne, Aunt Chris, and Rabbi." A nickname given to Robert by Grace because he knew more about the Old Testament than God himself. "Sit down. Can I get you something to drink?"

"Thanks, Grace. What do you have?"

"Soda, wine, and water." We placed our orders, and Grace turned, entering the tiny, albeit compact, kitchen. Even though there were adequate windows, the only view the clapboard side of the buildings that surrounded the house. There were three units, and the kids had an upper level.

"How was your trip down?" my son asked. "Was there much traffic?"

"Surprisingly, there was very little. I guess everyone was already settled in to where they were going. I assume not many folks travel on Christmas Eve."

After turning on the lights on their miniature, artificial tree, my son plopped onto the cushion of his favorite worn leather chair. Oh, how they loved and honored their tree. Year after year, Grace's college friend followed her into adulthood. She stood proudly, displaying all the loving ornaments collected over the years. Memories of special moments or people or both. Nothing fancy, just honesty.

Carrying a tray of cheese, fruit, and napkins, Grace entered the living space. "The church service starts at seven, but I think we should try to get there early. Is it really okay if Rob joins us?" She was speaking of her brother. We all loved Rob.

"Of course. Is he going to come to church?" I was hopeful.

Grace sat cross-legged on the floor. She placed the food and drinks on a table. "No, he will come down later." Secretly, I wished he could join us. He lit up the room, even more so than the Christmas lights.

My son's greatest joy in life is derived from sharing stories about his mother. Recounting anecdotes about me, those odd little quirks, such as asking silly questions, or the fact I repeat stories. He calls them *momisms*. An example would be the ever-present concern as to why sidewalks in Manhattan sparkle. If you have never walked the sidewalks in the city, you are unaware of the phenomenon. They look as if millions of diamonds were crushed, the dust dropped on the walkway. Of course, there was no diamond dust, but I always wanted to know. "Jamie, what causes the sidewalks to look like that?" I mean, I really wanted to know.

Through clenched teeth, as usual, he would answer, "I don't know, and I don't care, as usual."

What I recall of that night, a distinct night, is that it would be the last time we would all be together. After a blessed time in the beautiful church, the candlelight singing of "Silent Night," the joy of our faith, the celebration of the birth of our Savior, our little family, filled with love and hope anew, headed for a communal celebration.

Outside, the night was clear and chilly. "Merry Christmas! It's not too far to the restaurant. How about if we walk? The place is on the ocean, and beautiful with super Italian food." She paused, turned, and asked my husband, "Are you up for a walk, Rabbi?"

"Sure." He pulled his coat tight across his chest.

All around us, folks greeted each other with a "Merry Christmas." Families hugged their children as parents smiled down on them. Chatter commenced about plans, love, cookies, and all those things happy families discuss. How I envied families who live out their entire lives without drama.

Grace was right; the walk was reasonable and pleasant, even with the winter chill pinching at our exposed skin. I felt a heightened awareness of celebration. Passing homes and the numerous Victorian bed-and-breakfast danced beside the inhabitants as embraces were exchanged. Winter wind muffled voices singing traditional music as the world, and this little corner of that world celebrated the birth of a loving Savior.

"We're almost there," Grace called out. "The restaurant is right there at the end of the boardwalk."

Outside the restaurant, a block of light fell onto the sidewalk through the bank of windows. Jamie held the door open for us to enter.

Removing our coats, we observed an enticing, authentic Italian décor. Arched doorways greeted us, and a beautiful chandelier made from wine bottles cast images on the ceiling, walls, and floor. Walls painted in yellow tones ranging from sandy beige to golden mustard hues so familiar in the Mediterranean. All those memories of Italy came forth. Even though I was unable to share that experience with my family, at least sharing this hint of what we experienced was a gift.

"Hey, Ms. Sommers, are you sure you don't mind me joining you?" Rob asked, joining us. Grace's brother was charismatic. Gifted with the ability to make everyone he met feel special.

"Rob, I love that you're here. Of course, you do know I am now Mrs. Wright, not Ms. Sommers," I teased.

"So you teach Old Testament, that's great." He spoke to Robert. Then turned his attention to me. "Anne, did you tell Robert you ran the 5K in Central Park and came in dead last?"

Jamie jumped in. "Aunt Chris, is it true you won the world championship for the world's fastest remote changer?"

"So I hear the torture has begun." Everyone laughed at my statement. Our method of showing love was to tease.

"Robert, be honest. Does my mother's constant questioning drive you insane?" My son topped off the questioning.

"Jamie, I need to go home with her, so I take the fifth."

Later in the evening, our tummies full, spirits soaring, and reasoning a tad altered from the vino, the kindly waitress presented the check. I reached for it. For the first time in my life, I could pay. So much of my early life, I lived paycheck to paycheck. An immense sensation of success and accomplishment overcame me. Anne, who was once considered by some a throwaway child, was now able to handle a very expensive meal. I was not in this alone, thanks to God.

"I want a picture of all of you before we leave. Okay?" I watched as everyone rolled their eyes at my request. Forever taking pictures, another one of those annoying *momisms*. I should have taken the picture of them mid-eyeroll—that would have served them right.

Everyone positioned themselves to ensure their image was in the frame. "Do I look okay?" I asked.

"Anne, you're fine." More than a hint of annoyance from Grace. More eye-rolling.

"Okay, smile," our waitress directed. *Click.* "Let me take another one, just in case." *Click.* The kindly woman called out, "*Buon Natale!*"

We walked the boardwalk. The night was cold with a wind off the ocean blowing fiercely inland as we strolled on the weathered boards, savoring the moment. Tonight was a very special Christmas Eve. Normalcy had returned. I was surrounded by folks I loved.

*****

Robert went to his daughter's on Christmas. He had borrowed my son's truck. I was unwilling to chance an altercation especially during this season of goodness and light. I must admit it was easier to just surrender. Even though I was resentful, I would not be able to spend Christmas with Robert. Conversely, this meant I was able to spend alone time with my sissy. We could hang out in our pajamas all day if we wanted.

"I understand completely why you are not joining Robert," Chris said. "No more drama, especially at Christmas. I know you wish things were different, but can I be honest? I must admit I am happy to have alone time with you."

"So what is happening with your hip? When will you have the second surgery?" My concern was genuine.

Sitting in her wingback chair, her face was slightly twisted. It was clear that she was in pain. She was a warrior who raised her shield, not allowing this ailment to destroy her. I want pain medications when a nail breaks. "I need to call him next month. I should know soon, I hope. It is getting increasingly difficult to manage. I know, let's change the subject. Let's talk about Mom." We both burst into laughter. That discussion brought up anger, love, fear, and a huge portion of rightful regrets.

After hours of laughing, crying, singing carols, and bringing up things from our past, we both admitted the favorite discussion topic was still our mom. Laughter soothes deep wounds, that is why so many comedians come from challenging life experiences.

We had been enjoying leftovers, chocolate chip cookies. And what goes with cookies? Wine.

"Well, at least I never ate worms. You would sit on the sidewalk, in front of Grandma's, and scoop up a big handful. Yummy, down they went." I started to gag thinking about it. "Now that is what I call an eating disorder." I teased her.

"No, you just painted your crib in BM. How artistic," she countered.

We shared good stuff, sister stuff, secret stuff, scary stuff, not to be shared with anyone. Chris and I stuck together like Velcro against the outside world.

It was Robert's knock that delivered us back to the present. Leaving the past in the past, at least for this night. One glance told me this man was tired. "Did you have a nice time?"

He fell onto the couch. "Yes, it was very nice. You will need to excuse me, but I am exhausted. Okay if I go to bed?"

"Of course. I'll be in soon."

He rose, leaned in, and I kissed him. "Good night, brother-in-law," Sissy said, leaning in for her kiss.

He entered the bedroom. Chris and I stayed up for a while longer, but before too long, the yawns commenced. Chris stood up slowly, leaning on the table for support. "I am beginning to hurt, so time for me to take my meds and get some sleep. I am so happy you are here."

Soon, the household lay still. The only sound was the *tick, tick, tick* of a clock lulling me to sleep.

27

Our life was rich. We were active members in our church, even hosting a small group. Folks of all ages attended, including two young actors. We sang at the Hollywood Bowl on Easter. I continued to work, as well as volunteer at the Anne Douglas Center, the product of Michael Douglas's mother, on skid row. I loved it. These women were on the longest journey of their lives. From addiction and homelessness to an intimate relationship with themselves and God. The transformation was undeniable. I received far more than I gave.

One night, I was surrounded by people society had tossed away. Homeless. Addicted. Filthy creatures. They shared a life lived in filth. Lives existed in union with the rats that crawled through the streets, struggling for survival as much as these souls did on a daily basis. The stench of urine, vomit, garbage, and human waste attacked my senses. Cardboard boxes served as homes. Although the more fortunate beings resided in tents on the streets surrounded by hundreds of tormented souls. Men and women with mental illnesses left untreated, caught up in the addictions, many who had no frame of reference except to continue the life of those who gave them life.

A beautiful spirit, a woman of the streets, had received news about her family member. News you and I simply could not relate to or absorb. She cried silent tears. Her view of the world was horrific.

"May I sit with you?" I asked, silently expecting her to resort back to her street behavior. Surprisingly, she remained silent. Asking permission again, she nodded. I sat and took hold of her left hand. Our fingers entwined as I said, "Father God, please protect this beautiful lady, provide the wisdom she needs as she stands at the crossroads of her life. Hold her fast to the principles and faith that will allow her to change the only life she has ever known. Let this night be different from any other. I ask this in the name of your Son, amen."

My feelings of inadequacy almost brought me to my knees. If only I could just flee, like a coward to return to my comfortable, safe, affluent life. But instead, we connected on a deep level.

"Sweetie, look up. Keep your eyes focused above. Come on, look up."

She obliged. "What?"

"There is beauty, even here. Look at that sky. The night is calm, the stars glint to remind you there is a greater power than we know here. We must believe. Keep looking upward, talk to your creator, and rest in his promises. Can you do that?"

Her tears were her acknowledgment. I prayed a personal prayer that God would provide for her what this life had failed to supply.

Later, back inside I asked the group. "Listen, is anyone interested in making gingerbread houses for Christmas?" I called out. To my surprise, there was a universal agreement—some spoken in a loud, street-smart fashion, others were a raised finger, and others stared. "Okay, then we will schedule it, and we can lay them out for your families when they come for Christmas."

"Hey, you come with me? Come to my room." The woman barked at me, an order more than a request. Her manner set by her home on Skid Row. The weak did not survive.

"I'll be right back." My response. I turned and headed down the hall of the mission. It was very clean and attractive. Perhaps the only real home these women ever had. Seeing the pastor ahead of me, I called out to him. "Listen, one of the women asked me to come to her room. Is that permitted? I sure don't want to do anything that is against the rules."

He granted me permission, and I went back into the living spaces. I joined this woman as she walked to her room. At the side of her bed, a well-made bed, a neat room with a Bible on the bedtable, she began to speak.

"My mother loved making jewelry with beads, especially adding heart-shaped beads." She lifted a beautiful, multicolored necklace. I observed every fifth bead was one that was shaped like a heart. "Well, Mom died in April. Before she did, she gave this to me. I watched you, and I know your heart is real, not one of those fakes, so this is for you." She handed me the treasure, a gift from her departed mother.

I was touched but refused. That is, until I saw the need in her eyes to give. Acceptance was more important to her, for her growth and walk, than me. This woman who had nothing gave me the gift of love, passed on from her dead mother. What a blessing.

*****

There were still the ebbs and flow of my husband's relationship with his daughter. There were times I could hear her screaming over the phone, and then there would be what I called the I-love-you-gram. A selfie with "I love you" sent via e-mail. When she called, I left the room to afford privacy. But honestly to avoid hearing conversations about situations that just didn't exist.

Summer was winding down, although in SoCal, there is little distinction in seasons.

"Robert," I called to him. Dressed in jeans and T-shirt and bare feet, I was dusting the furniture.

I heard his footsteps. "I'm here—stop yelling."

"Sorry, I didn't realize I was yelling." My response dripped with sarcasm. "Can we talk about our vacation? Please, sit down."

Robert was determined to go back East and get his Airstream up and running. Then we could drive up and down the East Coast.

"Anne, why are we still talking about this? I thought we settled it." He paused. "I made arrangements to have all new tires, to have it cleaned—a complete overhaul."

Tossing the dustcloth on the table, I took a seat. "Who is going to drive? You know I can't, and your driving has been off." I knew what was coming next.

His voice was forceful. "I can drive just fine."

"Please listen to me. You are hitting curbs, coming back home with scratches on the car that you don't know how you got them. Listen, why don't we make alternative plans? Okay? If we decide the motorhome is not roadworthy, we will sleep in it and travel by car to see sights or visit. I am doing this for you because you want to see the motor home again and travel around New Jersey, but I want to go to Key West for a few days. Once we lock in the dates, I will make the plane reservations. We can stay at a lovely bed-and-breakfast I know. Agree?"

"Sounds good. I was thinking about mid-October."

"Great. We have a plan. Chris said we are welcome to stay there. You can go down and check out the motorhome with your daughter. That way, you can spend time with her."

*****

A month later, we arrived in New Jersey. October in the East is beautiful, but ever since my Jason died in October, it was just a painful reminder.

This day, my mind was filled with restless thoughts. Robert was at his daughter's condo close to the storage site. He would stay with her for a day or two, then she would drive him to the site to check out the condition of the motorhome. Secretly, perhaps not so quietly, I hoped the vehicle would not be street-worthy so we could just use it as a home base to save money. There were some nice camping sites that would be desirable for us to stay in. Wooded hiking trails, lakes, boating, and other attractions. I had spent a lot of time doing my homework in preparation of the trip. Robert had done nothing.

As was the case when Chris and I were together, we would go for a ride—it was always to the same place.

"Spruce Run is nearly empty. I hate seeing it like this." Chris steered her Bug into the boat launch area and parked.

"But look at the trees. They are beautiful reflecting in the water over there." I pointed to the far shore of the reservoir.

"So what are your plans?" she asked.

Releasing a great gush of air, I responded, "I wish I knew. Robert loves his motor home, and I would love to grant him one last fling, but it needs a good deal of work. Plus, who is going to drive it? As I told you, his driving is poor. Don't tell him that though. If we don't drive it, we will use it as a home base so we won't need to spend money on motels and food. I am praying for the latter. As you know, me driving something that big would be impossible. I have some concern about Robert in many areas. His memory is getting worse, his mood is changing, he is tired a good deal, and well, he is just different."

My phone vibrated. "Hello, young man. How are you doing?" It was good to hear Robert's voice. I listened. I could hear his daughter in the background coaxing him. Controlling the situation, once again. "What do you mean you and Colleen decided to sell the motorhome?" Anger grew in me. I don't think I was ever so angry. I listened. "Yes, Robert, you and I discussed selling it, but did it occur to you to call your wife? We were going to stay at the campgrounds in the motorhome even if driving was not an acceptable option. Did you forget? I spent weeks planning this trip. Now you and *your daughter* decided what to do next. Are you kidding me?" I yelled, disconnected him.

Chris, my confidant, knew the situation. "I can't believe they made such a decision without you. You're his wife. Dollie, I am so sorry."

"Welcome to my world." I started to cry. "All my work, my planning is gone." This had been the pattern. This was not normal behavior between a father and daughter. What was this hold she had on him? She ran our marriage behind the scenes. Using her father's password allowed her to follow us. Although time has passed knowing she read our private e-mail exchanges is such a transgression.

Despite my protest, my explanation, my recount of the plans regarding the motorhome, he protested. "We decided to sell the motorhome if it required too much work." Of course, he left out the fact that we, husband and wife, would discuss the next steps. Sadly, the decision was made without me.

There was nothing to be done but accept the situation. Again. There were too many people in this marriage. For reasons long before I came into his life, a relationship was cemented between father and daughter that even a jackhammer could not penetrate. Like all those folks preceding me, I was an outsider in a relationship unlike any I have ever known or will ever know. Any information was always second-hand, delivered through family members to me.

Money, a very sensitive area with me, was in question now. All previous plans were tossed out the window. Colleen and Robert, together, decided to alter plans.

"Dollie, don't let this ruin all your plans," Chris offered.

"Chris, I have tried so hard to keep the peace, to make the best of this situation, but I feel like a third wheel in my marriage. Why would he make decisions without me? Who does that?"

"I have no idea. At least none that makes any rational sense. But don't let this ruin your plans. Deal with everything when you get back to LA."

When he returned, I said nothing more about the incident. Several phone conversations resulted in the same ending. I wished the words I wanted to say didn't fail me at times. This inability to see things as they actually were are part of his Asperger's and other factors that occurred long before I entered the picture.

Visiting my friends, sailing, exploring failed to bring me joy. Robert's daughter was always with us. Just a phone call away, and call she did. Key West promised to be my panacea. I knew what I wanted and needed to do. This leg of the trip was about me.

Key West was the beginning of the end. A plethora of emotions took hold residing in my mind and body. Fear engulfed me as soon as we stepped off the plane. Humidity enveloped us. If there is one condition I hate, it is humidity.

We checked into our B and B owned and operated by a Cuban couple. There was a main facility and other smaller buildings on the property. "I love it. Look, Robert, there is a net over the bed. And wine! Don't you love the shabby chic décor? Just my taste." I exclaimed, lifting my bag onto the luggage rack. Robert grunted, sat on the bed. Seconds later, he was lying down, eyes closed. "Do you want to take a little nap before we go eat?" My question went unanswered. It was obvious he was asleep. We never did go out. Robert was unable to move, too tired and very weak. Scrawling a note to let Robert know I was going to pick us up something to eat, I left.

Stepping off the porch, I headed up Duval Street in search for food, alone. Robert remained asleep, never eating. There was something amiss.

The next morning, we awoke to blinding rain. Robert was awake, sitting at his computer. He had work to do for school, and that is what he was doing, even on our vacation. "Good morning, you really conked out last night." He grunted. I observed a man, sitting in front of his laptop, staring at the screen as if it was a foreign object.

"Robert, what's up?" No response. I repeated my question. Finally, he said, "I don't know how to turn this damn thing on." I was scared. My offer to help resulted in an onslaught of abuse. I assume he was as concerned as I was.

"I forgot some of my meds," he snapped.

After reviewing his medications, I knew what meds were omitted.

My dream vacation was becoming nightmare. I will go to pharmacy, call doctor, and hopefully they will be phoned in. I stepped out into the pouring rain, wandered the streets in search of the drugstore. Even when the rain lifted his energy, and ability to walk was declining. Confusion was constant. Several times as we were walking, he would grab a lamppost. Even with the correct medications, there was no difference.

"Robert, I am going to go next door to Key West Butterfly and Nature Conservatory. Do you want to come?" I asked.

"No, I want to rest." He rolled toward the window and fluffed his pillows.

Stepping inside the conservatory, I felt transported. Brilliant blues, yellows, scarlets, and multicolored insects floated amid tropical plants, colorful plants and man-made waterfalls. Occasionally, like a whisper of color, these insects would land on my arm.

"Mommy, look, that lady has some on her arms."

"If you stand still, maybe you can have one sit on you," I said. He smiled broadly.

My gaze shifted to the mother. "What is that aroma—smells like jasmine?" The mother shrugged. I stayed awhile longer, then decided to head back to the B and B.

Within minutes, I was sitting on the crisp, painted white porch, surrounded by tropical flowers and aromas that teased the senses. The property hosted hidden coves flanked by arches covered with vines illuminated by miniature lights, white wrought iron chairs and tables that held flickering candles. Couples drank wine, rested in hammocks tied between trees swayed in the first breezes from the ocean.

I decided to place a call to my son. "I am still very worried about Robert. I am hoping his behavior is the result of messing up his medications. Maybe I need to set them up from now on." Cell phone to my ear, I listened as my son voiced his concern. "I will. As soon as we get home, I will make an appointment with his doctor. If he has been messing up his medications, that could be at the root of his aberrant behavior. At least, I hope so. We were able to visit the Hemingway House, Mallory Square and drive a golf cart around the key. All the time, Robert was tired and appeared lost. I have a picture of him where he looks as if he had arrived from a galaxy far, far away. I am teasing but wait until you see the picture." It was so great to speak with my son. "Of course, Colleen came with us. One night, Robert suggested we go to a certain restaurant; it was quite a walk. Robert held my hand but twisted my arm back causing me discomfort. I was used as human cane. I learned as we dined that this was a restaurant Colleen liked. Their specialty, oysters and clams, neither of which I like. I felt like leaving him there to figure out how to get home. Love you, bye." I hated to hang up. I needed to return to caregiver.

A week later, back in California, we sat in the doctor's waiting room. My anxiety was elevated.

"Robert?" the nurse called. We rose and followed the cheery woman into a room near the back. She provided a few instructions and left. The entire exam lasted about thirty minutes. She started with a physical exam, at which time she asked broad questions to gain a history. When he answered incorrectly, I would shake my head out of his sight.

"Anne, is that how you remember it? What did you do about the missing medication?" she would ask, allowing me to supply accurate info without causing him distress or embarrassment.

"Actually, it was a little different. I walked to a drug store in Key West and were able to obtain to get what we needed."

"Good. Is that how it went, Robert?"

"Oh, yeah, I remember now."

"I think what is needed now is a complete workup at University of California Los Angeles. I will call them and make arrangements. You will be there for quite a while, I'm afraid. If you have any questions, just give me a call, okay?" I nodded.

The ride home was agonizing. The words *dementia* ringing in my mind. Married just two years, and I had dealt with so much. Plus, I felt I was deceived by Robert. He freely discussed every illness he ever had, but he never told me about *organic brain disease*. He was forgetful even early on. Questioning his daughter, she assured me he was just "the absentminded professor." I accepted that answer. Too trusting Anne.

"Can we go to McDonald's in Malibu?" he asked. His love of fast foods was as powerful as a magnet to metal. "We can sit on the seawall," he continued.

"What?" Lost in thought, I didn't hear what he had asked. He repeated his request. "Sure, you and your junk food." Thankful for the opportunity to escape what I was feeling, I complied. I pulled into the fast food drive through. I disliked driving, the result of jobs that required a great deal of my time on the road. Finally, someone else would take over. Unfortunately, when Robert began to come home with unexplained dents, I took over the task.

Even though sitting on rocks was not like sitting on a cloud, viewing the ocean was worth it. For a few minutes, I was transformed to a kinder, gentler time with my husband.

*****

My life for the next year consisted of watching my husband's physical and mental status spiral downward. Periods of alertness would be followed by periods of confusion. Unable to work, my time was spent taking Robert to the doctors, driving everywhere, helping him off the floor, monitoring all his activities. He could perform teaching, but it was getting increasingly difficult. By the end of the second year, he was physically and emotionally depleted. My health was greatly impacted.

"Thank you for allowing me to spend some time with you both," the social worker who came to our home stated. There was an accent I couldn't identify, but it was pleasurable. She was a black woman with extremely short hair. She looked like a model. Her visit was arranged by one of the numerous services for families dealing with dementia.

"I would like to arrange some services to help you," she stated, her eyes meeting mine. "I think you could use some help. At least, allow you to go shopping, attend church, or just take a walk. It has been my experience that often the caregivers suffer more than their charge." She turned toward Robert. "How does that sound to you?"

"No, I don't want anyone here. I can go with Anne if she needs to go out. If I get tired, I can sleep in the car." His logic, distorted. "I can drive her around if needed. She doesn't like to drive very much, do you, hon?"

"Not so much." I was thoroughly exhausted—just answering robbed me of energy.

After an hour, her questions answered, the kind lady said, "You are certainly living down the rabbit hole. A suicide, foreclosure, Robert, your illness occurred in such a brief time, you have been through much. I suggest you figure out a way to have a break, a respite. We can talk more about it in a few days. In the meantime, think about your options. Okay?" She rose, and I shook her hand, as did Robert. She left. I was alone again.

Even though Robert's daughter and I had no relationship, I always kept her informed not only in the good times but when there was a health issue. Communication was via e-mail; that was the safest. She was his daughter, therefore, she should be advised. Falls were now occurring with greater frequency. The latest fall required hospitalization and surgery.

"Colleen, this is Anne," I spoke into the phone. I went outside to make the call so Robert wouldn't interject. Silence. I repeated my greeting adding "did you hear me?" Barely audible, she answered. I explained how it happened: trips to doctors, his discomfort, the plan for his care. After I finished, there was absolute silence. Once again, I asked, "Are you there, did you hear me?" After several seconds, "yes" was her only response. Once again, I was aggravated. "I have no idea how to communicate to you. I feel as if I am speaking into a dead phone. No questions, no comments. Well, this is for you." I hung up.

A few weeks later, surgery and rehab over, I was driving north on the Pacific Coast Highway. We were returning from two doctor appointments when my cell rang—it was my sister. The phone was put on speaker. Chris had an infected hip that was not healing. Years earlier, she had hip replacements. One was no problem; the second, nothing but concerns. "I think you have been taking too many antibiotics. I am very concerned." I listened as she explained the challenges she faced, but not one to focus on self, she quickly turned the conversation on me.

"I am attempting to talk Robert into allowing me time for a respite. He is unwilling."

Forgetting she was on speaker, she voiced her opinion, including how selfish she thought he was behaving. "Why can't he go to his daughter's? I mean, she is in his life too much anyway. Why not let her share in all this?"

In addition to Robert's health issues, there were episodes of assaulting me physically or spitting on me. An increase in confusion with the resulting loss of his driving privilege by his physician. Diagnosis: dementia. I wouldn't let him drive, so I asked the MD to verbally take away his license so he couldn't go after me.

"I am not going to Colleen's. I don't want to go to her house, I can't go." His tone was indicative of the birth of angry outburst; spitting or hitting was a concern, especially because I was driving.

Chris was direct, abrupt, and firm. "Robert, you do this for Dollie. If you love her, you will go without making her feel upset." My family always referred to me as Dollie, a name given me as a child. I liked it.

"I'll go," he surrendered.

What was the "why" he didn't want to go to his daughters? Another unanswered question, although I certainly had my suspicions. I had heard much about her treatment of her father, even as a young adult from members of his family.

A few weeks later, we were at LAX. The traffic was insane, especially for those of us unfamiliar with the terminal.

"Robert, please don't read the signs." I pleaded. I slid into a narrow spot on the second level.

"Okay, here we are. Let's get you settled. I'll grab your suitcase." Exiting the car, I grabbed his suitcase from its resting place, and guided my husband, a brilliant man, had reverted to the logic of a child.

"Anne, please don't make me go. Please." My husband, a respected professor, was physically upset. He suddenly was unable to walk. He leaned on the cars we passed. I needed to seek assistance from another couple heading toward the elevator.

"Here you go," the caring couple stated, pushing a wheelchair. Robert took a seat.

"Thank you so much." My smile and words were authentic. Thank God for caring people.

"Hon, are you ready?" I asked as I pushed the chair forward. Without a word, I helped him take a seat. Never did I see my husband so despondent. His eyes lacked depth; not unlike Kevin. Could it be the absence of Anne caused concern? I was his soft place to land. And with his volatile relationship with his daughter, he knew her present semblance of calm could change in a heartbeat.

"Hi, can you help us?" I asked someone in a uniform. He smiled, made a call.

An attractive woman, with a huge smile approached us. "Afternoon, how can I help?"

I needed to communicate without embarrassing my husband. "Well, this good-looking young man is precious cargo, so I am entrusting him to you. His ambulation is a little off, so he will need assistance to be seated. His daughter will greet him at the destination. Please make certain this letter is handed to his daughter. Vital information is enclosed."

I leaned over, kissed my husband, winked to the woman. "Make certain you take good care of him."

Slowly, he was rolled away. Tears formed, knowing he didn't want to go.

Driving up the PCH toward home, I felt a plethora of emotions. Guilt. Sadness. Fear. Love. Honor. Could he be in danger? No, of course not. I would be proven wrong.

I learned much later that the first thing she did was obtain a POA. How? The man had dementia.

The ball was in play.

When I learned Chris was going to have surgery, I asked Colleen if Robert could stay with her longer. It was important to me to be able to care for my sister who had long been neglected. I lived in LA; she was in New Jersey, and so much of my focus was on Robert. Two people I cared about both needed me and were on different sides of the country. Now I would be able to help Chris.

I returned to California after her surgery. It was in April, the month of Robert's birth. I had just returned from the UPS office where I sent a present to him. He was still in New Jersey because I was having major stress-related health concerns and was advised I could not take care of Robert. Opening our mailbox, I saw the formal envelope from an attorney in New Jersey. The contents stated that Colleen, acting on behalf of Robert, was seeking a separation on grounds of irreconcilable differences. My longest journey was about to begin. He didn't want a divorce, nor did I. There was a list of what *she* wanted, including a portion of the condo I purchased a year after my son died.

28

I felt as if I were hit in the heart. We had never spoken about a separation. The terms were his daughter's, allegedly on his behalf, seeking a portion of the assets in my condominium. A home I purchased on my own and have been paying for twenty-five years! A place I moved a year after my son died in an attempt to move on and escape the pain of living in the house we had shared. I called my husband. I realized now why, when I tried to speak with her about returning to California, I never heard back anything from her.

Instantly, I placed a call to his cell phone. "Robert, it's me. What on earth are these separation papers about? I just returned from sending you a birthday present and come home to a letter from an attorney." I was in tears, devastated, exhausted. I felt like a fool—again.

"That's a mistake. Forget about it. Throw the papers out. I don't want a divorce. I love you." His voice raised.

"These are legal documents. I can't ignore them. Why are you doing this?" I knew it wasn't him, but his daughter, especially when I reviewed the list of material items. And the outrageous cause of the action: irreconcilable differences.

"Rip them up." The phone went dead. A usual event, especially if his daughter was around. As wild as this sounds, all conversations were on speaker phone if she was home. So when she was not pleased with the flow of the conversation, she hung up. Since I met Robert, phone calls were on speaker phone with her and from her. I was informed this was a lifelong pattern. It was a method of control.

For three consecutive days, I placed a call to my husband. Each time I called him, it was to ask the same question. Why was I being sued for separation? Each and every call I placed, I always received the same response: "It is a mistake. I love you. I don't want a divorce." On day 4, he was angry, insisting it was a mistake. I don't believe I ever heard him so upset.

On day 5, instead of the usual sound of a ringing phone, I heard: "The AT&T subscriber you are trying to reach is unavailable." That was the last phone call I had with him. I continued to call, and I continued to receive the same message. I just couldn't believe someone would do something so unkind. Not just to me but to Robert. Abuse, that is what it was. He wanted his wife; she blocked him. Now I realize why he didn't want to go to her house, pleading with me to stay home. I imagine her phone calls to him in SoCal; she began her destruction of Anne.

Calls placed to Colleen's house went unreturned. Weeks passed, and I decided to call the police. They went to the house, and after several weeks, I was able to speak with him. But he was on speaker, the conversation monitored. This was insane behavior. My mother recorded conversations; now my conversations were on speaker. Mother and Colleen had so much in common.

"Robert, I was so worried about you. Why did your daughter cut off communication with you?" But I knew the answer. She had a goal, a motive, and he was stating he didn't want a divorce. His comments in direct opposition to her goals.

"What are you talking about, Anne? Why did you have the police come here?"

I explained to him, but I don't think he fully understood; or, perhaps, he was once again just defending his daughter.

He spoke into the phone, his voice soft, the tone used when he was in a position of confrontation. He was shutting down. "I am confused."

In the background, I heard his daughter speak, "Tell her I got a POA." This said with such pride, as if something benevolent was achieved instead of the antithesis. An action so devious, personally I would have been acutely ashamed. All I could think of was *How?* He has been diagnosed with dementia. Three years prior, when he first started to show signs, I obtained a POA while he was still capable of making somewhat wise decisions. I did things the right way, the legal way, but it didn't matter.

Alone, health issues, all finances cut off, my car insurance was not paid, and on and on. Even though I was still married to Robert and unable to work because of my diminished health problems. Colleen now had what she wanted: control of Robert's accounts. I was cut off, she changed his account, stopped paying for my car insurance. I thank God I didn't have an accident. What kind of person puts another person in a position that could destroy them? My social security check didn't cover the rent and mortgage payments. My tenant left, so I was now paying for my home in New Jersey. I needed relief, but instead, I was kicked when I was down. "Who does this?" I asked my sister on what became daily phone calls. I listened, adding, "What is her motive? Is it just control? Money? You know who she reminds me of? Mom, exactly. I really can't go through that again. I loved her. Tried to help her and the whole family."

"Dollie, don't go down that pity slide—it will only lead you to a dark place. This is not about you. You did nothing wrong but show him and that family love. Now we know why he didn't want to go there." I said goodbye and hung up. I knew she was correct.

I called a lawyer in LA. A really terrific person who helped me in the past, free of charge! Her office was in Beverly Hills in a beautiful building. She reviewed the documents, took information from me, and then stated if neither party wants a divorce; it was a nonissue. Once again, no charge. I liked her immensely. I left feeling tired but comforted by her words. "I must admit, Anne, this is the first time I ever heard of a divorce 'by proxy'. This is crazy."

The next time we spoke, she informed me she had received information from Colleen's lawyer who presented her client as a victim. What? I didn't know on that day my fate was sealed. The life I had—sunsets, a husband, my friends in LA, my mission work, my church, and so much more—was over. I needed to move from LA. Why? Because someone wanted things and control, but what I suspect she wanted was love. Isn't that what we all want in the end?

*****

Months later, after packing up the entire contents of my condo on my own, I loaded up my two little felines, got into my Lexus, and headed for New Jersey. Alone. My beautiful sister was suffering in the hospital, my husband's daughter was suing me for divorce, and the life I loved five years earlier was just a memory. I had not chosen wisely because I was not at peace; in fact, I was in turmoil. One must make decisions based on head and heart. Not just heart. I ignored the red flags: her interference before our marriage, during and after. She wanted my social security number. Let's not forget our first contact. "Shut up Anne and get off the phone."

Driving beside the beautiful Colorado River, with my two sleeping felines nestled in the back, my phone rang. I had finally stopped crying. I had received many calls from concerned family and friends. Let's be honest, driving cross-country, alone, as a mature woman without any designated plan was foolhardy. I was running on fear, desperation, fatigue, loneliness, with a sprinkle of hope brought to light through prayer.

"Hon, I don't know where I will be tonight," I answered my son.

"I was thinking about meeting you halfway—you know, fly in and meet you so you don't need to drive alone. But I can't do that if I don't know where you will be. This is ridiculous. Everyone is worried, Mom—not knowing where you are moment to moment. And your stupid phone keeps shutting down."

Off to the left, the river and the road made a sharp turn. I was so distracted, I almost went off the road. "I promise to call you as soon as I check in tonight. I will try to have a plan, but because I am attempting to make time, I am driving until fatigue takes over. Listen, what's going on with Aunt Chris?"

My sister had her second surgery and had nothing but complications. Constant infections, drainage, pain, wound vac, and of course, the continued use of a myriad of antibiotics. That was a prime concern of mine all this time. I had spoken to her surgeon before leaving California to express my concern. After so long on antibiotics, they took out the hip, had a stretcher inserted, and then she needed another hip replacement. She almost died during that procedure. Now she was back in a different hospital. Before I left, most of my calls to the hospital went unmet. There had been no word from the MD, and the hospital staff was vague. I was frustrated and concerned.

"Aunt Chris is not doing well. I finally spoke with someone. They said she has nonalcoholic cirrhosis of the liver. Mom, one person makes it sound as if she is dying, another talk about her recovery, another says something different. It makes me furious. I threatened to bring in a lawyer."

"Dying? Oh, Jamie, she can't die." A wave of despair washed over me. I went blind to my surroundings, picturing my baby sister's face. A lifetime of suffering at the hands of others; now, because of poor decisions, her body was betraying her.

"Mom? Mom? Are you there?" my son called out.

"Yeah, I can't believe it. I wonder how long it will take me to get home. God, she can't die before I get home."

"I almost didn't tell you because I am worried about you driving." I knew that tone. Concern and annoyance that I have not provided him with an itinerary of my travels. He was right on both counts.

I pulled over. "Jamie, I promise you, I will be careful. She needs me, and dear God, I need to see her." I was holding back the tears I had been shedding for seven hundred miles and just laid to rest. Now they were back.

"Mom, you better keep in touch. We don't need to worry about you too." He hung up, allowing me to cry freely.

I arrived too late on a Thursday in New Jersey to visit. Regrettably, it was after ten when I entered her sweet apartment. This place was a reflection of her personality. Family pictures, cat toys, birdhouses, even an oven cover with birdhouses, and the rolypoly cows my Jason gave her one year watched me as I entered the kitchen. What I wanted, and needed, was a glass or two of wine. But for this night, I would need to go without. My feline children wandered throughout her place, checking every corner, inhaling the scent of her cat. I so needed a drink, and that said, needing a drink is an indicator of a problem. Unfortunately, drinking had become a nightly routine over the past several months, since the threatened divorce, the move, my declining health, financial situation, and my inability to speak with my husband and so much more. But it was my sister's surgery and complications that were the driver.

After nine hours on the road, I was too tired to shower. I fell into bed exhausted. In the morning, I jumped into the car and headed to the hospital. I needed to see my sister. Entering her room, I forced myself to smile, a characteristic instilled in me many years earlier. I didn't want Chris to see my concern. There she was sitting up in bed.

"What's wrong with your hair?" Chris asked from her hospital bed. This woman, who knew that her sister suffered from a wounded image problem, a lady who received most comments about her appearance as a dart to self-esteem, was now being criticized by her protector.

After I kissed my hero, the string to my kite, I pulled on my ability to make a joke even in the darkest of times. "I just drove twenty-eight hundred miles in four days, staying at motels even Norman Bates wouldn't stay in, with Harper and Pickles, unable to take a shower or wash my hair just to see my sister—and that is the first thing you have to say?"

I so wanted to cry but held back, pulling on my defense mechanisms. Humor. She looked terrible. The sister I loved and needed would never have made such a comment. Her filtering system was failing, along with her ability to reason. Toxins were building up in her system, impacting cognition. Something was wrong. How does this happen? I was so tired of unanswered questions.

"Your hair looks crazy." She added, "And where are your eyebrows?" My sister would never, ever say anything unkind, especially to her over-sensitive sister under normal circumstances.

I ignored her probing questions related to my disheveled appearance. "How are you feeling? What does the doctor say?" She was my focus, not my appearance.

"I feel okay. Not certain when I will leave. Everybody here thinks you are a pest. I suspect you will receive some nasty looks from the staff. You have not exactly made friends here with all your calls, complaints, and demands. I don't know what's going on. No one has seen me for weeks. They are moving me to another floor, and I don't want to be moved."

My sister's neuro functioning was impaired. Her kidneys were not functioning, nor her liver. "Chris, I don't care what they think. I was across the country, and I was kept in the dark. No one would speak with me, and in fact, some folks were rude. You know how I get when someone I love is not receiving the care they deserve. I can be their worst nightmare."

Shifting in bed, she asked me for a drink. I moved closer to her. Her eyes were absent of understanding. My sister, my Chris, was gone. My concerns were heightened by some of her remarks, as they were not consistent with the facts. She had hip surgery, and now, she was acutely ill.

"Why didn't you come see me sooner?"

I repeated the facts, but she didn't have a clear understanding. She actually became agitated that it took me so long to visit. Reality was not even a distant relative. Her behavior became increasingly belligerent. Requests were made that were completely unobtainable. Leaving was the only option in this scenario. I was angry, incredibly angry, but at whom? God? The doctors? Me? Her? The body that was failing?

My furniture was delivered to my condo on the hottest day recorded in New Jersey in years. It was 105 degrees, and my air conditioner was not functioning. Over six thousand dollars in missing or broken items occurred during the move. So as I was dealing with the move, Chris's illness, my own health issues, financial losses, I then had to file a claim, take pictures, and identify actual cost of items if possible. I would explore the Internet for comparable items of items lost or damaged with a cost affixed to the articles. To add more stress, of course, there were time constraints for submission. The first claim was lost, so I needed to resend. In the months that followed, I was informed they settled for seventy-nine dollars!

I sent Robert's daughter an e-mail. "Colleen, I am asking politely. Please tell me where my husband is." I learned he was now in a facility, but she was hiding him from me, threatening me, in fact. Her response was to take care of the divorce issue. Being forced to leave my beautiful home in California to move back to New Jersey, my money was depleted, and my health was tenuous. *Lord, is this another test, because I think I just might fail.* I believe I was as close to a complete breakdown as one can be. I felt helpless and hopeless. I prayed often but continued to try to do things on my own strength.

I received a certified letter a few weeks later—a printed copy of her e-mail to me. Once again, pushing the "let's get moving on the divorce" agenda. After that came another official document from her lawyer—the insanity of being sued for divorce, not from my husband, but his daughter. The letter from the attorney was threatening. If I attempted to locate my husband, she would file a restraining order. Of course, that was a complete falsehood, but for this lady, it scared me. After that, every time there was a knock on the door, fear gripped me. This was my plunge down the rabbit hole. Unfortunately, this journey was all too familiar. Chris was seriously ill, but I needed to obtain a lawyer (without money), complete paperwork, and visit my sister. This woman, who in my opinion, had similar characteristics of my mother was informed she had deprived me of time with my sister. And my husband. Why? An attempt to gain material items and money? What was her motive? This sad woman, like my mother, with much to offer, got offtrack and wandered in the darkness. Both sought the same thing. Love and acceptance, but was it their personality disorders that blocked their progress? To this day, I pray for this woman. For her, life was black or white. Love versus hate. No middle ground.

On a visit to my sister, now in a nursing home, her cognition was extremely impaired.

"How do you think I am? Just great! You were supposed to take me home. I waited all morning. I hate it here. Let's go." This bloated, mean-tempered woman was a stranger. Chris was gone. Her worst nightmare had come to life. Transferred to a nursing home for rehab, she was miserable and so confused. The toxin buildup was impacting her cognition. When she was like this, my visits were brief. She became increasingly frustrated and mean.

"Is that woman still in the hall, that phony nurse? She spies on me. I call and call for pain medication, but she just laughs and walks by." She stopped, and then bellowed, "I know you are out there, you bitch. I told my sister about you, so don't try anything. You don't want to mess with Dollie. Right?"

"Right!" I smiled in a shared but false camaraderie. "How is your pain level?"

Her look was intense. I was suddenly glass, and she was looking through me. "How do you think it is? Why do you ask such fucking questions? Where is Jamie? He was here this morning, and even though I called him, he didn't come into the room. I thought he was going to take me home. I want to see my cat." Chris ranted.

My heart was breaking. She would never see her cat again, nor would she go home—her life was ebbing away. I answered the best I could. Then stated, "Hon, I need to go." I made up some lie, knowing she wouldn't remember. I also knew that she would have moments when she was clear. I prayed that tomorrow might be different. I left, walked through the facility, and stepped out into the heat and humidity only New Jersey summers offer. I cut across the lawn under the maple tree, heading toward the parking lot. I melted into the driver's seat and started the car as my head fell back onto the headrest. Without warning, a waterfall of tears fell. I can't lose her—if she was gone, I would fly away or crash to the earth like a kite in the wind. She was my voice of reason, my port in a storm, and my storage vault of secrets.

*****

I visited daily.

"Dr. Wiener was in this morning. I love him so much. He thinks I am doing very well. He doesn't understand why I can't eat but am gaining weight." Her response was clear.

"You have not eaten since I have been back—your weight gain is fluid. Look"—I pressed on the lower leg, showed her the indentation, and said—"that is pitting edema, Chris. I'll talk with him before I leave if he is still here. If not, I will call."

We continued to speak for a while, Chris in her bed, me in a side chair. As the visit played on, she began to drift again. "Tell those people to go home now—the party is over." There were no people in the room. Hallucinations presented before the visit ended.

I stepped into the hall and turned right. There were tiles on the floor, handrails, floral boarders on the walls, and a faint smell of cleaning products and urine blended. As I reached the nurses' office area, I saw Chris's doctor in the distance. Catching a glimpse of me, he approached. "Hi, Anne. I am glad I ran into you. I was going to call you later. Can you step in here for a minute?" He pointed to the office. "I want to give you an update on your sister." He took a seat.

"Of course," I answered, lowering myself into the chair. "You do know Chris has a huge crush on you, don't you?"

A hint of a smile formed, fading quickly. "I am putting your sister on hospice. She is not getting better, and her labs are all over the place. We are not exactly sure what is happening besides her diagnosis of nonalcoholic cirrhosis of the liver. One by one, her systems seem to be shutting down."

"How does this happen? How does hip surgery turn into a death sentence? This doesn't make sense. In the past month, one story fades and another told. Now she is dying?" I started to cry. As I walked down the hall, the word *hospice* beating inside my skull, I thought about my stepdaughter suing me for divorce. I wanted to know why? Like so much in my life I knew, this would just be more missing pieces in the puzzle of my life. I loved God and his children. There was no intentional hurt cast upon another, and yet, so much hurt had been cast upon me and those I love.

I visited Chris every day, except when she was agitated. In between visits, unpacking, dealing with legal issues related to Colleen's divorce action, attempting to locate my husband, filling out forms for the moving company who broke and lost over six thousand dollars of my possessions, I was fighting a devastating depression, an illness that began to attack me while still living in my beloved California. I would ask God each night to take me home. I served no purpose, as everything and almost everyone I loved was gone.

*****

ALL THE MISSING PIECES

In early September, I was awakened by the sounds of my landline ringing, then my cell, then my landline. If I didn't answer, then I wouldn't hear the words I knew awaited me. When I saw Chris the day before, she was barely responsive. She had a little cough, and my touch hurt her—often the sign that the end is near. I kissed her, told her I loved her, then in the car, I prayed God would take her. He did.

I am unable to explain the pain I felt, the confusion and terrible sense of loneliness. What do I do now? Why do evil persons live on, and someone like my beautiful sister leaves us so soon?

"Hi, Anne, have a seat. I want you to know something about me. I am a believer in God first, I am a man second, and I am a lawyer last. Now, tell me about what's going on." Those were the words spoken by the attorney I needed to hire to prevent a travesty of justice to prevail.

How can a person force a divorce on a man with dementia, who doesn't even know he is getting a divorce? Forcing his wife to spend money she doesn't have to defend herself so this party can gain material possessions? Is this justice? Is this the law of the land?

"My husband's daughter is suing me for divorce. Neither of us want it. But her original separation agreement listed items, money, and even the cat. My sister just died, and I am beyond stressed. I have lost so much. My sister was my touchstone, my anchor, and except for my son, I am alone. She was the voice of reason in my head." I was so fidgety and scattered, a miracle for me was just forming a coherent sentence. I was as close to a complete breakdown as one can be. My health, both emotional and physical, were suffering as well.

"Anne, if you will allow me, I will take care of you like your sister did. I think we can go after her for my fees because this is a frivolous case." The retainer agreement was signed. I handed him a check, compliments of my sister, a small insurance policy she left to me to make my life easier. Instead, I am paying a lawyer with the little money my blessed sister gave me. Money left me by an angel was spent on defending myself against someone who was very ill and cruel.

On the way home, I felt much better. I would win the case, not spend much money, and justice would prevail. For the first time in a long time, I felt I had someone in my corner. He claimed to be a man of faith.

The phone rang one afternoon; it was Robert's brother. "Hi there, sister-in-law. I just had an interesting call from Robert's daughter." He went on telling me all the details of his strange call from his niece. "I wasn't even sure why she called me. She was crying and talking about a chair I had that she wanted me to ship to her. I couldn't believe it. Can you imagine? I don't hear from her for years, now I was supposed to ship a piece of furniture across the country. But the good news is I did learn where Robert is." He paused, possibly for effect.

"Okay, tell me," my voice rising in tone and strength.

"He is in Pennsauken in a place named Bentley," in a commanding voice he stated authoritatively, "Now, go call your lawyer and go see your husband." The relationship between uncle and niece had been severed a long time ago. It appeared most relationships with her were severed over the years. Sad, indeed.

I had promised to keep Robert safe, and I felt as if I had failed. But I did the best I could. Unfortunately, he made no such commitment. He allowed his daughter to say and do whatever she wanted, and he never defended me, ever. Avoid conflict at all cost.

My attorney placed a call to the facility. He made it very clear, as Robert's wife, I had every right to visit my husband despite Colleen's attorney's attempts to block me. I was threatened with a restraining order if I attempted to locate him. If he was amenable to the visit, they couldn't stop it. I learned later that a restraining order is difficult to obtain. There must be some proof of abuse. Of course, in my case, there was none.

*****

I will never forget the day I pulled up to a building in an industrial area in southern New Jersey. I was terrified. But with a prayer on my lips, I entered. Of course, not knowing my husband's location, I needed to stop at the receptionist's desk. The looks I received were piercing as I searched for his room. I felt like I was walking the last mile. This was my first visit with my husband in many months.

I entered his room, and he was being tended to by a caregiver. He looked at me and said, "Who are you?" He looked terrible. The light that was once my husband had been turned out. There was no evidence of the man I kissed goodbye over a year ago. The man I shared a romantic meal with on the ocean in California, who flirted with me, who cried when he left me. He had dementia then, but it was obvious the disease had pulled him down, like quicksand. He had lost his footing in the land of reality.

"I'm Annie, your wife." Saying those words to this shell of a man took the greatest of effort. I had become the master of pretense, a chameleon able to transform into whatever situation I am placed. I smiled when I wanted to cry and exuded confidence when inside, insecurity loomed. In that moment, with almost all of what I held dear was gone, the effort to appear strong, when I was weaker than ever before, caused tachycardia and profound vertigo. Silently, I prayed for strength. There was no way I could deal with this on my own.

"My wife? Well, kiss me then." He sounded like a little boy. I kissed the face of a man I no longer knew. I kissed a stranger. He was but a mere shadow of the man I surrendered to his daughter. My heart was broken.

I was robbed. He was robbed. He had slipped away and left in his place. Was this being? A being with no memory of the wonderful life we shared. Sure, there were problems, mostly from outside influences, but we had good times. His memory was erased. Erased because there was no Annie to visit, no one to remind him of the time we spent together.

29

Months passed, and my money was low. Five years ago, my credit was excellent; credit card debt, almost nonexistent; health, perfect; lived in paradise; and my beautiful sister was alive. I applied for job after job online. In California, I was making decent money, but now I couldn't get Walmart to call me back. I had shingles, severe asthma attacks, a concussion—the list goes on.

"I couldn't think of one reason to get up. Everything and almost everyone I loved was gone. Watching TV has become my drug of choice," I shared with my adopted mom, Ms. Mary on the phone one afternoon. God placed this wonderful woman in my life to lavish the love, the wisdom, the guidance that I never received. We had met at work many years ago. Both nurses, we connected at a level that is ordained by the Father. Her heart was pure, loving, open, and generous. And she loved me even with my flaws.

Mary was beautiful. Not just physically but inward as well. Her hair, now white, was kept short. For a woman her age, she boasted a figure that still turned men's heads. The greatest accomplishment we can have is to be the type of person others strive to emulate. That describes my Mary. She is the ladder I climb to reach true happiness in the pursuit of bringing joy into the lives of others.

One day, on a visit to her, she said to me, "You are such a little girl, innocent, trusting, and easily hurt. You cannot accept one immutable fact. That is, there is evil in the world. People who will hurt you just because they can and, of course, add mental illness to the stew, and you have a tasty meal of destruction for them and anyone who ingests their lies." Her smile and caring gaze delivered a wave of compassion directly to my heart. "Do you want something to eat? Some cake? A sandwich?"

I was much younger than my dear friend, but she had the energy of folks half her age. I sat on the couch in her apartment savoring the love she dished out so freely. She lived in a senior living apartment. Three compact rooms crowded now with all of Mary's special keepsakes and oversized furniture.

"No, I'm fine." I remained seated on the sofa, gazing around at pictures of family, Bibles, dolls, photo albums. A woman of mature years but a spirit of youth.

In the doorway of the kitchen area, she said, "How about something to drink. Coffee? Soda? Water?"

"If you have diet soda, that would be great."

She turned, stopped, and came back. "You look so pretty. I love your lovely blonde hair."

"Thanks." I knew her compliment was sincere.

Minutes later, my friend placed a tray with cookies, cakes, and soda on the table before me. I was not surprised. Mary loved to nurture, and food was always comforting.

She turned and took a seat across from me, slightly to the right. "Anne, you know God is in charge. He will bring about his plan to His glory. You have survived much worse. You will get through this and come out shining as you always do."

"I just don't understand why. Why did God take my sister? Why did Robert's daughter lie about me, telling everyone I abused Robert? I am treated so horrifically when I visit. They monitor me and have called the daughter when I am there. Crazy. You know me. You remember me writing someone up for abuse of a patient. I spent my life fighting against abuse. Now I am on the defending side. Mary, am I unlovable? Is God mad at me? My questions do not appear to have answers."

"I love you, and so many others do as well. You know that, don't you?" Her words and smile were as soothing as my precious Pacific Ocean.

"I guess I am having a pity party, and because I love you, I invited you." We both started to laugh, a bit of a strained laugh for me. I was deep in a hole that I feared I would never climb out of. But Mary's soothing manner, as all good mothers do, helped comfort me, offering a ray of hope.

"Anne, I don't think you have truly grieved the death of Chris. You were so close, and now she is gone."

Shifting uncomfortably, knowing she was right, I said, "I agree. I cannot accept it." Intellectually, I know she is gone but to honor her loss, accept it as fact, leaves me alone.

"Oh, I want to show you something." My friend rose, sifted through some papers in a drawer, and pulled out a piece of paper. She began to read. This was a poem she wrote. A glimpse into the soul of my friend. Beautiful and comforting like a cup of cocoa on a cold winter's day. My Mary.

"That is beautiful. Could I have a copy?" I knew the answer before her lips moved. With my Mary, it was always a yes.

After several hours, I left. Hope, a least a teaspoonful, had been restored. The ride back from Pennsylvania to New Jersey was peaceful as I listened to the tones of Andrea Bocelli. Life is like music. It rises and then falls, then rises up again.

The second year since I was forced to move back, losses continued. Rob, the young man I wrote about, Grace's brother, was diagnosed with CUP, cancer of unknown primary. That was in May. In September, he died. There will always be a hole in the space he occupied. He died almost to the day my sister went home the year before. Then my dear friend, who has been fighting cancer, lost her fight. Her adopted daughter will now be raised by her grandmother. Three deaths in less than two years. During all this time, I was in and out of court thanks to the frivolous divorce suit that impacted every area of my life. Seventeen thousand dollars spent on lawyers to fight a divorce that should have never made it to the courts. I had shingles, elevated blood pressure, and bill collectors calling night and day, with the threat of losing my home.

I continued my visits with my husband, always so happy to see his Annie. The visits remained difficult with the treatment from some of the staff, mostly management. They had been informed I was seeking the divorce, threw him out of the house, and God knows what else.

The day I went to court the first time, I had to deal with the pain of shingles—another result of constant stress. There would be no divorce. But it was not over yet. His daughter was very angry.

Then, in October, another date was set to go to court. My very special friend Lynne accompanied me the first time, but this time, it was just me, my attorney, and an associate. My attorney Howard spoke. His word's kind but with a pinch of caution. "Wait here. I'll be back soon. I need to meet with them. This is all good. After today, it will be over. No divorce."

Robert's daughter looked furious. Everything she sought after was about to end. I needed to learn how this woman paid her attorney. I suspect she used her father's money to hire an attorney to obtain a divorce he didn't want. Afterward, when the case was overturned, I left the courtroom and went to a really nice restaurant with my group. Was it actually over? The case was dropped. No divorce, and the POA was back in my hands. Or was it? The fight was ongoing.

The first full day of spring was my birthday. Snow covered the earth, grabbing to tree branches in a desperate attempt to keep from falling. I was working again. The organization I worked for prior to moving to California called me to learn if I was interested in coming back. A friend had mentioned to the CEO that I was looking for work. Life was calmer, although the same splinter remained in my side.

My husband now lives just minutes from me in a nursing home. Jamie helped me move him in in May. Although I still yearn for my previous life in California, I am attempting to grow where God planted me.

30

After church, I walked around town admiring the bountiful homage to the end of summer as fall's brilliance bounced from the river that snaked through our little town. I was sad. Still am, I guess. You see, I need to bid farewell to my past. A past that held a good deal of pain. To bid farewell to a mother held captive by mental illness, a woman I loved but who was unable to return that love. Sheer frustration on her behalf forced her to do and say acts focused on destroying me. But I will abandon those memoires. God knows I have carried them long enough. I shall, instead, remember her fantastic sense of humor, her quick mind and creativity. I will leave behind negative memories of a father who failed that role in so many ways. A man-child with a volatile temper that just wanted what I had: to be loved.

There were many people who hurt me, but I know that hurting people *hurt* people. I will pray for those folks still here and celebrate those who have passed. But most of all, I will celebrate and fight to retain the positive memories and, with time, dismiss the ugliness. I smile now thinking of my brother, strumming his guitar and singing "Mr. Bojangles." My sons and I decorating a tree with handmade ornaments and a star made from the lid of a pizza box covered in tinfoil. So many good memories that will allow the brilliance of life to shine.

Since I began writing, I have relived every single ugliness, sadness, and evil that entered my life. Memories that all came crashing down on me like a freight train.

Every day there is a sunset, and I choose to be present for as many as I am allowed. The past is just that: in the past. I will not allow it to cripple me in the future. There are many leftovers, unfair acts from Colleen and Colleen's lawyer. Lies. Abuse. Deceit. Crippling financial losses. Pain. Confusion. Fear. Everything inflicted upon me as a result of one act. I married her father.

Today, I visited my husband, a brilliant, kind man held at bay by a disease. All that is left is a dear man who thinks he is an African-American Christian Buddhist who sees images of animals on his ceilings. When he cannot remember my name—that occurs almost every visit—he calls me Penelope Poopcidoodle. There is an identification of the face, but all memories of sailing, flying, hiking, singing at the Hollywood Bowl, Napa Valley vineyards, missions, Catalina Island, BBQs, listening to the ocean while in bed—gone. That really is a crime punishable by eradication, eradication of the disease.

Seasons have faded one into another. I said goodbye to 2017, allowing a new year to take its place. A new president is in office. My husband continues to decline, ever so slowly bidding farewell to precious memories. Life continues to propel me forward.

Despite the changes, there is one constant. My life is still a mystery to me. My attempt to complete the puzzle of my existence without the pieces cannot be done.

Today, a sunny Sunday mid-January afforded me the opportunity and privacy for introspection. Do I need to know the answers to the whys in my life? No. Where there are questions, missing pieces, there was the opportunity for growth. Why did Mother not love me? I have struggled with that question, but I know, deep within, it doesn't matter. Despite everything, I loved her, although I hated her actions.

"Hi, hon. What's up?" My thoughts interrupted momentarily by the familiar voice of my son on the phone.

"Just checking in. This was a good trip. Robert has really declined. I give you so much credit for taking such good care of him despite everything you have been through."

"Jim, I really can't talk now but, please, give me a call before you leave for LA tomorrow. Okay? Love you. Bye." We hung up.

Family. That's what is important. Not doing to him what was done to me is my goal. As usual, I ruminated for months about my next steps. Afterall, I required a path to peace after a lifetime of tumult. In late April I retired. My life appeared to be on track. Credit restored, Robert was safe, my son settled with a terrific woman and my health restored. Most importantly, I was loved. This day was coming to an end as I began to write my goals. Years ago, I learned the way to success is to have an action plan. Mine would hang on the refrigerator. My goals focused on completing another book, exercise, church involvement and, yes, painting. A new endeavor. Time to live, not just survive. Oops, gotta run. Don't want to be late for my first flying lesson. Scared? Sure. Excited? Absolutely.

EPILOGUE

Two years have passed since I wrote the end to my memoirs. My Robert went home. He is whole once. Knowing again the man as I did, I imagine he is engaged in conversation with Jesus about the Bible. I still miss my sister, my anchor. But I can't complain. She visits me nightly. And if I am fortunate, she brings my son. The nightmares are almost completely dissolved.

When I look at the picture of me as a baby, the little girl with the beautiful smile, holding a ball in her braceleted hand, regret washes over me. A sweet little girl with curly brown hair. A glance at that face held the promise of tomorrow. Unfortunately, her smile was wiped away by the very people, her parents, who should have provided love and safety. They couldn't give us something they didn't have. People have limitations. We need to recognize and accept them as they are or leave the situation if it is harmful. Not everyone has the capacity to love unconditionally. Some people should never have been parents.

If you have listened to Mozart's Serenade no. 13 for Strings in G Minor or my beloved Beethoven's Fur Elise, you can't help but think of our lives. Music builds to a crescendo, powerful, then gently fades. Is that not what life is? The music or the waves in the ocean lift you up, drops you, comes back again stirring your emotions. The music of life is powerful. Listen. Observe and take the ride. I promise you there will be drama, anger, peace, and soothing. Enjoy the ride. Listen to your inner voice, it might just be the voice of God.

I still face the residual financial concerns due to Colleen. Her actions cost me a future of travel, relaxation, and financial security. So where am I today? My focus is on what I have. People who love me, good health, a lovely home in a beautiful "Norman Rockwell" like community. Quaint town, waterfall, museum with a working watermill, ducks that wander into stores and well, even a Rubber Ducky Race each summer. It is beautiful. Even though my heart will always be in SoCal with my ocean view, I will grow where God planted me.

I am not the same person I was just a few short years ago. I no longer give folks the benefit of a doubt. I wait until they have proven worthy of my trust. My sister and Robert would always laugh at me. Robert would say, "Your sister is always trying to fix everybody even if they don't want it." Chris would respond, "Oh, don't you just love it when she rambles on about life not being fair?" They loved mocking me. So, now I say, until God calls me, I will wait to jump in to fix a problem. So far, no call.

The greatest gifts you can give someone who is suffering are your love, acceptance, and guidance. As a therapist told me about my mother and Robert's daughter, the greatest gift you can give them is to make them accountable for their actions. Ignoring inappropriate behaviors is like ignoring a lump on your breast. Inappropriate behavior is nurtured by your silence.

The greatest gift you can give yourself is to trust your feelings. I Need to repeat that. Trust your feelings. If something about a person just doesn't feel right. Trust yourself. If you are correct, you will know soon enough. People need to earn your trust. Don't do what I did all my life. I measured others by my yardstick. I assumed my kindness begets kindness. It doesn't. If there are red flags, don't ignore. I did.

I learned the hard way.

My future holds many possibilities.

ALL THE MISSING PIECES

ABOUT THE AUTHOR

Anne's humorous toolkit "surviving as a single parent" drew on her life's experiences. Raised in a dysfunctional family where abuse, addictions, and mental illness robbed her of a childhood, Anne is a widow, mother of two sons. Her younger boy died from a gunshot at fourteen years old. Questions continue regarding the events on that horrific day. Just more missing pieces in the puzzle of her life.

Anne's accomplishments as a registered nurse and rewards occurred regardless of numerous barriers. Despite keeping God at a distance, he was always there. She wrote *All the Missing Pieces* for self but primarily to enlighten suffering lost men and women. The current tumult in our society was the impetus. Mental illness is just that, an illness. Time to bring it out of closet and help the sufferer.

CPSIA information can be obtained
at www.ICGtesting.com
Printed in the USA
BVHW032137130520
579682BV00001B/38